# 25 DAYS TO ADEN

# 25 DAYS TO ADEN

## MICHAEL KNIGHTS

PROFILE
EDITIONS

First published in Great Britain in 2023 by
Profile Editions, an imprint of
Profile Books Ltd
29 Cloth Fair
London
EC1A 7JQ
*www.profileeditions.com*

Copyright © Michael Knights, 2023
Cover image © Stuart Brown

1 3 5 7 9 10 8 6 4 2

Typeset in Garamond by MacGuru Ltd
Printed and bound in Great Britain by
Clays Ltd, Elcograf S.p.A.

A CIP catalogue record for this book is available from the British Library.

ISBN 978 1 80081 509 4
eISBN 978 1 80081 510 0

*This book is dedicated to:*

Lieutenant Abdulaziz Sarhan Saleh Al Kaabi
Sergeant Saif Youssef Ahmed Al Falasi
First Corporal Juma Jawhar Juma Al Hammadi
First Corporal Khalid Mohammed Abdullah Al Shehhi
First Corporal Fahim Saeed Ahmed Al Habsi

# NOTES ON THE COVER ILLUSTRATION

The image on the front cover is a painting by Stuart Brown, one of two such official commissioned war paintings from the Aden operation that hang in the entrance of the UAE Presidential Guard headquarters at Mahawe, Abu Dhabi. It shows the 'helocast' insertion of the first eight Presidential Guard special operators and their Zodiacs off the coast of Aden on 13 April 2015. Tracer bullets can be seen lighting up the sky on their original intended rendezvous (RV) site, forcing them to motor two additional nerve-wracking hours in the darkened sea to their secondary RV.

Some licence has necessarily been taken to make the painting more illustrative. The actual night of 13 April was extremely dark and overcast. The choppers were moving fast over the water, not hovering. By the time the swimmers had breached the surface after jumping into the warm waters, the Chinook helicopters were actually already heading into the distance. Overall, the painting wonderfully conveys the dynamism and drama of the moment, and contains some superb details, such as the armament of the first group with AK-47s, to better blend in as Yemeni Resistance fighters.

# CONTENTS

# LIST OF MAPS

# List of Maps

# GLOSSARY

| | |
|---|---|
| ADSB | Abu Dhabi Ship Building |
| AESA | Active Electronically Scanned Antenna, a sophisticated radar developed jointly by the US and the UAE for service in the UAE and US F-16 multi-role aircraft |
| AQAP | Al-Qaeda in the Arabian Peninsula |
| ATGM | Anti-Tank Guided Missile |
| ATO | Air Tasking Order, the pre-written first 72-hours of an air campaign |
| BMP | The famous Russian infantry fighting vehicle, derived from Boyevaya Mashina Pekhoty (BMP) |
| Chassis | Yemeni parlance for a pick-up truck |
| CIMIC | Civil–Military Cooperation, usually involving military provision of humanitarian support |
| CSAR | Combat Search and Rescue (pronounced 'see-sar'), the recovery of downed aircrew |
| CTU | Counter-Terrorism Unit, a Yemeni commando unit trained by the US but seized by the Huthis |
| CSF | Central Security Forces, a Yemeni paramilitary trained by the US but seized by the Huthis |
| DJ | shorthand for Djibouti, UAE military forces |

DOP        Drop-Off Point, where a helicopter or ship drops troops into the sea

Dushka      A 12.7-mm or 14.5-mm heavy-machine gun, derived from the Russian Degtyaryova-Shpagina Krupnokaliberny (Dshk)

EFP         Explosively Formed Penetrator, an Iranian-designed anti-armour warhead

FLIR        Forward-Looking Infrared, a heat-sensing optical device

FLOSY      Front for the Liberation of South Yemen, an anti-British liberation movement in 1960s Aden

GBU        General Bomb Unit, the body of a bomb, to which precision-guidance kits may be added

GPC        General People's Congress – the ruling party of Yemen from 1978-2011

HALO      High-Altitude Low-Opening, a parachute insertion technique

IED         Improvised Explosive Device, an explosive mine or booby trap

ISR         Intelligence, Surveillance and Reconnaissance, military parlance for military sensors

IRGC       Islamic Revolutionary Guard Corps, the Iranian armed force committed to exporting the Islamic Revolution

IRGC-QF    Islamic Revolutionary Guard Corps Quds Force, the department of IRGC that works covertly with partner groups to export the Islamic Revolution

JAC        Joint Aviation Command, the UAE's joint helicopter forces

| JOC | Joint Operations Command, the UAE's strategic coordination headquarters |
| JSOC | Joint Special Operations Command, the US' special forces |
| JTF | Joint Task Force, an organization that is temporary, fusing together multiple units to perform a mission |
| JTAC | Joint Terminal Attack Controller, a highly-trained operative who can direct air and artillery strikes and arrange the movement of aircraft within a set airspace |
| KLE | Key Leader Engagement, military parlance for managing relations with the commanders of partner forces or civilian leaders |
| KIT | Kornet Interdiction Team, UAE parlance (developed in Aden in 2015) for a Kornet anti-tank guided missile sent out on offensive patrols to harass enemy forces at long range |
| LCU | Landing Craft Utility, a smaller landing craft designed to carry troops and vehicles |
| LST | Landing Ship Tank, a larger landing craft that often has opening doors to allow 'roll-on, roll off' operations, even on shallow beaches |
| LAW | Light Anti-Tank Weapons, shoulder-launched, single-use, unguided anti-tank rockets |
| LRTV | Long-Range Thermal Video, a sensor system |
| MANPADS | Man-Portable Air Defence System, a shoulder-launched anti-aircraft heat-seeking missile |
| MRC | Military Regional Command, the geographic military commands used in Yemen |

# Glossary

MRAP — Mine-Resistant Ambush-Protected, a level of armouring intended to protect occupants against small arms fire and mine blasts from below

M-ATV — Mine-Resistant Ambush-Protected All-Terrain Vehicle, a lighter MRAP variant optimized for off-road performance

NLF — National Liberation Front, an anti-British liberation movement in 1960s Aden

OMLT — Operational Mentor and Liaison Team, pronounced 'omelette', an Australian and NATO practice from Afghanistan

ORBAT — Order of Battle, a listing of the units in a combat force

PDRY — People's Democratic Republic of Yemen, the post-British, pre-unification state that existed in Aden and much of southern and eastern Yemen between 1967 and 1990

PSO — Political Security Organisation, the main intelligence organization in Yemen

PG — Presidential Guard, the UAE's elite military special operations unit

Popular Committees — The neighbourhood-level organizational unit of small Yemeni resistance fighters in Aden

Resistance — The anti-Houthi resistance fighters in Aden, supported by the Yemeni government and organized by the Resistance Council

RV — Rendezvous, military parlance for a pre-arranged meeting point and time

| | |
|---|---|
| RHIB | Rigid-Hulled Inflatable Boats, pronounced 'rib', a military speedboat |
| RPG | Rocket-Propelled Grenade, a reloadable or single-use, shoulder-launched, unguided anti-tank or anti-personnel rocket |
| SH | Safe House, a covert operating location used by special operations forces |
| SOC | Special Operations Command, the UAE's special operations command |
| TCMOC | Training and Civil Military Operations Centre, a headquarters developed to support post-liberation stabilization in Aden |
| USMC | US Marine Corps |
| UCT | Universal Coordinated Time, also known as 'Zulu', that corresponds to Greenwich Mean Time, and which aids time-coordination for forces operating across time zones |
| ZSU | Military parlance for anti-aircraft cannon, pronounced 'shoe', derived from the Russian |

# ACKNOWLEDGEMENTS

This book is about a small country sending its army, navy and air force to fight a long way from home in a tough mission where no one expected them to succeed on their own. Just such a conflict had left a strong impression on me as a child in Britain, watching the 1982 Falklands War and the fate of our soldiers, sailors and airmen unfold on the news when I would return home from school each day.

This is the story of just such a hard-earned victory at the limits of a nation's endurance – the first major solo operation undertaken by the armed forces of the United Arab Emirates (UAE) and the critical final 25 days of the campaign to liberate Aden by Eid al-Fitr in 2015. Telling the inspiring story of the Aden campaign in 2015 would require the collective effort of a large number of people, whom I would like to thank here.

The UAE Armed Forces are a learning military and I should first extend my gratitude to the leadership of the armed forces for their strong support for this book. Emiratis do not tend to discuss military and security affairs, especially not with outsiders, but in this case the military leadership adopted a visionary approach in order to accurately record the history of the Aden campaign and allow future generations of UAE soldiers and citizens to learn from the operation.

The UAE Ministry of Foreign Affairs and International

Cooperation also deserves my deep gratitude for their support on the diplomatic and international aspects of this history. Thank you all for trusting me to tell this proud story.

In the course of researching and writing this book I spent hundreds of hours interviewing and living alongside UAE military personnel. In many cases, I gathered their stories while they were deployed on other battlefronts in Yemen, during my visits to the frontlines, and they kindly gave their evenings and down-time to retell the story of Aden from their perspectives. In addition to sharing their history with me, they kept me safe during my visits and I am eternally grateful to them for their hospitality and protection. I also want to recognize my friend and colleague Alex Almeida for his comradeship on those visits into Yemen and for his unstinting attention to detail as we watched the war unfold.

Special thanks go to the uncles of the book – Jaber L. of the UAE Ministry of Defence; Peter Jones of Profile Publishing; international man of mystery Rashid al Mizrouei; and Abu Iskander.

Last but definitely not least, I want to thank all my Yemeni friends in Aden and other parts of Yemen – those who survived and those who did not – for their support of the book. Yemeni journalist Salah al-Obeidi made an especially important contribution to Aden's history and to this book with his courageous battlefield photography.

There are too many UAE service-persons to thank individually, and security considerations prevent me from naming serving officers in any case, but I want to collectively thank all the people who shared their stories with me, which was often the first time they had talked to anyone about the war. Reliving the conflict seemed to help them process thoughts and feelings that had been buried since 2015 and I hope they keep talking about the war with each other and their families, to the extent security allows.

It is fitting that the last word goes to one of those exceptional young people, who reflected on his war experience as a 27-year-old UAE soldier, with no battle experience, by saying:

> After this operation, a real war, my mentality changed completely. I was brought up in this country, with good living standards and education, and then I was suddenly in a war zone, away from my friends and family, my kids. It's lonely and makes you appreciate life. I saw poverty and suffering in Yemen. It made me appreciate more the need to protect our home.

# PREFACE

*Zero Dark Thirty, 13 April 2015.*

*Aden's outer harbour.*

*The dark interior of the Chinook is packed with men and kit. The interior looks like a mess of padding and straps, metal struts and panels, but everything is exactly where it is supposed to be and everything is there for a reason.*

*The only sound that can be heard is the discordant high-pitched whining and thrumming, as every single thing in the chopper rattles and clatters with the vibration of the twin rotors overhead. After an hour in the Chinook, the soldiers don't hear the engine sound anymore – it is just white noise in an otherwise soundless environment.*

*Seven men stand alongside two Zodiacs, 15-foot-long inflatable boats that they are readying to push into the sea. Each boat is carefully packed with strapped-down equipment: bulging backpacks, AK-47s, ammunition, waterproofed night-vision devices and radios.*

*The men are young, muscular and dressed in grey-blue T-shirts and tan shorts, thin life preservers and swimming flippers hanging on their utility belts. They are trying to look casual but they're excited to finally be on their way after many false starts. They look like American or British special forces, but they're not – they are elite pathfinders of the UAE's Presidential Guard Special*

Operations Command. *They are veterans of dozens of missions in Afghanistan, the Balkans or Somalia.*

*A loadmaster in a baggy beige jumpsuit, bulbous helmet and night-vision gear is shuffling around the back ramp. He is tethered to the chopper by a long safety strap and he strenuously cranes his neck, looking to the left and right of the hovering helicopter, checking for anything below. Two door gunners are leaning out of their windows into the darkness, piercing the night with their night-vision googles. In the gap between their goggles and the bandanas covering their cheeks, each of their eyes is precisely spotlighted by an eerie grey-green light. They look like robots with coldly glowing eyes.*

*Silently, using a green chem-light, the chief signals 'GO', and the three men closest to the ramp begin roaring with exertion as they shunt the 400 pounds of dead weight over the edge. The Zodiac goes out engine-first, has to land the right way up, and the folded-up outboard engine cannot be damaged or the mission may be scrubbed. The sea is zipping by as the three men drop off the rear ramp to land close – but not too close – to the falling Zodiac.*

*The commander, Salem, watches his second team heft the other Zodiac off the fast-moving Chinook. The men walk off the ramp, dropping into the sea with their arms by their sides. No-one hears the WHAPP!! as the Zodiac smacks down into the water and the three wranglers go in after it.*

*No one knows this but Salem has never done a so-called 'helo-cast' insertion before, nor do they know that his old injury has returned on this of all days, and puffed his knee up like a football. But he could not miss this mission. Even after 20 years in the army, he is full of adrenalin. This mission is like a gift at the end of a military life. Not a Mickey Mouse mission: the best thing he could offer his country. All this lets him forget the danger that is right in front of him, lets him 'go to the land where the devils are', as he later puts it.*

*Salem steps off the ramp but will never remember falling or hitting the water. The sea is warm. By the time Salem regains the surface, the Chinook looks far away, a black moving shape in the distance. Whompwhompwhompwhompwhompwhomp. Silence.*

*The stars are very bright and clear. Feeling a little dazed, like he did after his first solo parachute jump, Salem looks around. He hears the sound of a motor starting. Good, someone's on the boat already. He swims towards the sound.*

*Sergeant Ahmed roughly pulls him up into the boat. Soon all three swimmers are on board and the other boat flicks a thumbs-up. Their four made it. Kneeling behind their own wet bergens – a British army term for backpack – men quietly insert curved magazines into AK-47s. Usually they would sport custom-rigged M4 carbines, but the AK was picked for the mission to allow the team to blend in with the Yemenis. Now they use them from behind the cover of their packs to scan the forward arc as the boats turn towards the land.*

*Salem scans the dark and forbidding coastline. Small lights shine from individual houses along the shore. Car headlights slowly crawl in the distance. To the right is the city of Aden and the dark outline of the extinct volcano at Crater, which towers over the city. Somewhere far to the left, too far away to worry about, there are tracer bullets arcing into the sky or bouncing off the ground at strange angles. Seconds later a staccato tapping sound echoes over the water.*

*Looking out to sea, Salem worries about the squat black shapes dotted along the horizon. They're tankers and cargo ships owned by the notorious Yemeni businessman Ahmed Issa, and any of these ships might have heard the helicopter and sent a report to the Houthis, the Iranian-backed militias besieging Aden city. Salem had heard a lot about the ease with which Yemenis sold information to the highest bidder, or sometimes to multiple sides at the same time. The team needed to get moving.*

The signaller checks the radio and hands the headset to Salem.

'Striptease, Striptease,' says Salem – the codeword that the mission will proceed, a private joke between commanders. Time to get underway. Hand signals send the two boats away at low power.

Salem takes a compass reading and searches for visual references all around as the GPS powers up. The tiny unpopulated shoal of rocks dead ahead – codename 'Hyde Park' – is the rendezvous with the resistance boat, but where are they? Salem calls the agent on his Thuraya phone.

'Don't worry. We're coming,' the agent says.

Salem is not reassured.

'Stop!! Stop!!' hisses Ahmed to the trooper on the outboard. The tension in his voice speaks of something unexpected and unwelcome. A bright flash of light lashes their faces. A spotlight. 'We're exposed,' thinks Salem, and his heart sinks.

Half-blinded after taking the full glare, Ahmed raises his AK-47 and levels it at the light, which shears left and right in the choppy waters, urgently searching for them. He means to shoot out the light.

'No!!' snaps Salem with a growl. 'Hold your fire!! Reverse!! Slowly ...'

In the split second since being blinded by the searchlight, Salem knows that they could never win a firefight in a couple of flimsy inflatables. The boats would sink. They would all be killed. Evasion is their only hope now.

This book preserves for history the battle of Aden in 2015, the true story of Yemeni Resistance fighters and elite forces from the United Arab Emirates (UAE) battling a ruthless and fascinating invader, the Iran-backed Houthi tribesmen of northern Yemen. The following chapters are an operational recounting of the liberation of Aden, related by the participants and meticulously fact checked.

The backdrop of the story is the romantic but mouldering port-city of Aden, built up by the Victorian British into one of the busiest ports in the world as late as the 1950s and then run into the ground by corruption, factionalism and war. The story will span the heights of the towering 700-foot volcanic cliffs of Crater to the quaintly British concrete 'flats' of Mualla, from the beach resorts of Gold Mohur to the old British Petroleum refinery of Little Aden, and from the dense alleys of the old tribal souk of Sheikh Uthman to the half-built urban sprawl and roundabouts of Dar Saad and Mansoura.

This is the history of Arabs drawing a line in the sand to stop Iran and her militias from gaining a beachhead on the Arabian Peninsula, where they were within striking distance of Islam's holiest sites, Makkah and Medina. They would also be positioned to cut off the Suez Canal and 20 per cent of world oil shipments. In the words of one special forces soldier, it is a story of Arab elite forces 'fighting a ghost from the mountain, next to the world's most important seaway'.

The story is also about a race against time: the desperate effort to liberate Aden before the Houthis could consolidate their hold through military victory or by exploiting well-intentioned ceasefires being negotiated by the international community. The heart of the tale is the frantic final weeks of the liberation that took place during the month of Ramadan in 2015, when UAE commanders were told they had 25 days to take Aden.

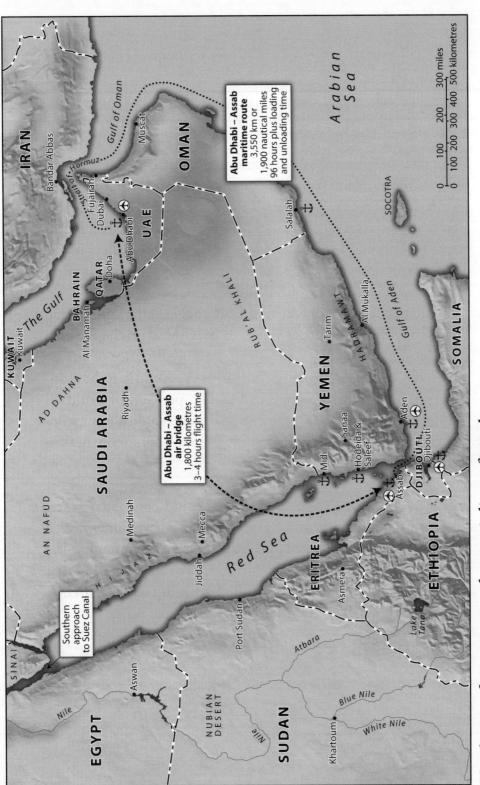

**Abu Dhabi – Assab maritime route**
3,550 km or 1,900 nautical miles 96 hours plus loading and unloading time

**Abu Dhabi – Assab air bridge**
1,800 kilometres 3–4 hours flight time

Southern approach to Suez Canal

IRAN

Bandar Abbas

Strait of Hormuz

Gulf of Oman

Muscat

OMAN

UAE

Fujairah

Dubai

Abu Dhabi

QATAR

Doha

BAHRAIN

Al Manamah

KUWAIT

Kuwait

The Gulf

AD DAHNA

Riyadh

SAUDI ARABIA

AN NAFUD

Medinah

Mecca

H I J A Z

Jiddah

Red Sea

RUB' AL KHALI

YEMEN

Tarim

HADRAMAWT

Al Mukalla

Sanaa

Midi

Hodeida & Saleef

Salalah

Arabian Sea

SOCOTRA

Gulf of Aden

Aden

Assab

DJIBOUTI

Djibouti

SOMALIA

ERITREA

Asmera

ETHIOPIA

Lake Tana

Blue Nile

White Nile

Atbara

SUDAN

Khartoum

Port Sudan

NUBIAN DESERT

Nile

Aswan

EGYPT

SINAI

0   100   200   300 miles
0   100  200  300  400  500 kilometres

**The theatre of operations and strategic lines of supply**

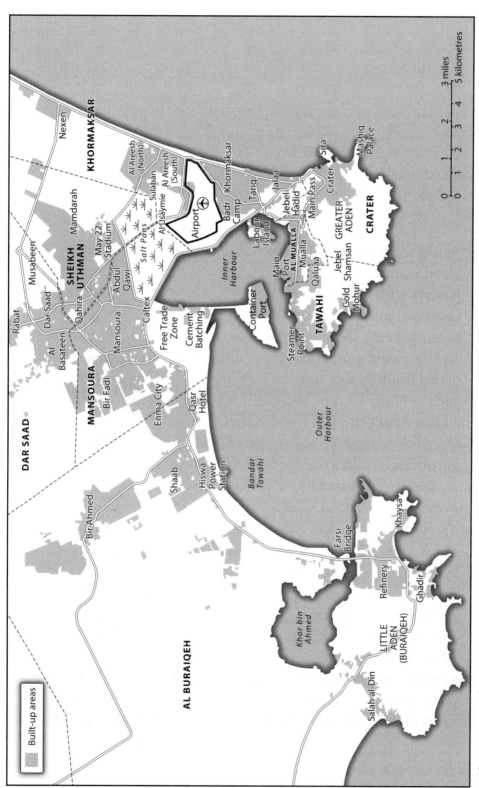

Aden city and its environs

# I

# WAR COMES TO ADEN

Across the world, if it is known at all, Yemen is a dimly under-stood country. It's regarded as a place of danger and crushing poverty with more guns than people, a land of curved daggers (*jambiya*) in the belt and the addictive, chewable leaf *qat* in a bulging cheek. Those who like geography will be able to place it on a map: the southernmost tip of the Arabian Peninsula, bor-dering Saudi Arabia and Oman, with coastlines on the Red Sea and the Gulf of Aden. Those with a good recall of world events will inevitably think of war and terrorism, most prominently Al Qaeda's bombing of the destroyer USS *Cole* in Aden's harbour in 2000, which killed 17 American sailors.

It wasn't always this way. People from outside the Arab world have been fascinated by Yemen since Roman times, when *Arabia Felix* (blessed Arabia) first became known to Europe-ans as an exotic land of luxuries and aromatic spices. Visited by great seafaring empires – Chinese, Indian, Portuguese and British – Yemeni ports such as Aden and Mokha became known worldwide as centres of trade in frankincense, myrrh, coffee and cinnamon. The opening of the Suez Canal, in 1869, placed Yemen's ports on the newest global trade highway, resulting in a century of growth until Aden was among the world's busiest ports, perhaps even surpassing New York as late as the 1950s.

While Westerners only knew the coastal fringes of Yemen,

Arabs were intimately connected to the interior of al-Yaman (the south, meaning southern Arabia) since long before recorded history. Indeed, the tribes of Arabia sprang from Yemen and grand Arabian empires existed in Yemen over 2,000 years ago. The Sabeans were the greatest, known in the Roman and European worlds as the home of the famed Queen of Sheba. The Marib Dam is perhaps the most famous and oldest archaeological wonder in the Arab world, created around 2,300 years before the birth of the Prophet Muhammad. The Prophet himself was fond of the Yemenites, saying of them: 'They have the kindest and gentlest hearts of all. Faith is Yemeni, wisdom is Yemeni.'

Yet Yemenis also held themselves apart from the Arab world, keeping back something unique about themselves. The interior of Yemen remained an obscure backwater even as the other parts of the Arab world became known. The Yemenis were distinct from those Arabs from al-Najd (the 'uplands') and al-Sham (the north). They held tightly to linguistic, cultural and architectural holdovers from the pre-Islamic past, and their writers for the last thousand years have dwelt on the melancholy of their faded glory. Yemenis are famously proud, independent, hospitable and individualistic.

Yemenis – and particularly the tribes of the interior – are also famed as fighters. Yemenis served proudly in the vanguard of the Islamic Conquest of the Arab world in the seventh century of the Christian calendar, and they have rarely known peace. As one Arab diplomat told the author: 'the "forever war" is the normal state of affairs in Yemen. There are only short truces in the fighting that never stops.' If tribes are not warring internally or with each other, it was only because they were fighting external occupiers – Turks, Egyptians and Britons. The two post-colonial states in Yemen – the northern Yemen Arab Republic and the southern People's Democratic Republic of Yemen – unified in

1990 but were soon internally warring again in a bloody two-month civil war in 1994. Six internal wars were fought between the post-civil-war Yemeni state and the Houthi tribes in northern Yemen from 2004–2010. When the Yemeni government collapsed in 2011, during the chaos of the Arab Spring, it set the stage for a new and devastating war four years later. The man who lost his power in the Arab Spring – and also the architect of the new war in 2015 – was an inveterate schemer called Ali Abdullah Saleh.

## Dancing on the Heads of Snakes

From 1978–2011, President Ali Abdullah Saleh presided over first northern Yemen, until 1990, and then over the reunified north and south of the country after 1994. Ali Abdullah was said to be able to 'dance on the heads of snakes', meaning that he was uniquely capable of staying one step ahead of the various factions vying for control of different parts of Yemen. These included followers of the Muslim Brotherhood (called Al-Islah in Yemen), Salafist tribesmen spread across Yemen, and southerners still smarting from their defeat and humiliation in the 1994 civil war. But, above all, Saleh had to stay on top of deadly rivals from inside his own Hashid tribal confederation and within his own political party, the General People's Congress (GPC).

Ali Abdullah could only survive in this byzantine game of thrones because he had a foot in many camps. He was a prominent member of the Afaash clan of the Sanhan tribe of the dominant Hashidi tribal confederation. The Sanhan tribe solidified its grip on northern Yemen through a stable intra-tribal compact known as 'the covenant' (Al Ahd), which was agreed in 1978. According to a classified US government diplomatic cable exposed by WikiLeaks, the 'covenant' involved a written agreement that the Hashid confederation writ large would 'stand together under Saleh's leadership' until it was the turn of (then) Brigadier General Ali Mohsen al-Qadhi al-Ahmar (commander of Yemen's armoured forces and a more senior tribal figure from the rival Qadhi clan of the Sanhan tribe).

Of course, Ali Abdullah Saleh made sure this handover never occurred, instead seeding the military, and especially his powerful Republican Guard, with relatives from his own Afaash clan. In 1999, Saleh began to prepare a constitutional change that would allow him to extend his term as president, and he was clearly grooming his son, the head of the Republican Guard Ahmed Ali, to take over from him after his death. While Ali Mohsen fought six gruelling wars against the northern Houthis and grew closer to the Muslim Brotherhood, Ali Abdullah plotted against and undermined Ali Mohsen and his Qadhi clan-dominated 1st Armoured Division. Indeed, when Brigadier General Mohammed Ismail al-Qadhi, one of Ali Mohsen's relatives and a key subordinate, clashed with Saleh over control of an important base, the general and his staff died shortly after in a mysterious 1999 helicopter crash and Saleh's forces smoothly took over the base.

Yet for all his successes, by the time the Arab Spring occurred in 2011, Saleh had perilously narrowed his power base to his Afaash clan and its close confederates. The pendulum swung against him as young protestors sought to bring down Saleh, the only president they had known in their lifetime. Ali Mohsen and his loyalists in the military joined with resentful Hashid confederation tribes and urban protestors to force Saleh's removal. Old grudges were swiftly revisited: in February 2010, Ali Mohsen was nearly killed in a Saudi Arabian airstrike that, it is strongly believed, was deliberately mis-targeted on Ali Mohsen's coordinates by a treacherous Ali Abdullah. On 3 June 2011,

Saleh received his repayment, being badly wounded in a mysterious missile strike on his palace, where he was penned in by Ali Mohsen's forces. After the strike, Ali Mohsen's troops protected and supported the new acting president, Vice President Abd-Rabo Mansour al-Hadi, also a former general.

For the first time in 34 years, Ali Abdullah found himself on the outside of the corridors of power, but he was not remotely done with 'dancing on the heads of snakes'. Instead, he found new snakes. Like a lot of restless intriguers, he would prove dangerous until the moment he died. As the new UN-recognised interim government under Hadi sought (in 2012–2014) to remove Saleh loyalists from the military, Ali Abdullah ordered his men to lie low and stockpile heavy weaponry outside the view of the state, while Saleh looked for some new friends. He found them in the unlikeliest – yet most logical – of places: the enemies of the new UN-backed Hadi government and of Ali Mohsen, namely the Houthi rebels, tribes who had fought the government in the six wars from 2004–2010. An alliance between the Houthis and Saleh was not as unthinkable as it seemed. Though Ali Abdullah Saleh had presided over the country during the six anti-Houthi wars, the Houthis knew that the real drivers of those wars were Ali Mohsen and his coterie of Al Islah-linked generals. Like the Houthis, Saleh was a northerner. By birth at least (if not by practice) he was also a Zaydi, the Houthi's branch of Islam. Behind closed doors, the alliance was struck that would spark Yemen's most devastating war.

# II

# STRANGE BEDFELLOWS: THE HOUTHIS AND SALEH

The Houthis are an Arab clan whose base is in the Marran Mountains, a range that separates the northern Yemeni province of Saada from the south-western fringes of Saudi Arabia. Members of the Houthi clan consider themselves to be *sadah* (descendants of the Prophet) and their modern patriarch was a respected religious scholar, Badr al-Din al-Houthi, an influential preacher until his death in 2010. The Houthi's Zaydi sect of Islam venerates Ali as the legitimate heir to the Prophet, and they are doctrinally closest to Fiver Shia Muslims (as opposed to the more prevalent Twelver Shiism dominant in Iran, Iraq and Lebanon). The Houthis rose to prominence in the aftermath of the fall of the Zaydi imamate (which ruled northern Yemen for almost a millennia, from 897–1962 AD (or 284–1384 AH in the Muslim calendar). Their growth came from a thirst to return the Zaydis to their former prominence.

By the 1980s, the political decline of Zaydism and the Houthi *sadah* was answered with a new call for Zaydi revival, championed most actively by Badr al-Din al-Houthi and taken up by his prominent sons Hussein, Yahya, Mohammed and Abdulmalik. In the 1990s, Badr al-Din al-Houthi and his sons built a powerful, cross-cutting social network around the Zaydi revivalist movement that included intermarriage with tribal and *sadah* families. Badr al-Din built up the 'Believing Youth' (Muntada al-Shahabal-Mumin) summer camps and social pro-grammes, and a political party.

The obvious similarities between the growing Houthi movement and Lebanese Hezbollah were not coincidental: the Houthis worked very closely with Hezbollah when developing both the structure of their organisation (called Ansar Allah, Partisans of God) and their television station, Al-Masirah, 'The Journey', which was based in Lebanese Hezbollah's stronghold of Dhahiya in Beirut. After the collapse of Saleh's government in the 2011 Arab Spring, the Houthis began to rapidly fill the power vacuum in northern Yemen, and an early priority had been to pressure the intelligence services into releasing all the Lebanese citizens who had been held since 2010 under suspi-cion of conducting Hezbollah activities. Hezbollah advised the Houthis how to expand, and the Houthis helped Hezbollah in return, one hand washing the other.

The Houthis also drew on an increasingly close relationship with Iran and her Islamic Revolutionary Guard Corps Quds Force (IRGC-QF), the overseas paramilitary arm of the Islamic Revolution. Iran's interest in Yemen seems to have been piqued when Saudi Arabia intervened in the sixth anti-Houthi war in late 2009, at which time an Iranian intelligence-gathering ship took up station in the Red Sea near Eritrea's Dahlak Islands, on the same latitude as the Saudi-Yemeni border and the Yemeni port of Midi. Arms shipments between Iran and the Houthis began in October 2009 and accelerated after November 2011, when the Yemeni government lost Midi port to the Houthis in the chaos after the Arab Spring.

There is no telling how many shipments of arms and person-nel entered Yemen via this Houthi-friendly port, but the January 2013 interception of the Jihan-1 dhow suggests a powerful post-2011 effort by Iran to arm Ansar Allah in the same manner that Iran armed Lebanese Hezbollah. Intercepted off Yemen's coast by the destroyer USS *Farragut*, the Jihan-1 carried exactly the same kinds of Iranian-provided arms that Israel had previously intercepted off the coasts of Lebanon, such as Iranian-made rockets, armour-piercing roadside bombs called Explosively Formed Penetrators (EFPs), Iranian copies of Russian Kornet anti-armour missiles, Iranian AM-50 sniper rifles, Iranian-made C4 explosives, and anti-shipping missile variants only operated by Iran and Lebanese Hezbollah.

Revolutionary Guard and Lebanese Hezbollah advisors sharpened the post-Arab Spring ambitions of the Houthis, convincing them that the Zaydi revival could restore the lost power of the Imamate, which had ruled Yemen for all but 52 of the previous 1,207 years. Ambitious plans were laid for the defeat of Ali Mohsen, the takeover of the Yemeni capital Sanaa and the ousting of the UN-backed President Abd-Rabo Mansour al-Hadi. Hezbollah mentored the group on the mechanics of the takeover. Mareike Brandt, the respected historian of Yemen, noted in her 2013 book *Tribes and Politics in Yemen: A History of the Houthi Conflict* that 'parallels in the Hezbollah takeover of West Beirut in 2008 and the Houthi grab of power in 2014 also suggest some exchange on military strategy'. Brandt reflected on the virtuoso political-military moves undertaken by the Houthis, remarking: 'The Houthi rebellion works through carefully developed plans and brilliant moves on the chessboard. They rely on alliances, both secret and openly visible.'

## Ali Abdullah Saleh and the Houthis

One such alliance was with the ousted Ali Abdullah Saleh and his loyalists from the Republican Guard, though it was hardly a meeting of minds – just a way for Saleh to avenge himself on his enemies. To ensure good behaviour, the Houthis fell back on the age-old tribal tactic of the imamate: taking hostages from the families of senior officers, even including Saleh's closest relatives, for instance, the wife and children of his nephew Tariq Saleh, who remain under Houthi control at the time of writing. As Houthi politburo member Mohammed al Bukhaiti told Reuters after Ali Abdullah's conspiracy became public, 'He's not doing it out of love for us, but fear.'

Once the Houthis and Ali Abdullah Saleh had committed to working together, their cooperation was smooth and ruthlessly effective. On 9 July 2014, Saleh loyalists literally opened the gates of the headquarters of 310 Armoured Brigade of Ali Mohsen's 1st Armoured Division in Amran (in northern Yemen), allowing the Houthis to flood in and kill the unit commander, Brigadier General Hamid al Qushaibi, a friend of Ali Mohsen's. In August and September, the Houthis began to infiltrate military units into Sanaa, eventually undertaking an efficient coup on 21 September, corralling political and military leaders inside their palaces and barracks. President Hadi and his Minister of Defence Major General Mahmoud al Subaihi were placed under house arrest, and the Yemeni military was subordinated to a new central committee of Houthis and Saleh generals. Hadi's presidential guard – the remnants of Saleh's Republican Guard – stayed in their barracks and did not intervene. All resisting locations were shelled by the Houthis, including the Al-Islah headquarters and the Iman University. Even the state television studios were shelled, with the terrified staff reporting the attack live on screen from their shaking building.

Thanks to Ali Abdullah Saleh's backroom machinations with his former military subordinates, the Houthi-led coup in September 2014 placed large parts of the Yemeni military under

Houthi control. Fuelled by military modernisation, oil exports and Soviet advisors, the Yemeni military had grown substantially larger under Saleh, from the token force of 3,000 troops in the early 1970s to around 130,000 personnel by 2012, with perhaps half this number actually serving on a regular basis due to widespread corruption. New forces such as the Counter-Terrorism Unit (CTU) of the Ministry of Interior's Central Security Forces were also built with post-9/11 American counter-terrorism aid, and they were quickly placed under Afassh clan Saleh loyalists.

All of this now defaulted back to Ali Abdullah. There was simply too little time between Saleh's downfall in 2012 and the coup of September 2014 to undo decades of infiltration and properly purge Saleh's people from key military units. The leadership of the United Yemeni Air Force had been painstakingly hand-picked by Saleh and put under his half-brother Mohammed Saleh Abdullah's command for over a decade. Now, the air force, with its ramshackle collection of MiG-29 fighters and Su-22 and F-5E fighter-bombers plus Russian-built helicopters, quickly sided with Saleh. In November 2014, Saleh loyalists chanted at their Hadi-appointed commanders to 'leave, leave, leave!' Saleh's chosen men were back in charge of the elite CTU and the US-trained Hard Missions Unit of the Yemeni Special Operations Forces. The US government was preparing contingency plans to shut down the US embassy in Sanaa and the counter-terrorism base at Al-Anad, north of Aden, recognising that the changes occurring daily were not just turning back the clock to the Saleh era but were increasingly a handover of Yemen's most powerful weapons to the Iran-backed Houthis.

## The Republican Guard–Houthi Hybrid

Despite mutual distrust between leaders, the Houthi partnership with Saleh's military networks was not as uncomfortable for both sides as one might imagine. Since Saleh's fall from power, the air force had refused Hadi's occasional orders to bomb Houthi areas. The Republican Guard, Saleh's praetorian force, modelled on Saddam Hussein's own guard divisions, had been kept largely separate from the anti-Houthi war. Indeed, strong rumours even suggested that Saleh had quietly used the guard to resupply the Houthis as they fought Saleh's rival, Ali Mohsen – a version of the age-old 'the enemy of my enemy is my friend'. According to the excellent investigative research by American writer Lucas Winter, leaked Yemeni government documents show that the Republican Guard was rapidly turned into a 'Republican Guard–Houthi hybrid' force in late 2014 through the installation of hundreds of veteran Houthi fighters at all levels of the guard. The Republican Guard – a reinforced armoured division with under-command heli-borne commando units – came under the joint command of Saleh loyalist Major General Ali al-Jaifi and Abdulkhaliq al-Houthi, the brother of the Houthi spiritual and political leader Abdulmalik, and arguably the best Houthi battlefield commander.

As important to Yemen's neighbours, the Houthis had also gained control of the country's most advanced strategic weapons. These included around 18 Soviet-built SS-1B Scud missiles and around 45 North Korean Hwasong-6 missiles, each capable of lobbing more than 800 kg of high explosives hundreds of kilometres into Saudi Arabia. Yemen also had around 24 newer Soviet-built short-range ballistic missiles known as SS-21 Scarabs or (in Russia) Tochkas, which could throw a far larger warhead (2,000 kg) up to 70 km away with great accuracy – enough, for instance, to devastate oil-loading facilities, power and desalination stations, or civilian airports in the southern Saudi cities of Jazan or Najran. The Houthis also gained control of hundreds of surface-to-air missiles, anti-shipping missiles and mines capable of closing the Red Sea to international shipping, and also an air force that still operated over 50 modern combat aircraft. Indeed, controlling Yemen's Red Sea ports, the Houthis became the proud recipients of new Russian-overhauled Sukhoi jet fighter-bombers as soon as they were shipped back to Yemen via Hodeidah port in late 2014.

The strategic missiles were probably the last straw, setting Saudi Arabia on the road to military intervention. A reported 133 Saudis had died in the intense fighting on the Saudi-Yemeni border in 2010, in which the Saudi military was an active combatant against the Houthis for the first time. In the intervening years until 2014, Saudi Arabia had built up its military capabilities facing Yemen in order to avenge the blow. Now the Houthis were positioned to rain Scuds down on the kingdom, as Saddam Hussein had done in 1991. In October 2014, Riyadh received intelligence from US agencies that the Houthis were moving Scuds from their cave shelters in Sanaa up towards the Saudi border. War was only narrowly averted in the month after the Houthis took Sanaa, with Riyadh warning its key allies to prepare for conflict but recognising that the time was not right, and that the coalition had not been built or prepared for war.

## Striking a Death Blow Against Hadi

The Houthis were also readying themselves for the next stage of the conflict. Since the days of Imam Yahya in the first half of the twentieth century, the northern *sadah* had their eye on reincorporating southern and eastern Yemen, if and when the British departed. Now, in 2015, important parts of Yemen were still outside their control. In the east, the city of Marib and its oil and gas resources were still guarded by five Yemeni army brigades loyal to Ali Mohsen, who was now based in Marib. The Houthis controlled the Red Sea oil export terminals at Al Saleef but not the oilfields at the other end of the east–west export pipeline in Marib. Without Marib, the new Houthi statelet would be without the oil money needed to rule. Nor did the Houthis control all of Yemen's Red Sea coast. Three Yemeni army and coastal defence brigades held the Bab el-Mandeb, a critical maritime choke point that commanded all Red Sea traffic moving north or south from Suez. And nor did the Houthis rule the populous southern cities of Ibb, Taizz and Aden. Parts of seven Yemeni army brigades remained outside of Houthi control in southern Yemen, though most of them were engaged in a desperate struggle to prevent Al Qaeda in the Arabian Peninsula (AQAP) from exploiting the chaos to take over small cities like Zinjibar and Jaar. The common feature in all these areas was the surreptitious influence of Ali Abdullah Saleh, whose military networks still marbled every major unit with potential traitors. With Saleh's help, the Houthis calculated, they could secure more defections and collapse more army units. All that was needed was a final push.

Preparations began at the end of 2014 for the long-range offensives that would be required in 2015 to finish off the scattered remnants of the UN-backed Hadi government – which styled itself the 'legitimacy government'. A delegation of Houthi and Saleh-loyalist officers visited Iran at the start of 2015, headed by two of the most revered Houthi military commanders, Yahya Abdullah Al Razzami and Yusuf al-Madani. In three days of meetings, they visited the Islamic Revolutionary Guard Corps (IRGC), the Basij (a popular mobilisation militia), and the Iranian Ministry of Defence. The Iranian officers spoke proudly of four Arab capitals now under the control of the Islamic Revolution: Beirut, Baghdad, Damascus and Sanaa. Offers of assistance were made to support future offensive operations against Hadi forces, including spare parts for key offensive weapons such as the Republican Guard's T-72 tanks. An IRGC logistics expert was detailed to visit Yemen and assess the fuel and ammunition needs of the Houthi–Saleh forces. If successful in controlling all of Yemen, the Iranian hosts told the Houthi–Saleh delegation that they could expect to receive the mind-boggling sum of 3–5 billion dollars' worth of aid over five years.

Back in northern Yemen, Houthi advisors and Republican Guard soldiers were being melded together into what Lucas Winter characterised as a 'hybrid Houthi-Republican Guard force ... composed of ideologically motivated irregular fighters working alongside operators of heavy weaponry and professionally trained commanders.' Helicopter commando units and special forces from the Republican Guard were mixed with fighters from elite Houthi formations known as the Al Hussein 'rapid intervention units' and Abdulkhaliq al-Houthi's Ashura Battalion. Most of the forces were formerly Saleh's men, but their primary loyalty quickly began to shift when subjected to the indoctrination provided by Houthi instructors and when Houthi dominance over the Saleh officer corps was demonstrated on a daily basis. As would be shown later when Houthi–Saleh prisoners were questioned, the troops sent to overrun government-controlled areas in the south were told they were being sent to fight Al Qaeda.

IRGC and Lebanese Hezbollah advisors helped plan the swift overrun of southern and eastern Yemen in the same way they had advised the Houthis how to seize Red Sea ports and the capital, Sanaa. A powerful Iranian resupply effort was initiated in February 2015 when Tehran announced the commencement of an air bridge between Iran and Sanaa. A twice-daily shuttle service was launched by Mahan Air, a government-controlled airline used by the IRGC Quds Force to ferry trainers and equipment to Lebanon and Syria. Two daily return flights brought in Lebanese Hezbollah and Iranian trainers (and a small number of Iranian pilots) and brought out and back around 300 Yemenis who visited Iran for training. Military cargoes also arrived by air and sea. One Iranian cargo ship unloaded 180 tonnes of military equipment and ammunition at Al Saleef under conditions of tight security. Iranian fuel tankers also docked at another port, Hodeida, giving the Houthis (who lacked a refinery) on-hand fuel reserves for long-range vehicle movements.

# III

# OPENING SHOTS

As final preparations were underway, the Houthis' hand was forced by the escape from house arrest of President Hadi. In late February, Hadi was spirited away from Sanaa to Aden, followed in early March by his defence minister, Major General Mahmoud al-Subaihi. When safely in Aden, Hadi retracted his 21 September 2014 letter of resignation, which he had been forced to sign. Hadi declared the Houthi coup illegal and designated Aden as the temporary capital of Yemen. Controlling oil and gas resources in Marib, Shabwa and Hadramaut, plus the ports of Aden and Mukalla, Hadi's next move would likely be to transfer the Central Bank of Yemen's operations to its branch in Aden. The Houthi-controlled north would be a country without an income. US Ambassador to Yemen Matt Tueller met Hadi in the Mashiq Presidential Palace in Aden, and all the Gulf States (barring Oman) agreed to transfer their embassies to Aden. These Arab monarchies were laying down a red line. Saudi Arabia warned the Houthi-led forces not to attack the government's new seat in southern Yemen, the last toehold for anti-Houthi forces.

**The Plan to Seize the South**

Ali Abdullah Saleh had different ideas and was preparing to

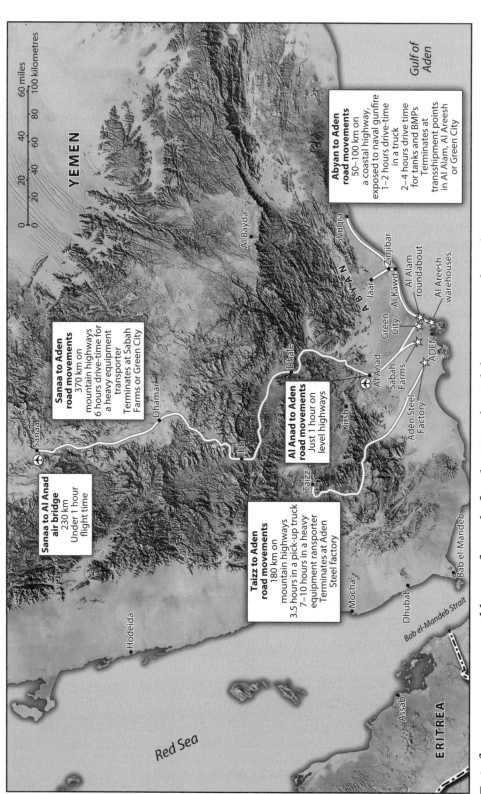

**Sanaa to Al Anad air bridge**
230 km
Under 1 hour flight time

**Sanaa to Aden road movements**
370 km on mountain highways
6 hours drive-time for a heavy equipment transporter
Terminates at Sabah Farms or Green City

**Al Anad to Aden road movements**
Just 1 hour on level highways

**Taizz to Aden road movements**
180 km on mountain highways
3.5 hours in a pick-up truck
7–10 hours in a heavy equipment transporter
Terminates at Aden Steel factory

**Abyan to Aden road movements**
50–100 km on a coastal highway, exposed to naval gunfire
1–2 hours drive-time in a truck
2–4 hours drive time for tanks and BMPs
Terminates at transshipment points in Al Alam, Al Areesh or Green City

YEMEN

*Gulf of Aden*

*Red Sea*

ERITREA

Hodeida

Sanaa

Dhamar

Al Bayda

Ibb

Dhale

Kirsh

Taizz

Al Anad

Sabah Farms

Aden Steel Factory

ADEN

Green City

Al Kawd

Jaar

Zinjibar

Al Alam roundabout

Al Areesh warehouses

Shuqra

A B Y A N

Mocha

Dhubab

Bab el-Mandeb

*Bab el-Mandeb Strait*

Assab

60 miles
100 kilometres

0    20    40    60    80

0    20    40    60

Reinforcement routes and lines of supply for the Houthi-Saleh invasion of southern Yemen hand Aden to the Houthis on a silver platter. Saleh loyalists in various military units in Aden, Abyan, Taizz and Bab el-Mandeb were approached in advance of the southwards drive of the Houthi–Republican Guard vehicle columns. The plan was broadly to encourage military units to mutiny in favour of the Houthis and to offer no resistance to their next phase of expansion. Saleh publicly boasted in early March that he would 'drive Hadi into the sea'.

Yet one of the plan's key elements was placed in jeopardy when the newly arrived President Hadi began to purge pro-Saleh officers from command of the Central Security Forces (CSF) in Aden on 18 March. Hadi had many faults but failing to protect his own powerbase was not one of them. As soon as he had arrived in Aden, he began looking for potential rivals and Houthi sympathisers. The CSF was known to be a pro-Saleh force and its northerner commander Colonel Abdul Hafez al Saqqaf had, for many weeks, been receiving reinforcements from the CSF bases in northern Yemen. Hadi decided to nip this potential fifth column in the bud.

Hadi's survival instincts were spot-on. Al Saqqaf had indeed been secretly ordered by Saleh to seize the Aden International Airport, into which Houthi–Saleh forces would be flown from Sanaa. The new faces showing up at his CSF base, Camp Sulaban, were Saleh and Houthi infiltrators sent to the south to prepare the attack. They were perfectly positioned for a strike on the airport, located just 1 km north of the runway.

When dismissed by Hadi's presidential order on 18 March, al Saqqaf refused to step down and, instead, accelerated his plans to move against the airport. The forces rallied at Camp Sulaban, which had once been the old British base known as Radfan Camp. With hasty coordination, an attempted airstrike was launched by one of Ali Abdullah Saleh's Su-22M fighter-bombers from Al Daylami airbase in Sanaa. The strike targeted Hadi's presumed location in Al Mashiq Palace at dusk on 18 March, but Hadi – ever slippery – was not where the putschists expected him to be. In the early hours of 19 March al Saqqaf led his blue-camouflaged CSF troops to the airport in an improvised attack that quickly unravelled.

As dawn broke, fighting began on the eastern end of the tarmac and around the Fateh (Victory) base at the northern side of the airport, the old Champion Lines built by the British Royal Air Force. Al Saqqaf's men tried to rush the air traffic control tower but three of them were gunned down by alert sentries. Using a ZSU-23 anti-aircraft cannon on a flatbed truck, al Saqqaf began a bombardment of the airport that killed four civilians and wounded 14 others. Next, al Saqqaf's men began firing B-10 recoilless rifles, Katyusha rockets and heavy machine-guns (known as Dushkas). Hadi's presidential aircraft, an ageing Boeing 747, was damaged in the crossfire and would never fly again. A Yemenia flight to Cairo had boarded its 96 passengers but was unable to take off, so the terrified crew and passengers used the plane's emergency slides to exit and ran wildly towards the terminal.

Hadi's Minister of Defence, Mahmoud al Subaihi, and the president's brother, Nasser Mansour Hadi, mustered a counter-attacking force led by their bodyguard units that overpowered al Saqqaf's troopers by sheer weight of small arms fire. Thousands of bright shining brass shell casings littered the airport's apron as the sun rose out of the sea to the east of the runway. Al Subaihi pushed the CSF back into their camp and then bombarded Camp Sulaban with mortar and Rocket-Propelled Grenade (RPG) fire until dusk. Not for the last time in the Aden campaign, the battlefield quieted in the late afternoon as soldiers settled down to chew *qat* and talk through the events of the day. And not for the last time, the result of a skirmish would be determined by the cowardice of a commander, with al Saqqaf slipping away during the early hours of 20 March to drive northwards towards other Saleh loyalists, leaving his men behind. On his way to surrender to the governor of Lahj province, 30 km to the north, al Saqqaf's convoy was shot at when it ran a checkpoint. One vehicle in the convoy rolled at high speed, killing its four occupants, but al Saqqaf's bullet-riddled vehicle escaped, albeit with a dead bodyguard seated alongside the fleeing commander.

## Al Anad: Stepping Stone to Aden

This setback did not stop the coming offensive. On 21 March, the Houthi Revolutionary Command Committee declared a 'state of general mobilisation' against 'terrorist forces' in southern and eastern Yemen. The wheels of the plan turned smoothly. Mainly Houthi-manned columns struck eastwards towards Marib, where Saleh knew he would find no allies among Ali Mohsen's forces. Pro-Saleh commanders in the major cities of Ibb, Taizz, Bab el-Mandeb, Aden and Abyan were warned to be ready to link up with Houthi–Republican Guard forces driving southwards. In the offensive against Hadi's seat of government-in-exile in Aden, the initial key objective would be Al Anad airbase, 50 km north of Aden, where the attackers hoped to find the tanks and heavy weapons needed to seize the southern port city.

For decades, the Saleh regime had been adept at rapidly switching forces from the north of Yemen to Aden whenever southerners looked likely to revolt or secede, helicoptering elite forces to Aden and Al Anad to hold ground until convoys of tanks arrived on wheeled heavy equipment transporters. The same methods would be tried again in 2015. Having lost access to Aden airport, the coven of Saleh, Houthi and Iranian planners recognised that Al Anad had become doubly important to the plan to seize Aden. Al Anad had been expanded in the mid-1970s by the old Soviet-backed People's Democratic Republic of Yemen (PDRY) – the pre-unification south – in order to accommodate Russian Tu-95 Bear-D bombers. The Cold War mission of the Bears was to hunt US aircraft carrier battle groups with nuclear-armed cruise missiles, and to shadow the British-leased base at Diego Garcia archipelago in the Indian Ocean. The huge Bear bombers needed every metre of the huge 2,900-metre runway at Al Anad to get airborne in Yemen's thick superheated air.

By March 2015, a different superpower was resident in Al Anad, which was the forward base for a hundred-person counter-terrorism task force of the US Joint Special Operations Command (JSOC) and the Central Intelligence Agency's MQ-9 Reaper armed drones. Yemen always seemed on the edge of boiling over to the Americans, but Al Anad had got even weirder since the Arab Spring in 2011. Some Saleh-loyalist air force and special forces units at Al Anad had simply refused to demobilise or to leave since Saleh's fall in 2011. Unsettling signs of an impending mutiny increased after the Houthis took Sanaa in February 2015, and Houthi propaganda channels seemed to have insider access to video footage from air force units based at Al Anad. The United States prepared to depart, with the customary shredding and burning of classified documents.

On 21 March, just hours after the Houthi 'state of general mobilisation', part of the garrison at Al Anad mutinied in favour of Saleh. As scattered fighting broke out across the airbase, the US special forces and drone units undertook an emergency evacuation, effectively shutting down the main US base in the 'war on terror' in Yemen. US helicopters and light aircraft clattered away into the distance, headed for other US sites in Djibouti, where their terrorist-hunting mission would refocus on Somalia now that southern Yemen had become a fully-fledged war zone. Saleh-loyalist helicopter crews at Al Anad sent their Mi-17 helicopters northwards to begin a shuttle service between the Houthi areas and Al Anad. On the roads, advance parties of Abdulkhaliq al Houthi's Ashura battalions had been driving south from the Houthi-held territory since the early hours, packed together in the flatbeds of Hiluxes. These veteran troops started the day wrapped tightly in their scarves in the chilly pre-dawn ride to the south, and would be warmed by the rising sun by the time they were halfway to Al Anad. The race to control the stepping stone to Aden was in full swing.

Saleh had one more delicious slice of revenge in store for Hadi: he made good on his promise to drive the UN-backed president into the sea. After failing to kill Hadi in the 19 March 2015 airstrike on the Al Mashiq Palace, Saleh's air force did not stop trying. Further Su-22 fighter-bomber sorties launched from Sanaa struck locations where Hadi was believed to be present; three times on 20 March and four times on 21 March. Though decades old, Saleh's Sukhoi fighter-bombers were sturdy war beasts. With analogue dials and heavy on the stick, with no fancy fly-by-wire controls, the Su-22 was hardly cutting-edge, but it could heft a heavy load of rocket pods, bombs and cannons. Seventeen Sukhoi sorties dumped their loads on known leadership locations in Aden.

The strikes were getting closer each time, suggesting that traitors close to Hadi were leaking his position as he moved from place to place. On 23 March, Hadi was evacuated by sea by his brother Nasser Mansour and UAE special forces from the Aden consulate guard force, a chaotic scene where a gaggle of white armoured SUVs were crammed onto a tiny pier at the Sira yacht club. Hadi was unceremoniously bundled onto a motor-launch and sent off to Mukalla, and from there to Oman, and finally to Riyadh. The Al Mashiq Palace was thoroughly looted before Hadi even made landfall at his first friendly port. Generators, gold-painted furniture and even window frames were all loaded onto pick-up trucks (*chassis* in the Yemeni parlance) by opportunistic citizens. But most of the men of Aden had other priorities, namely preparing the defence of their city.

# IV

# THE SOUTH RESISTS

There is a reason that the Houthi–Saleh offensive suffered its first setback in Aden, and why Saleh found Aden's southern soldiers less receptive than many northerners. For generations, Aden had been the capital of Yemen's south, and the heart of resistance against occupation by outsiders. For hundreds of years, the Adenese looked to the sea for prosperity and only looked backwards, over their shoulders at the interior, with fear. Not much good came from the north. And the southerners could be fierce fighters when they wished.

It was no surprise in the late 1950s when the British Empire had a hard time suppressing tough tribal militias in Radfan, Lahj, to the north of Aden city, but the city folk proved to be even more trouble. In the 1960s, two Aden-based insurgent groups, the National Liberation Front (NLF) and the Front for the Liberation of South Yemen (FLOSY), grew out of local trade unions and anti-colonial Arab nationalist circles. These groups saw the British out, with the last Royal Marines leaving on 30 November 1967. Then, decades later, the PDRY fought a brief but bloody six-week war against Saleh's military in 1994 to try (unsuccessfully) to reverse the 1990s unification of north and south, ultimately suffering defeat and the occupation and looting of Aden by northern troops. The southerners did not forgive or forget, coining the battle-cry: 'My country, my country is South Arabia, and the capital of the Republic is Aden.'


## A Southern Insurgency

Resistance re-emerged in the 2000s as the northern Saleh government sucked Aden dry by putting northerners in charge of its ports, industries and land sales. Saleh demobilised many proud Adenese military officers and sent them unemployed onto the streets. In time, these soldiers formed protest groups that became insurgent cells. By 2010, just before the Arab Spring, a new guerrilla war was being waged by southern men. This short period of insurgency is worth exploring because it provided some of the roots of the resistance that Aden would mount against the Houthi–Saleh forces in 2015.

The potential for armed revolt had been growing in the south since 2005, when retired army officers first began to collectively approach Saleh's southern governors with petitions for the reinstatement of military pensions, land grants and their positions within the military. A free officer's movement named 'The Armies of Liberation Movement' formed in 2007 and undertook some small explosive attacks against oil tanks and government trucking. The regime's main intelligence service, the Political Security Organisation (PSO), began a dirty war of assassinations and arrests against both retired soldiers and the civilian protestors of the separatist Southern Movement (al-Hirak al-Arabiya al-Janubia, or al-Hirak). As one Southern Movement official told the author in 2010: 'Our people are in the same jails as the retired officers. The two groups are beginning to join together.'

In the lead-up to the Arab Spring and the fall of Saleh's government, the south witnessed real insurgency once more.

Southern militants began to develop semi-rural 'no-go zones' in which it is difficult for the Saleh forces to act freely. Graffiti sprang up calling insurgent operating areas 'al-Janub al-Har' (the liberated south) and the PDRY flag was once again openly flown and inscribed onto mountainside rocks and walls. In contrast, intimidation attacks on Saleh's security forces made such units reticent to fly the Republic of Yemen flag on government bases and checkpoints. On 1 April 2010, under cover of a demonstration, a crude Improvised Explosive Device (IED) was used to breach a wall at a PSO prison in Dhale, allowing 40 southern separatists to escape. Elsewhere, insurgents took Saleh's soldiers hostage to be used to secure the release of southern detainees.

The southern insurgency even took a crack at Saleh himself. When Ali Abdullah visited Aden on 13 May 2010, the PSO got wind of an assassination attempt and his security detail sent motorcades in two different directions on the return journey to confuse potential attackers. The two land convoys were both attacked as they left the south, one by a fierce ambush that combined small arms and RPG fire, and the other struck by two roadside bombs hidden in garbage by the side of the highway, one of which had cleverly been built into an abandoned television. Of course, Saleh had sent his pawns to die, while he himself had travelled unnoticed up to Sanaa by helicopter. This time, he had flown over the heads of snakes.

**Defensive Arrangements**

The people of Aden and nearby territories were harder for Saleh and the Houthis to crack precisely because these southerners had an ideology and a distinct identity from the northerners who attacked once again in March 2015. The Adenese were ready to resist and were not shy about warning any outsiders against interference. Even Hadi was told to limit his ambitions when he arrived in Aden as a president in exile, with Southern Movement leader Ali al Saadi warning in a television interview: 'We seek independence and liberation of the south. Hadi will be a loser if he tries to oppose our peaceful approach towards independence.' By late March, Hadi had fled, and Aden stood on its own with powerful enemy forces bearing down on it, alone but in charge of its own destiny at least.

The first efforts to defend Aden were rudimentary and saw the different parts of the anti-Houthi resistance act largely independently of each other. Months earlier, the city's notables set up a Resistance Council. 'We sensed as soon as Sanaa fell: we're next, they're coming for us,' one council member recounted. The Resistance Council loosely drew together 26 neighbourhood-level militia commanders, some drawn from former military officers of the PDRY and some civilians prominent in their urban neighbourhood mosques or leaders of tribal groups from the hardscrabble farms at the edges of the city.

These forces had been active since late 2014 because local leaders wanted to ward off chaos, looting and particularly Al-Qaeda efforts to exploit instability to control neighbourhoods – which had happened during the Arab Spring in 2011 and which was happening again now up the coast in Abyan towns like Zinjibar and Jaar. Drawing these groups together, the Resistance Council had a few self-imposed rules, probably with an eye to securing support from the Arab Gulf States. Resistance Council members had to formally resign any involvement with Al Islah, the Muslim Brotherhood's main front group in Yemen. As recounted by Hani bin Braykh, a veteran Salafi commander with friendly ties to the UAE: 'Our ideology was against Al Qaeda and the Muslim Brotherhood.'

From the outset, Resistance leaders expressed few doubts

about the Houthis' intentions: their southern push was seen as an invasion by a northern force but, worse, it seemed to have international and sectarian dimensions too. Some of the Adenese militia leaders such as Hani bin Braykh and Hashim Sayyed had fought the Houthis in the north during the previous six wars. They respected them as an enemy but also saw them as Zaydi (Shiite) sectarians serving a Shiite Iranian agenda that had no place in the mainly Shafei (Sunni) south of Yemen.

As luck would have it, many of these more combat-experienced anti-Houthi fighters were outside Aden when the battle began. Hani bin Braykh was in Cairo, and it took a week to recall him and send him, first by land (a failed effort via Saudi Arabia) and then by a 14-hour sea voyage, to Aden. Veteran Salafi fighter Hashim Sayyed took an even more dramatic route back to Aden. As the city was attacked, he had been called away to Zinjibar with his Salafi fighters to answer a desperate plea to fight Al Qaeda's efforts to exploit the power vacuum. When a call came to hurry to Mukayris, further to the east, to repel an Al Qaeda attack, Hashim Sayyed found that it was a ruse to draw him into one of Saleh's traps, whereupon he was ambushed by Houthi–Republican Guard forces. After two days trekking inland, he made it to a tiny coastal village called Khabur al Muraqshi, near Shuqra, that the enemy had bypassed. There he found a boat that would take him back to Sira, in Greater Aden, which was still within friendly lines at the time.

In the absence of Hani bin Braykh and Hashim Sayyed, other Salafi commanders had stepped up to rally the defence. Sheikhs Ali Salman, Sabr al-Nejdi and Ali Jabr set up the first Resistance Council headquarters at the May 22 school in Shekh Uthman – optimistically named after the day of unification in 1990, one of many Aden sites to be called after this date. They gathered money to buy food and *qat* for the fighters, and to attract former soldiers who could operate heavy weapons and armoured vehicles. Aden's television stations ran talk shows to rally the residents to arms, and the city's mosques began to call on young men to prepare themselves for war. For now, with no clear leadership, the Resistance Council's factions would each defend their parts of the city of Aden with their light weapons, typically just AK-47s, and it was still hoped that the trained professional Yemeni army could shield the city from a direct ground assault.

Hadi's military men were aiming to do just that, using Al Anad as their main blocking position. Control of the airbase, its aircraft and armament depots was split between pro-Saleh and anti-Houthi forces still answering orders from Hadi's Minister of Defence Major General Mahmoud al Subaihi. A Yemeni Army officer from Hadi's inner circle, al Subaihi was made of tougher stuff than Hadi himself. Born in Lahj, close to Al Anad, al Subaihi had served much of his career there, as head of the 201 Mechanised Infantry Brigade of the Yemeni Army and later as the head of the Al Anad regional command. He intimately knew the terrain and the need to secure Al Anad at all costs, for it contained large vehicle parks of T-55 and T-62 tanks, plus BMP-1 tracked armoured vehicles of the 314 Armoured Brigade, one of Ali Mohsen's old 1st Armoured Division units that had been sent south to serve as a shield for Aden if the Houthis attacked again.

Yet, al Subaihi also knew that he could not risk just driving up to Al Anad and expecting the troops there to rally to him. It was clear that the garrison was divided between Saleh defectors and Hadi loyalists, so al Subaihi wanted to arrive at the head of an imposing force, in order to flip the garrison firmly onto his side. The plan was to gather as many armoured vehicles as possible from the small 31 Armoured Brigade base of Bir Ahmed, on Aden's northern fringe and 20 km south of Al Anad. The base had been commandeered by Brigadier General Fadhil Hassan Khalil, an old subordinate of Ali Mohsen's from the 1st Armoured Division. Khalil knew 31 Armoured Brigade because he had fought alongside them in the tough battles against Al Qaeda in Zinjibar in the late summer of 2011, which took place even as the Arab Spring unfolded in Yemen's cities. Khalil knew al Subaihi as well: the defence minister had also been a brigade commander (of the 201 Mechanised Brigade) in that desperate fight at Zinjibar, which had seen Yemeni forces encircled and only resupplied with para-dropped ammunition delivered by US Air Force planes. A final comrade from the Zinjibar days also joined the trio, Brigadier General Faisal Rajab, who had led the 119 Infantry Brigade through the same hard fighting, cutting his force out of one Al-Qaeda encirclement after another.

Only 30 of the 70 T-55s and T-62s at Bir Ahmed were operational – 'runners' in tank-officer parlance. Almost forgotten in their maze of sand berms, the brigade's tanks – like almost all military equipment in Yemen – had been left to bake in the sun and rust in the humid nights with almost no maintenance or protection against the climate. But nowhere near 30 tank crews could be scraped together, nor fuel, so the three commanders set off on 24 March with what amounted to a reinforced company of 15 tanks, 12 BMPs, plus pick-up trucks filled with *jundis* – foot soldiers with AKs, heavy machine guns and RPGs.

The old warrior al Subaihi confidently predicted to locals that he would turn back 'the Iranians' but by the time the tanks had trundled up the highway towards Hawta, just south of Al Anad, the way was already blocked. A fast-moving Houthi–Republican Guard vanguard had arrived a day earlier by helicopter and *chassis*, followed by a large column of truck-mounted Houthi Ashura Battalion and Republican Guard

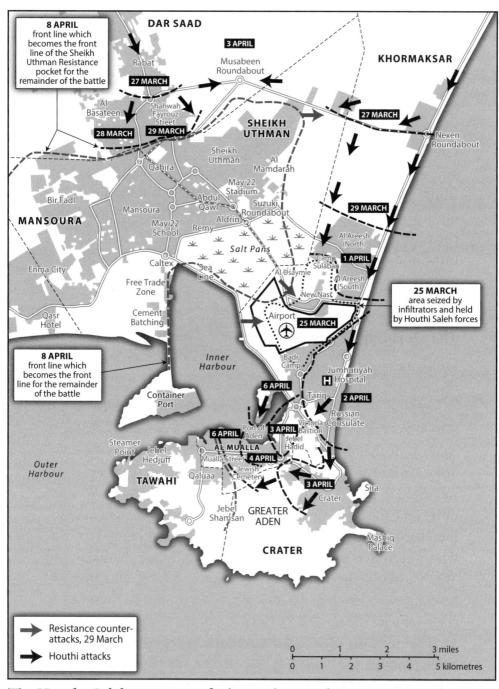

**DAR SAAD**

**KHORMAKSAR**

**8 APRIL** front line which becomes the front line of the Sheikh Uthman Resistance pocket for the remainder of the battle

**3 APRIL**

Rabat

Musabeen Roundabout

**27 MARCH**

**27 MARCH**

Al Basateen

Shahwah Fayrouz Street

**SHEIKH UTHMAN**

Nexen Roundabout

**28 MARCH**    **29 MARCH**

Sheikh Uthman

Al Mamdarah

Qahira

**29 MARCH**

May 22 Stadium

**MANSOURA**

Bir Fadl

Abdul Qawi

Suzuki Roundabout

Mansoura

Aldrin

May 22 School

Remy

Al Areesh (North)

Salt Pans

Camp Sulaban

**1 APRIL**

Enma City

Caltex

Sea Line

Al Usaymie

Al Areesh (South)

Free Trade Zone

New Nasr

**25 MARCH** area seized by infiltrators and held by Houthi Saleh forces

Qasr Hotel

Cement Batching

Airport

**25 MARCH**

**8 APRIL** front line which becomes the front line for the remainder of the battle

*Inner Harbour*

Badr Camp

Jumhuriyah Hospital

**H**

Container Port

**6 APRIL**

Tariq

**2 APRIL**

Russian Consulate

Steamer Point

Jebel Hedjuff

**6 APRIL**

Port of Aden

Victoria Bastion

**3 APRIL**

Jebel Hadid

*Outer Harbour*

**AL MUALLA**

Mualla Street

**4 APRIL**

**TAWAHI**

Qaluaa

Jewish Cemetery

**3 APRIL**

Crater

Sira

Jebel Shamsan

**GREATER ADEN**

Mashiq Palace

**CRATER**

→ Resistance counter-attacks, 29 March

→ Houthi attacks

0    1    2    3 miles
0   1   2   3   4   5 kilometres

The Houthi-Saleh conquest of Khormaksar and Crater, 25 March to 8 April 2015 troops under the command of Abdulkhaliq al Houthi. Al Anad had fallen to them without a fight, and Republican Guard tank crews were flown down to the airbase to operate armoured vehicles from the large tank park. The Houthi columns also brought fuel with them, so the gas-guzzling armour could come to life. The attack on Aden even had local air support: Al Anad's Czech-built L-39 armed trainer jets were fuelled and armed and sent to support the Houthi–Saleh forces advancing on the Aden front. Al Subaihi and his small band fought a delaying action on the highway in Hawta on 24 March but they were overrun the following day and all but Fadhil Hassan Khalil were captured and sent back to Sanaa to face a victor's justice and years of imprisonment.

## The Storming of Khormaksar

On that exact day, 25 March, a second column of Houthi–Saleh forces stormed into Aden via the other main approach, on the coastal highway from Abyan. As fate would have it, their armoured vehicles had been seized from al Subaihi's old unit, the 201 Mechanised Brigade, including dozens of BMP-1s; squat Soviet infantry fighting vehicles with a stubby 73 mm cannon mounted in their low turrets. Considered cramped by Western observers, the BMPs were designed to fit eight Russians in absolute discomfort and had no problem fitting that many Yemenis, who were often wiry and very lightly equipped. Unlike Cold War Russians, the Houthis were happy to let it all hang out, keeping every hatch and firing port open to vent the heat inside their vehicles.

The previous night, 24 March, five truckloads of Houthi–Saleh commandos had already infiltrated the Khormaksar side of the city. Here, the airport sat at the neck of the isthmus linking the mainland to 'Greater Aden', comprising the neigh-bourhoods of Crater (a literal volcanic crater with 1,000-foot cliffs on its inner edge) and the port districts of Mualla, Qaluaa and Tawahi. Pro-Saleh officers snuck around military camps in the city like thieves in the night, trying to convince units of the Aden-based 39 Armoured Brigade and 120 Air Defence Brigade to defect. Large-scale fighting erupted in Khormaksar on 25 March as these infiltrators linked up with the incoming columns from Abyan. Cell phone service was cut from the pro-vider's headquarters in Sanaa, plunging the Resistance into even greater uncertainty. The lightly armed Resistance Council units quickly ran out of ammunition and lacked RPGs or other means to stop the enemy armour. The 39 Armoured Brigade base at Camp Badr, adjacent and south of the airport, was split between the invaders and defenders, with the former securing most of the heavy weapons.

Desperate for arms, mobs of young Yemeni men overran the Jebel Hadid Military Zone, a modern-day air defence camp set up on the mountain that towered over Crater, Mualla and the Inner Harbour. A naturally strong defensive position with imposing ramparts, Jebel Hadid had been fortified by the Otto-mans and later by the British, including a strongpoint called Victoria Bastion, which commanded the isthmus leading to the old city. Jebel Hadid once again became vital to the defence of Aden, as Resistance fighters seized whatever arms and equip-ment they could find. With civilians rollicking all over the arsenal, accidents were bound to happen. First signs of fire and then explosions issued from the Jebel Hadid, becoming louder and stronger, until they shook the city. The arms depots let off shocking sharp cracks of high explosive, echoing booms across the city, and spewing dusty grey clouds across the towering hills of volcanic rock. In trying desperately to loot the arsenal, the

Resistance had destroyed their only major store of arms and explosives.

It looked like the city must fall. But at that moment, in New York, the United Nations heard a call from President Hadi, then en route to Riyadh from Oman, for urgent military assistance. Hadi told the UN Security Council to authorise 'willing countries that wish to help Yemen to provide immediate support for the legitimate authority by all means and measures to protect Yemen and deter the Houthi aggression'. The Arab League heard the same message that day and its most important members approved a military response. Help was coming, but the Adenese needed to hang on for just a few weeks so that help could come from the Arab States.

# V

# THE UAE DRAWS A LINE IN THE SAND

Unlike Yemen, almost everyone in the world had some impression of the United Arab Emirates (UAE) by 2015. An elective monarchy, formed from a federation of seven emirates in 1971, the country was ruled by a Federal Supreme Council of the seven emirs of: Abu Dhabi (the capital), Ajman, Dubai, Fujairah, Ras Al Khaimah, Sharjah and Umm Al Quwain. This country of 1.4 million Emirati citizens and 7.8 million non-citizen guests had become a bustling centre of investment, tourism and logistics by the start of the twenty-first century. The UAE was a young nation but a busy one. It would be this young, ambitious nation and its equally young and impressive military that would make the most profound and positive impact on the war in Yemen, starting with the desperate struggle to save Aden.

The previous autumn, the UAE's senior diplomats had been in New York for the United Nations General Assembly (UNGA) just as Sanaa was falling to the Houthis. UNGA began on 16 September and was only five days into its three-week programme when the Houthi coup collapsed Hadi's UN-backed government. To the Saudis, Yemen was a neighbour, a perennial source of threat and a constant concern. In the same way that the United States might have looked at Mexico or Cuba during the Cold War – as too close to America for the Russians to fully control – the Saudis could not tolerate an Iranian beachhead on the Arabian Peninsula.

At the time, the UAE's diplomats were told by the Saudis: 'The danger is real; we are probably going to war in Yemen.' Though the crisis moment passed, it served as a warning – conflict might be coming, perhaps with very little notice. Civil war drew closer as the Houthis formally declared their opposition to the UN-backed Hadi government on 6 February 2015, followed by Hadi's escape to Aden and his statement of ongoing resistance by the 'legitimacy government' from its new base in Aden. The UAE military began to sharpen up contingency plans, including a rudimentary Crisis Action Plan that would allow the country to go onto a war footing within 36 hours.

Urgency was further sharpened by the 19 March efforts to overthrow Hadi's control of Aden, and apparently even to kill Hadi by airstrike. On 21 March, the Gulf leaders met in Riyadh, at the invitation of the newly crowned Saudi king, Salman bin Abdulaziz Al Saud. On 22 March, the French-chaired UN Security Council condemned, 'in the strongest terms, the airstrikes against the Presidential Palace in Aden and attacks at the international airport', referring to the Houthi–Saleh plots against Hadi. Calling out the Houthi–Saleh power base, the Council urged 'non-state actors to withdraw from government institutions, including in the south of Yemen, and to refrain from any attempts to take over such institutions'.

By the evening of 23 March, with Hadi driven out of Aden, the UAE's military chiefs of staff were ordered to prepare for action in Yemen, at the very least involving an air campaign and a naval blockade by Saudi Arabia, the UAE, Kuwait, Bahrain, Egypt, Jordan, Morocco and Qatar. Late on 25 March, as Houthi–Saleh fighters were clawing their way into Aden city, the UAE joined its allies in answering Yemen's call for help. Lieutenant General Mohammed bin Zayed (hereafter MBZ), then the Crown Prince of Abu Dhabi and Deputy Supreme Commander of the UAE Armed Forces, informed his commanders that the coalition would begin airstrikes that night, and that the UAE Air Force would be at the forefront of those operations.

## The Calculus of Intervention

The decision to take the UAE into war was made neither lightly nor quickly. It was the last resort and came after six months of fruitless efforts to get the United Nations and other partners to freeze or reverse the Houthi's creeping takeover of Yemen. 'We were not gung-ho about it,' noted Anwar Gargash, the UAE's Minister of State for Foreign Affairs. 'We really didn't want to go to war. We tried everything to avoid it.' Back on 28 March 2015, Gargash had told Al-Sharq Al-Awsat that the decision to take military action 'was not hasty, but was preceded by intense political efforts and sincere initiatives that were responded to by ingratitude and aggression. We decided on this remedy only after having knocked on all doors.'

In the end, however, diplomacy had not prevented the Houthis from overrunning Sanaa and there was no reason to believe diplomacy would stop them seizing the rest of Yemen now. For the UAE, it was simply inconceivable that the Emirates would *not* act in concert with its Gulf Cooperation Council (GCC) treaty partners. In 2011, as Bahrain faced the chaos of the Arab Spring, UAE police officers had been bussed into Manama alongside Saudi Arabian military forces to support the Bahraini government – and one, First Lieutenant Tariq Al Shehhi, had even been killed in a bombing. In 2015, the UAE again had no hesitation in backing Saudi Arabia and the other Arab states.

But, equally important, the UAE had its own cogent strategic narrative for joining – and ultimately shaping – the military intervention to support the UN-backed government, imperfect though that government clearly was. (UN Security Council Resolution 2216, issued on 14 April, 2015, imposed sanctions and travel banks on the top Huthi leaders and Huthi-commanded Yemeni Republican Guard commander for "undermining peace, security and stability" in Yemen.) The UAE connection to Yemen was multi-faceted. Many prominent UAE families had tribal connections to Yemen's eastern border with Oman. Many other Yemenis had gained Emirati citizenship after serving in the UAE police or had become successful businessmen in the Emirates, gaining fame as the Gulf's most prolific construction equipment magnates.

In recent years, the UAE's most urgent interest in southern Yemen was hunting the terrorist group Al Qaeda in the Arabian Peninsula or AQAP, which viewed Yemen as one of its most valuable bases and the UAE as one of its deadliest enemies. AQAP grew out of the Yemeni Arab-Afghan mujahedin who had fought in Afghanistan and also Al Islah party associates of Osama bin Laden, who himself was of Yemeni lineage. Indeed, Al Qaeda's first real attack came in Yemen, on 29 December 1992, when the group bombed the Gold Mohur hotel in Aden and the hotel parking lot. The attack killed two civilians but failed to harm the intended target: US military personnel transiting Yemen as part of Operation Restore Hope in Somalia. Bin Laden continued to strengthen his ties to Yemen when a Hadramawt sheikh, Ahmad Abdulfattah As Sadah, married his daughter to bin Laden in 2001. According to Bin Laden's biographer, Patrick Bergen, one-fifth of the calls made from Afghanistan by bin Laden on his satellite phone were made to Yemen. Months later, Yemenis played prominent roles in the tragic 9/11 attacks, leading two of the three hijacker teams that turned airliners into suicide bombs and killed 2,977 people.

For the UAE, the threat posed by Yemeni-based terrorists was close to home. Al Qaeda's top maritime attack specialist, the prolific Saudi-Yemeni planner Abdulrahim Mohammed al

1. The ultimate rivals: General Ali Mohsen al Ahmar (left in grey shirt) and Ali Abdullah Saleh were ordained by their Hashid tribal confederation to share power, but instead spent their lives plotting to undermine and eliminate each other. Both tried to kill the other with airstrikes in 2009-2011. When purged from power in the Arab Spring of 2011, Ali Abdullah Saleh began to build ties with Ali Mohsen's most bitter military adversaries, the Houthi clans of northern Yemen. Saleh was famed for being able to 'dance on the heads of snakes', a reflection of his ability to keep various rival factions fighting each other, with him always on top. His ambition outstripped his capabilities and he was eventually murdered by his erstwhile Houthi allies on 4 December 2017. Ali Mohsen outlasted Saleh, remaining Vice President of Yemen for over four years after Saleh's death, only being removed from office in April 2022.

2. Abd-Rabo Mansour al Hadi, Saleh's vice president and another former general from Abyan, who replaced Saleh under the UN-backed Yemeni government from 2012-2022. Hadi was imprisoned by the Houthis and Saleh forces when they took over the Yemeni capital Sanaa in the coup of September 2014. He escaped to Aden and declared it his new seat of government. Saleh promised to drive Hadi into the sea, which he did by aiding the Houthi invasion of Aden in March 2015.

3. Houthi fighters in the flatbed of a *chassis* – Yemeni parlance for a pick-up truck, the most popular and reliable means of tactical transport. The fighters are young, some well under eighteen years old and thus categorized under UN rules as child soldiers. The fighter in the foreground has a bulging cheek full of qat, the chewable narcotic leaf that produces a talkative super-alert status of consciousness, akin to way too much coffee. On his Rocket-Propelled Grenade (RPG) warhead, the fighter has a sticker bearing the Houthi motto, the 'scream' (*al sarkha*): 'God is great, death to America, death to Israel, a curse upon the Jews, victory to Islam'.

4. Ali Abdullah Saleh's Republican Guard fighters, identifiable by their maroon beret. By Yemeni military standards, these were well-equipped troops with morale-boosting advantages in salary, accommodation and uniforms. Many of these young soldiers came from northern provinces where the Houthis were strong. They were easy to convert over to a Houthi-led force when their Republican Guard officers were undermined in front of the troops by Houthi 'supervisors'. Note the qat in the driver's cheek and the picture of Ali Abdullah Saleh in the background. Young Yemenis had known no president except Saleh, who had ruled most of Yemen since 1978.

5. The ZSU (pronounced "shoe"), or technically the ZSU-23-2, is a Russian-made 23mm twin-barrel anti-aircraft cannon that was the dominant heavy weapon in the Yemen war. Whether the twin- or single-barrel version, 23mm cannons showed up everywhere, usually firing single shots or short bursts. Weighing about 1,500 lbs when stripped of unnecessary components, they were mounted on flatbed trucks. Single-barrel 23mm guns were stripped down to just a gun, base and seat, weighing around 500 lbs, which allowed them to be manhandled over mountains, onto roofs and up the stairwells of buildings. The ZSU-23 could punch through any armoured vehicles on the Yemeni battlefield except main battle tanks

6. The Houthi "keys to heaven", a totem carried by Houthi fighters to ward off enemy bullets and assure the wearer admission to heaven. The same kind of keys were given to Iranian conscripts and child soldiers during the Iran-Iraq War. Note how the keys are basic, unadorned Yale door keys. By the end of the Aden battle, a large pile of such keys had been recovered from the battlefield.

7. A Houthi fighter in police uniform stands in front of an Airbus A310 of Iranian private airline Mahan Air at Sanaa International airport following its first flight to Yemen from Iran on 1 March, 2015. The air-bridge between Tehran and Sanaa operated 14 flights a week, bringing Iranian personnel, weapons and technology into Yemen, and taking Yemeni personnel to Iran for training. Iranian pilots, planners and logisticians aided the design and execution of the attack on Aden in March 2015. In 2019, Mahan Air was designated by the US Department of Treasury's Office of Foreign Asset Control for its support to the Islamic Revolutionary Guard Corps, a US-designated terrorist group.

8. Street fighting in Aden on April 8, 2015. The scene contains many of the staple features of resistance actions by the Popular Committees. The urban people who made up the Popular Committees were more akin to a 'neighbourhood watch', intended to prevent Al-Qaeda or the Islamic State from taking over Aden city, while the army were expected to keep the Houthis far away. Soon, these small militias were instead fighting the Houthi-Saleh armoured forces in the streets of Aden. 'Spray and pray' shooting techniques were widely used: un-aimed bursts of automatic fire that contributed to massive depletion of ammunition; one-handed firing (while running!), an extremely dangerous method of shooting; and (not shown here) the 'Beirut handshake', whereby the gun is held around a corner or over the top of hard cover, and fired in the rough direction of the enemy. Also typical of the battle, civilian observers gather to watch the fighting.

9. In June 2015, *VICE News* filmmaker Medyan Dairieh spent two weeks on the Dar Saad front with a Resistance group. This is screenshot from the excellent documentary, called 'The Siege of Aden' (released on July 27, 2015). It shows Popular Committee fighters manually reloading Kalashnikov magazines with loose rounds, underlining the rudimentary logistics of the force, which lacked even spare magazines. All the outer edges of Aden city are sparsely populated and studded with unfinished three- to six-storey buildings such as the one in the background.

10. Small arms ammunition is the lifeblood of modern skirmish warfare. The side that runs dry first is the side that will retreat and cede territory. Though Yemenis are proud fighters, it is perfectly acceptable for fighters to leave the battle when their ammunition is expended, after which their presence is seen as achieving nothing. This photograph from 27 March, 2015, shows Popular Committee fighters in Tawahi, Greater Aden, after they have filled the flatbed of their *chassis* with AK rounds. Of this haul, some might make it to the battlefront, but much would probably be squirrelled away as a form of currency, to be traded or sold later in the battle, or even years after the fighting ended.

11. This dramatic 28 March 2015 photograph shows the Jebel Hadid arms depot on fire after being carelessly looted by civilians and Resistance fighters. In high heat and with poor safety standards, any arms depot in Yemen presents acute danger, but especially so in the midst of a battle and when overrun by civilian militias. The rumble of explosives and the crack of ammunition 'cooking off' lasted for two days.

12. One of the few operational Resistance tanks shells the airport and Camp Badr on 29 April 2015. A smoke cloud billows over the airport in the distance, possibly the result of an air strike or a fire caused by the tank's shelling of the area.

13. Resistance fighters watch a friend shooting into the airport perimeter from the Sea Line causeway with a PKM machine-gun. The type was widely used as it was relatively light (about 20lbs or 10 kilogrammes) and fired an older type of Soviet rifle round (7.62x54mmR) for which there were more plentiful reserves. This may be the fighter's weapon or he may have dropped by to 'have a go' with the gun.

14. A 3 May 2015 image showing an armoured truck. Any Resistance commander wanted one for himself and they would make lavish promises of success if they could first attain this status symbol from the UAE. Numerous types were in action, mostly ancient Soviet-era Eastern Bloc wheeled armoured personnel carriers and scout cars.

15. A 27 April 2015 picture by Saleh al-Bayati of the defense of Tawahi. This 81mm mortar is being fired at a high angle, suggesting the Houthis are close, probably in open ground beyond the buildings in the background.

16. A Popular Committee RPG gunner poses for a photographer at Dar Saad on 9 May 2015. Yemenis are very photogenic people and this image captures the look of the Resistance fighters: lightly dressed due to the heat, they were generally young, fit and lean. They carried minimal or no "belt order" – ammunition pouches and webbing. An RPG gunner typically did not carry a secondary weapon such as an AK-type assault rifle, both for weight reasons and because small arms were in quite short supply. RPG gunners had to expose themselves to enemy fire in order to steady, aim and fire their launchers, and they were easily spotted due to the visible back-blast of the weapon. As a result, carrying an RPG was a badge of honour. In the background is one of Dar Saad's many four to six-story buildings, probably near the Shahida Fayrouz Street, which was an avenue of small hotels. The battle damage is typical of Aden: corner apartments and roof penthouses have drawn enemy fire, probably because Resistance fighters were using them as elevated firing positons. RPG, B-10 recoilless rifle and 23mm cannon fire has caused localized damage. Fire has gutted one apartment but left the rest of the breeze-block tower intact.

17. The devastated front line at Dar Saad, probably in the vicinity of Airplane Roundabout. Aden's skyline is dominated by three- to four-story grey and white-coloured buildings. In areas with sustained fighting, the multi-storey apartment complexes above the ground-floor shops were soon empty of residents, creating a lifeless, urban no-man's land where enemy patrols would prowl and clash. All glass was shattered quickly, creating massive numbers of dangerous openings from which snipers might shoot. Any large shell-hole might be used as a firing embrasure.

18. A fighting patrol returns bearing a wounded Resistance militiaman. Note that not all fighters carry guns, with the availability of AK-type rifles being less than 1:1 for much of the battle. This image, from later in the battle (16 July) shows what looks to be a small group of comrades working together to carry a wounded friend many hundreds of metres back from the frontline. At the start of the battle, the only real Intensive Care Unit (ICU) operating in Aden was the *Médecins Sans Frontières* emergency room at Al Wahda Hospital in Dar Saad. The UAE developed four more ICUs close to the front lines to stabilize battlefield casualties. Whereas a limb wound could easily kill or permanently cripple a fighter in the early battle period, the improvement in ambulance and stabilization capabilities gave the Resistance more confidence that they could survive a wound.

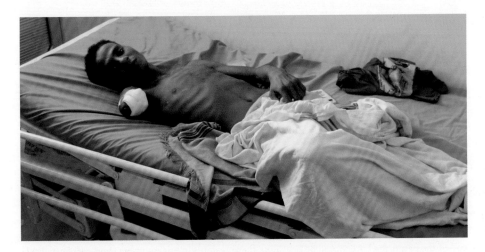

19. A wounded Yemeni lies in a hospital bed in the area of Sheikh Uthman, most probably in the May 22 Hospital. This August 2015 image shows the improved conditions of the late-battle hospitals, while the early battle saw wards and corridors over-spilling with wounded persons on the floors, with splashes and puddles of blood on all surfaces. One of the UAE's priorities in improving emergency rooms across Aden was the reduction in the number of amputations being undertaken early in the battle. By the end of the battle, many unnecessary amputations were being avoided and limbs saved.

20. UAE special forces operators and a Joint Terminal Attack Controller (JTAC) at one of the early Safe Houses. This is what modern war sometimes looks like. They use a Harris handheld secure radio, a Samsung, an iPhone, multiple Nokia phones, an iPad running a commercial mapping application, and the trusty notepad. At this stage, the JTACs had no full-motion video to watch. They looked at maps and pieced together the enemy position based on the live calls from Yemeni Resistance observers, then they asked circling Coalition pilots to confirm using their own sensor pods. Note the urn of super-sweet Karak - black loose tea leaves, crushed cardamom, saffron and lots of evaporated milk and sugar. Everything a JTAC needs to stay awake and in the fight.

21. The other end of the radio. As the Houthis could switch on and off cellphone service from Sanaa – or monitor it – tactical communications moved to low-power Motorola radios. By the end of the battle, the UAE would be providing these systems in huge numbers and even installing repeater stations to improve reception in areas where the Resistance were expected to advance. Both the Houthis and Resistance used these systems and listened to each other's broadcasts, and both sides used rudimentary codes. Note the status-symbol short AK variant of the commander, the so-called 'Krinkov'.

22. Two UAE Air Force and Air Defence Block 60 F-16s taking off from King Fahad Air Base in Taif in Saudi Arabia, bound for Yemen. These cutting-edge F-16s are more advanced than those flown by the US Air Force. On the wing-tips and outer under-wing 'hard points' are AIM-120 and AIM-9 air-to-air missiles. The mid-wing 'hard points' carry GBU-10 Paveway II 2,000lb laser-guided bombs. The bulges above the wings are conformal fuel tanks and large 370-gallon fuel tanks are carried on the inner under-wing 'hardpoints'. The under-fuselage 'hard points' carry Lantirn and Litening targeting and navigation pods. The nose contains the cutting-edge AN/APG-80 AESA radar, which the UAE jointly developed with the US Air Force, allowing both the US and UAE to field a more advanced sensor system.

23. The impact crater from a 2,000lb bomb at Imran. This bomb knocked out a T-62 tank that was driving towards Imran on 14 April 2015. It was one of the strikes guided in by 'Abdullah Hammer's' small special forces team almost as soon as they landed. The Yemeni Resistance leaders had been skeptical that 'eight men and a radio' could stop the Houthi advance. That changed after the team obliterated the Houthi tank attack with air strikes coordinated from a safe house 15 kilometres away from the battlefront. 'You were eight, but we looked at you like you were eight thousand,' a Resistance commander recalled.

24. Al Forsan operators on the *Al-Quwaisat* (A81) Landing Ship Tank (LST), which would become the command ship for the UAE Amphibious Task Force. The *Al-Quwaisat* and her crew were one of the unsung heroes of the Aden campaign, performing a huge multitude of vital tasks in the background. The *Al-Quwaisat* hosted the Al Forsan platoon that would eventually deploy into Aden, functioned as a drone landing zone, carrying logistics and humanitarian aid back and forth from Assab in Eritrea, and even served as a 'tethered goat' to lure enemy artillery out into the open when UAE aircraft could destroy it. In this image, the Al Forsan are being readied by their commanders for insertion into Aden. Note the US Marines t-shirt worn by one man: the Al Forsan and other Presidential Guard units train extensively with the elite US Marine Corps at their 29 Palms training centre in California.

25. The *Al-Quwaisat* was not designed to undertake the many roles she ultimately fulfilled, nor was she built to house three times its crew complement for months on end. As a result, the ship was hot, noisy, and overfilled with men, constantly moving and buffeted by wind and wave.

26. An intelligence fusion cell at the sharp end of modern warfare. The team is operating on the roof of one of the two safe houses during the preliminary fires that were intended to precede the first assault on the airport. They operate from the roof, below the level of the parapet, in order to get optimal signal reception and stay slightly cooler. UAE special operators and JTACs sit alongside their Yemeni counterparts, fusing together what Resistance fighters are reporting on the ground with the UAE's aerial view from above. With well over a dozen mobile phones and radios working in tandem, and with the help of commercial mapping applications, the JTACs oversee the dynamic targeting portion of the fire plan against Houthi forces at the airport, reacting to enemy movement and striking newly exposed Houthi-Saleh forces. Note the rips in the blue tarp, to stop it catching the wind and billowing like a sail.

27. The first meetings with the Resistance Council. When Lieutenant Colonel Salem D. arrived in Aden, within minutes of arriving at the safe house he was hosting a crowd of Resistance leaders. The Yemenis needed an older and higher-ranked figure than Major 'Abdullah Hammer' to serve as their liaison officer with the Emiratis. Salem stayed on as the stable face of the UAE throughout the campaign, almost from the start to the end. This continuity proved valuable in diagnosing the limitations of the Resistance and prescribing the 'protected mobility' required to turn them into an attacking force.

28. The famous 3 May 2015 image taken by a press photographer that first gave the world a detailed look at the mystery 'Arab special forces' who were on the ground in Aden, clinging to the tiny scraps of cover along the Sea Line causeway. Most observers thought they were Saudi or Egyptian marines. In fact, this shows UAE Al Forsan rangers with distinctive Ops-Core helmets, M4 carbines and an RG-6 40mm, six-shot, revolver-type grenade launcher that the Al Forsan used to deter Houthi snipers from approaching too closely through nearby bushes. Live footage shown by Al Jazeera added further detail, including the presence of FGM-148 Javelin anti-tank missiles – the same kind used to devastating effect against Russian forces in Ukraine in 2022. Note nearly 30 artillery or tank shell casings that appear to have been fired towards Houthi lines from the same position at an earlier point in the battle, perhaps by the tank shown in an earlier photograph in this book.

29. A superb 3 May 2015 battle photograph taken at the Sea Line causeway, 1.5 km southeast of Caltex Roundabout and 2.5 km northwest of the runway. At this point on the exposed causeway there is a line of concrete blocks that comprise the foundation for metal advertising billboards. These blocks are some of the only hard cover on the Sea Line and became the line of departure for numerous airport attacks. The billboards were also the fire support base for Resistance forces such as the B-10 recoilless rifle shown here. The B-10 is a 1950s-era Soviet-designed anti-tank weapon that fires an 82mm shell. Intended to be a towed weapon fired from a stable tripod mount, Yemenis of both sides in the war instead tended to use it as a monstrous 70-kilogramme shoulder-fired weapon. Inaccurate at over 400 metres even when being fired from a stable base, it was wildly uncontrollable when fired from the shoulder.

30. Yemen Resistance fighters defending a tiny and precarious lodgment at the western end of the runway, where the airport meets the Sea Line. There was little hard cover, forcing Resistance fighters to cling to each concrete bollard or short wall. These positions offered no protection from overhead fire, and the Houthis preceded their counter-attacks with 120mm mortar barrages to make such lodgements impossible to reinforce or defend. Note the fighter has a German G-3 assault rifle, which fires different (longer) cartridges to the Kalashnikovs carried by most fighters, a reminder of the logistics problems facing both sides in the battle.

31. Two T-62 tanks brought over by ferry to the Tawahi defensive pocket in early May 2015 as part of the desperate effort to prevent the fall of Greater Aden. The lead tank flies a Southern Movement flag, the symbol of southern resistance to northerners.

32. A Yemeni Resistance fighter fires his Russian PKM machine-gin into the air. This 12 April picture was probably taken in Mualla. It underlines the manner in which Resistance fighters used up vast quantities of ammunition in what is called 'celebration fire' after tactical victories. In fact, such gunfire had many potential motives and effects. Sometimes it was intended to put the enemy on notice and deter their advances. As often, the fire might be mourning a martyr, or celebrating the return of a prisoner or the safe return of a fighter to his family after a period of absence at the front. A football game on television might be the cause of fire, or a squabble between Resistance factions. The UAE learned that it was a good rule of thumb to assume about twenty per cent of ammunition would be wasted in celebration fire, with at least that much stolen to be sold or added to private hoards. The UAE troops also learned to send out patrols if such fire stopped, as it usually indicated some kind of unusual and worrying development.

Nashiri, kept a close watch on US warships leaving Jebel Ali port in Dubai on their way to Yemen. On 3 January 1999, al Nashiri's cell attempted to bomb the destroyer USS *Sullivans* in Aden harbour with a remote-control explosive-packed speedboat that thankfully foundered and sank. On the next attempt, al Nashiri succeeded. The 12 October 2000 attack on the USS *Cole* in Aden harbour forwent remote control and instead utilised a suicide attacker, who managed to blow a huge whole in the side of the *Cole*, causing 17 US fatalities and knocking the ship out of commission for over three years. On 6 October 2002, when al Nashiri sought to attack another US warship off the southern port of Ash Shihr, the UAE intelligence services picked up chatter about a new attack and warned the US, which diverted its transits away from Yemen. Al Nashiri was instead forced to attack a 'target of opportunity', the French-flagged oil tanker MV *Limburg*, and in doing so he exposed himself to UAE surveillance and was arrested in Dubai in October 2002 and handed over to the US.

In the years after, Yemen continued to act as a base for attacks on global transportation. The Saudi-Yemeni terrorist Ibrahim al Asiri was Al Qaeda's most talented bomb-maker, and he spent the late 2000s working out of AQAP's central Yemen redoubts. It was al Asiri who built a series of bombs designed to evade global aviation security checks. One was the 25 December 2009 liquid explosives 'underwear' bomb that aimed to destroy Northwest Airlines Flight 253 over Detroit. Another was the October 2010 cargo plane bomb plot, which sought to send explosive-filled printer cartridges via Dubai onto cargo flights to the UK. Al Asiri even turned his own brother, Ahmed, into a walking bomb, emplacing a suicide bomb inside his body to use in the 2009 assassination plot against Saudi Arabian Deputy Minister of Interior Prince Muhammad bin Nayef. (The Saudi official, known as MBN, was wounded in the attack, with his attacker exploding right next to him.) It was obvious that Al Qaeda would eventually turn its gaze directly on the UAE. As Yousif al Otaiba, the UAE ambassador to the United States, was later to reflect on: 'We don't believe in being sympathetic to extremists. Instead, we see extremism as an existential threat.'

The desire to confront Al Qaeda drew the UAE into a 12-year special forces and reconstruction mission in Afghanistan's Helmand province and into partnered operations with the US Joint Special Operations Command commandos in southeastern Yemen in response to al Asiri's bomb plots. The Emirates knew that Al Qaeda would quickly spread like cancer wherever it could exploit ungoverned space and chaos. As the Arab Spring collapsed the government in August 2011, AQAP tried to present itself as a new movement, Ansar al Sharia, in order to join with protestors and local tribes to seize Zinjibar, a small city of 20,000 residents in Abyan province. A senior AQAP member called Adil al Abab telegraphed his movement's ambition to penetrate the protests and take over when government control collapsed, noting in 2011: 'It is only a lack of money that has stopped us from entering Aden. Allah knows we were only a few days away from taking power there. But it will fall, first Zanzibar and then Aden.'

In 2015, the same thing was happening again. As Hadi and Houthi–Saleh forces fought each other, Al Qaeda and the fast-rising Islamic State were taking advantage. The Abyan towns of Jaar and Zinjibar were once again falling to the terrorists pouring down from the mountains to the north. Al Qaeda prison breaks were beginning to occur in major southern cities like Aden and Mukalla. In the latter port city, it even appeared that Saleh loyalists were deliberately engineering the handover of government-controlled military bases *to* Al Qaeda in order to weaken the Hadi government. Three Islamic State suicide bombings in Sanaa on 20 March 2015 killed 137 people and showed that they, too, had ambitions for Yemen. To prevent a jihadist caliphate from forming, such as the fate that had just befallen large swathes of Iraq and Syria in 2014, the UAE was ready and willing to put boots on the ground to firm up resistance to Al Qaeda in eastern and southern Yemen.

## Losing Yemen to Iran

The Houthis and their Iranian and Lebanese Hezbollah partners presented a newer and equally urgent threat to the UAE. The Islamic Republic of Iran had a chance when it emerged in 1979 to undo the Shah's illegal 1971 annexation of three UAE islands in the Gulf: Abu Musa, Greater Tunb and Lesser Tunb. Instead, post-Revolutionary Iran kept the islands, fortified them, and rained down anti-shipping missiles and naval mines on the UAE's shipping lanes during the 1980–88 Iran–Iraq War. In the intervening decades leading up to 2015, the IRGC rulers of Iran had shown themselves to be deeply hostile to the UAE and Saudi Arabia, so there was understandable alarm in Abu Dhabi when the Houthis grew ever closer to Iran and Hezbollah in 2010–2014. Hardened UAE diplomats were in deep shock that Ali Abdullah Saleh, who had once sent Yemeni units to fight Iran on Saddam Hussein's side in the Iran–Iraq War, could sell out so completely to Tehran, all to regain his throne in Yemen.

As a result, the Gulf Arabs drew a line in the sand. To them, the war in Yemen was about stopping Iran from gaining a foothold on the Arabian Peninsula, home to Islam's holiest sites, Makkah and Madina, and to the world's greatest concentration of oil reserves. The risks for global security were huge: Iran already overshadowed one of the world's greatest maritime straits, at Hormuz, and now it sought to dominate the Bab el-Mandeb and thus the southern approaches to the Suez Canal as well. Iran had given Lebanese Hezbollah advanced anti-shipping missiles such as the Iranian copy of the Chinese C-802, which Hezbollah used to cripple an Israeli Saar-5 corvette off the coast of Lebanon in 2006. The same missile warheads were now turning up in the Iranian shipments intercepted off Yemen.

In addition to Iran's ability to shut off 20 per cent of global oil supplies at the narrow Strait of Hormuz, control of the Bab el-Mandeb would give Iran a block on a further 12 per cent of global trade. Previous closures of the Suez Canal showed that the most affected countries – Pakistan, India, Kenya, China and the Eastern Mediterranean states – saw 20 per cent reductions in their economic activity while the sea lane was closed. Later, the blockage of the Suez Canal by the *Ever Given* cargo ship in 2021 provided an example of the potential costs to the global economy of losing Suez Canal trade, estimated by Lloyds List at £330 million an hour or £5.5 million a minute. The defensive action requested by Yemen's UN-backed government was thus legal, necessary and justified as Houthi–Saleh forces streamed southwards towards the Bab el-Mandeb and the port of Aden. As a Saudi special forces officer in Yemen told the author: 'If the Houthis take the south, you will be fighting a ghost from the mountain, next to the world's most important seaway.'

The Gulf States were used to America stepping up at such moments, but, in late 2014, the White House was partway through negotiating a nuclear deal with Iran that, it was hoped, would avert a regional war over Iran's nuclear ambitions. No help would come from Washington. Instead, for the first time, the Gulf States acted militarily on their own. After years of watching Iran growing stronger, they decided that enough was enough. The UAE's motive was defensive. Anwar Gargash, the UAE Minister of State for Foreign Affairs, told reporters months earlier: 'We can't be a stable house with brush fires all around us.' For the UAE, the choice was between doing something and doing nothing at this critical moment, and they chose to act. Later, Gargash reflected on the thinking within the leadership:

> After the Arab Spring and [the Islamic State in Iraq and Syria] and the chaos, what were we supposed to do? Sit and wait? Let the chaos spread, and just wait for the tsunami to get us? We had to manage our security environment and take matters into our own hands.

## The Air War Begins

It was hard for many Westerners to grasp that Saudi Arabia, the UAE and other coalition members could mount a large-scale, sustained air campaign on their own, but that is what unfolded when Operation Decisive Storm began in the early hours of 26 March 2015. Invoking Article 51 (self-defence) of the UN Charter and the Arab League and Joint Arab Defence Treaty, the Coalition began to execute a classic 72-hour Air Tasking Order (ATO). An ATO is an enormously complex timetable comprising the first three days' worth of pre-planned air strikes, which had been sorted into a prioritised programme by Saudi Arabian planners in the six months since the September 2014 war scare.

The air campaign would closely resemble the kinds of air campaigns the US had fought in 1991 in Iraq or against Serbia in 1999, and that was no coincidence. Ever since the 1990s, the Saudis had trained to emulate the American targeting of Iraq and Serbia from the air. American contractors filled the gaps in Saudi target lists, and the format was very familiar: first, the coalition gained air superiority by striking all known air force bases to destroy as many MiG-29s, Su-22s, F-5Es and L-39 armed trainers as possible.

The Gulf air forces also prioritised the destruction of enemy air defences by bombing identified SA-2 and SA-3 surface-to-air missile sites. On the second night, with greater safety to operate, the Coalition struck as many Houthi-held ammunition depots and surface-to-surface missile sites as they could, with the obvious intent of disarming the Houthi–Saleh conspiracy of as much military materiel as possible. The third day was spent re-striking areas that were not destroyed in the first two waves. Over 150 targets were attacked, with the Coalition employing 170 strike aircraft, which included 100 Saudi F-15S and Eurofighter Typhoon aircraft, 30 UAE F-16s and Mirage 2000-9s, and a mixture of Bahraini, Jordanian and Moroccan F-16s plus Kuwaiti F/A-18s and Sudanese Su-24s. The skies were clear for strike aircraft and Coalition aerial refuellers, and they were closed to Iranian resupply flights. In modern war, where control of the air is essential, the successful opening week of the war provided the necessary basis for all the subsequent operations that would follow.

While most observers were wondering how the Gulf States could launch such a major operation with minimal US participation (limited to refuelling support), MBZ was already thinking about the next challenge. The Coalition's Saudi spokesman Brigadier General Ahmed al Asiri had identified the 'main objective' of Operation Decisive Storm as 'protecting the government in Aden'. As a keen student of military history, the UAE's Deputy Supreme Commander knew that airpower alone did not win wars, and it could not save Aden. Only local ground forces could defend the city. At the very least, airpower needed ground observers to cue strike aircraft onto targets and minimise the risk of civilian casualties. As important, the coalition would need boots on the ground to bolster the morale of local resistance forces, gauge their resupply needs and gather 'ground-truth' on the local situation.

For this reason, on 23 March, the UAE chain of command had warned the Presidential Guard commander, Major General M (hereafter MGM) to make ready the UAE Special Operations Command (SOC) and Al-Forsan (commando) units for missions in Yemen. On 25 March, just hours before the air campaign began, MBZ directed his commanders that they should focus on preparing to insert special forces into Aden to mobilise and sustain local tribal militias and surviving pro-Hadi military units. Yemenis would lead the fighting, but the UAE would give them what they needed to keep resisting. MGM was told to be ready to insert UAE special forces within 'two to three weeks'.

The reason that the UAE Deputy Supreme Commander thought immediately of doing more than the minimum – specifically more than just air operations – was that he had built up small but capable ground forces that he trusted to get the job done. MBZ was a graduate of officer training at the Royal Military Academy Sandhurst in the UK, and he had served in both the Emiri Guard (forerunner to the Presidential Guard) and as a pilot officer in the UAE Air Force and Air Defence. In the 1990s, under the leadership of MBZ's father, Sheikh Zayed bin Sultan Al Nahyan, the UAE was a unique kind of Arab state building a unique kind of Arab military. The founder and father of the nation, Sheikh Zayed encouraged the development of a strong UAE military. Uniquely for a Gulf State, the UAE leadership neglected neither the human resources nor the technological aspects of military power. Like all the Gulf monarchies, the UAE Armed Forces would be equipped with advanced Western weapons, but in the UAE's case, those weapons would not be downgraded export versions of American or French systems, but rather the same *or better* versions than used in the US and French militaries. Thus, one of MBZ's first triumphs was to secure for the Emirates a more advanced version of the F-16 than even the US Air Force employed – the Block 60 – and the UAE was intimately involved in funding and designing the next-generation AN/APG-80 AESA (active electronically scanned antenna) radars that would be carried by the UAE F-16s, and (years later) would equip US F-16 fighter-bombers.

As MBZ learned in his interactions with Western militaries, including first-hand at Sandhurst, the best militaries are built on foundations such as tradition, nationalism, military pride and investment in people. Like all nations, the UAE had a class of military families for whom service is a tradition. Under Sheikh Zayed and his successors, the military became a more prestigious career with competitive pay and professional advancement opportunities. Just before the Yemen war, the experience of military service was broadened with the introduction of one-year compulsory national service for men in order to develop patriotism, service, discipline and physical fitness, although quite limited numbers went to Yemen, and none fought in the battle for Aden in 2015.

The first UAE warriors to go to Yemen were all volunteers and professionals, the hand-picked tip of the spear. These were the first products of the military reformer MBZ's new generation of officers and other ranks, rewarded and promoted to an unprecedented extent for merit and competence, not connections or tribal status. They could be trusted to go into a real shooting war because they took the effort to put their men through rigorous, realistic training, and because they groomed similarly promising subordinates to come up behind them as they progressed.

Though foreigners were expressly prohibited from serving at the front lines with the UAE Armed Forces, plenty of them did transfer their skills and experience through professional military education and training. This developed into a complete system by the late 2000s from pre-commissioning prep schools to overseas officer training at Sandhurst, West Point, Australia's Duntroon and France's St Cyr academies. Expatriate lecturers served at the National Defence College in Abu Dhabi and the Radban Academy, the latter of which taught interagency government skills and provided ongoing education to mid-level officers. Hands-on tactical training for ground forces took place at the US Marine Corps' 29 Palms training centre in California and the UAE's own al-Hamra pre-deployment training site, which again used Western trainers alongside Emiratis. The UAE Air Force and UAE Naval Force regularly participated in US and European exercises.

But the most effective training was that gained on real-world battlefields as the UAE Armed Forces served alongside Western militaries in coalition operations in Somalia, Lebanon, the Kosovo war, Afghanistan, Libya and the war against the Islamic State in Syria. As one Special Operations Command officer noted:

> In our courses, people just memorised the curriculum. Then you go into the reality of war and it's different – really murky, ambiguous. I learned more in my first year of real war than I did until then in my whole career in the military.

In particular, the UAE graduated a whole generation of soldiers through the 12-year deployment of UAE forces to Afghanistan alongside US and NATO units. As an unnamed UAE task force leader in Afghanistan told a *Washington Post* reporter in 2014, 'It really hardened our soldiers, it tested us like never before in a real environment.' Afghanistan saw the UAE contingent hone its local community engagement skills, leveraging its understanding of Islamic society and tribal culture. Afghanistan shaped the men who would become the captains, majors, lieutenant colonels, colonels and brigadiers who led the UAE forces in the Yemen war. They learned war-fighting culture, self-sacrifice and critical thinking on real battlefields. Because all of this was so different from the caricatured parade-ground militaries of the Gulf, the US military officers coined the affectionate nickname 'Little Sparta' for the UAE Armed Forces. This was a high compliment, underlining that the UAE was building a small, hard force that could win on the battlefield – like the Spartans of Ancient Greece.

For what the UAE had in mind, the UAE would not need to deploy large formations. The envisioned operations in southern Yemen would be an efficient employment of military force, blending special forces, rangers, airstrike controllers, air and helicopter forces, an amphibious assault force, and the sealift and airlift needed to get them to Yemen and keep them supplied. The core of the 'ready force' in March 2015 was the Presidential Guard, which consisted of the Special Operations Command; the Al-Forsan ranger battalion; and two ground units of the old Emiri Guard, the Khalifa bin Zayed 2nd Mechanised Brigade and the Reconnaissance Group. These well-armed units could draw on support weapons (Leclerc tanks and G-6 howitzers) seconded by the larger UAE Land Forces.

Overhead, the UAE Air Force could provide powerful dedicated air support when needed. UAE F-16 and Mirage crews were highly experienced by 2015, having each flown numerous long-range strike missions and aerial refuelling operations in Afghanistan, Syria and Libya. Their aircraft were cutting-edge, constantly updated with the newest upgrades, precision-guided munitions and sensor pods. The UAE had taken the far-sighted step of gaining NATO-standard qualification for its forward air observers, known as Joint Terminal Attack Controllers (JTACs) in the modern jargon, and the Presidential Guard had even built its own accredited JTAC training school – the Joint Fires Initiative – to increase the numbers of personnel from all services capable of directing airstrikes. This was all the more impressive because, after more than a century of alliance, the NATO countries had also developed precisely one JTAC academy.

Backing all this up, the UAE had the rare distinction among US partners of having invested in the right airlift and aerial refuelling capabilities to be self-deploying and self-sustaining, giving the Emirates global reach and independence of action. These systems – such as the C-17A Globemaster III heavy airlift aircraft and the air-to-air refuelling Airbus A330 Multi Role Tanker Transport (MRTT) – arrived just in the nick of time. Though some of these platforms had been in service for five years before the 2015 war, the whole complement of airlift and tankers was only fully assembled and incorporated into the force shortly before the war. The equipment was, by military standards, brand new and without too much wear and tear, but its use was comfortable and practised at the moment war began. In other words, a freshly equipped force that was ready to undertake the job. The ability to reach out and support friends would now be tested as the Houthis tried to break the will of the Yemeni government and the Adenese Resistance.

# VI

# NOT BY AIRPOWER ALONE

Mohammed bin Zayed's instincts about the crisis in Aden were proving to be spot-on. The Yemeni government and its remaining forces in Aden were willing to resist and might provide a resilient ground force, but they needed support and would not survive on their own. And airpower, while vital to the defence, would not be sufficient to dig the Houthis out of Aden before they entrenched themselves. The first weeks of street fighting in Aden gave a sense of the kind of battle that would be required to first hold the line, and then to liberate the city. The Houthis and Saleh had mounted neither a full-blown military assault on the city, nor a weak probe, but rather something in-between. After infiltrating Houthi and Saleh special forces into the city, the next step was to create a sense of chaos – as if Aden had already fallen – by activating these cells at neuralgic points across the city. Acting on Lebanese Hezbollah advice, the Houthis had used this 'nodal' approach before, seizing so-called 'hegemony points' in northern Yemeni cities to quickly splinter resistance into isolated pockets and gain a psychological advantage over adversaries.

In practical terms, this meant putting snipers on rooftops to dominate wide avenues and roundabouts with harassment fire and sending patrols out into the city with loudspeakers or knocking on doors to make the citizens aware of the takeover. As the Saleh government had previously done against the Houthis during the six wars, and indeed against restive southern cities, cell phone coverage was turned off from the main headquarters of telecommunications companies in Sanaa, increasing the feeling of isolation and the potential for panic. At this stage, it amounted to an enormous bluff: the same kind of bluff that any blitzkrieg tactic relies upon to convince an enemy they are beaten, when, in fact, they can still resist if they keep their heads.

In many ways, Aden is really two cities, not one, separated by the salt pans that once provided one of the city's richest exports. To the west of the 8 km square of shallow tidal drying pans are the sprawling slums of Shaikh Uthman: from east to west, Musabeen, Dar Saad, al Bastaeen and Bir Fadl. Well over half the population of Aden live in this largely unplanned metropolis, which grew out of the old tribal souks to the north of the twentieth-century port city. To the east of the salt pans, south of the airport, is the city proper. Adjacent to the airport is Khormaksar, which was once the British Royal Air Force canton in Aden, with street names drawn from British aviation history such as Viscount and Avro. After the British period, Khormaksar remained the diplomatic quarter of the PDRY and the seat of Aden University's premier and oldest departments. Known as a tombolo (or sandy isthmus), Khormaksar connected the volcanic Crater, in effect a tied island, to the mainland.

This made southern Khormaksar a choke point that needed to be forced if the Houthi–Saleh forces were to seize the most politically significant locations in what was known as Greater Aden – the Mashiq Palace in Crater and the main ports in Mualla and Tawahi.

The Houthi–Saleh force pushed from two directions. From the northwest, drawing on the arsenals at Al-Anad, one Houthi–Saleh front began probing and splintering the northern neighbourhoods on the Sheikh Uthman side. Standing in

their way were the Popular Committees of these densely populated neighbourhoods. At the northern edge to the Sheikh
Uthman side, at the Al Karaa Roundabout, the Popular Com-
mittee of Amjad Khaled was overrun by Houthi–Saleh tank
forces who drove straight through the lightly armed Resistance
outposts. The resistance rallied 1.5 km to the south in the Dar
Saad area, where the hotels of Shahwa Fayrouz Street (the main
north–south highway, R-17) were held by committees led by
Muhammad al Bukari and Ahmed Jalab. The western flank of
Shahwa Fayrouz Street was held by the Al Basateen Popular
Committees of Bassem al Mindhar and Abdalaziz Abu al Baraa.
The eastern flank of Dar Saad was held by Mumdara al Aden
Popular Committee commander Wissam al Futaisi.

These small resistance bands were not trained soldiers. As
local council member Mohammed Ali Saadi told US Vice News
reporters in the Dar Saad area: 'The defenders of this city are
university students, architects, writers, businessmen and civilians; we don't have an army with which to fight back against
the occupiers of our lands.' Though Yemen is a country where
there are more guns than people, many of those weapons were
hoarded by the few and used as currency and a means of gifting
patronage. Many of the city people of the Popular Committees
did not routinely own guns, and there was less than one AK-47
per man in the committees. The only heavy weapons they possessed were an occasional immobile tank, emplaced as a bunker,
a couple of intermittently mobile BMPs, and the odd salvaged
anti-aircraft cannon.

Nevertheless, the Houthis found the Sheikh Uthman area
hard to break and, ultimately, more trouble than it was worth.
The sheer physical size and population density of the area could
absorb many more thousands of troops than the Houthis or
Saleh possessed. The Popular Committees were clearly ready to

fight for their neighbourhoods and were not short of martyrs; either to the southern cause, or to the Salafist call to jihad that was chanted nightly from the minarets of Sheikh Uthman. Barricades were raised to make it harder for Houthi-operated armoured vehicles to drive straight through Dar Saad into the heart of Sheikh Uthman. Airpower proved quite effective against Houthi–Saleh tanks and BMPs on the wide avenues that segregated Sheikh Uthman's warren-like neighbourhoods.

The frontlines gelled, with a no-man's land of about 700 metres. Like all static urban front lines, this zone would be devastated in the coming months of bombardment and skirmishing, with neither side able to advance without taking heavy casualties. The Houthis lined up their single-largest concentration of tanks, BMPs, anti-aircraft cannons, mortars and B-10 recoilless rifles along the 2.5-km front and kept up a harassing fire on the densely populated Sheikh Uthman area, now swelled with the displaced persons of the northern suburbs. A Médecins Sans Frontières surgical team deployed to the Al Wahda Hospital, just 480 metres south of the frontline. Civilians learned to stay inside during the day as Sheikh Uthman began its four-month ordeal of fire. Thus began an urban siege with scenes reminiscent of other contemporary struggles such as Sarajevo, Grozny and Mariupol.

While the Sheikh Uthman zone held out, the main Houthi attack came on the Khormaksar side, drawing on the military arsenals of Al Kawd, Jaar and Zinjibar (50–60 km north-east on the coastal highway) and Shuqra (90 km away, on the same highway). As early as 25 March, the Houthi–Saleh forces already had a firm lodgement inside Khormaksar at the airport, and now they began to receive reinforcements from Houthi–Saleh forces from outside the city. Then, from 26 March to 2 April, Houthi–Saleh forces leapfrogged from one major landmark to another, using taller buildings to snipe and direct mortar fire.

It took nearly a week of heavy fighting for the invaders to clear 2 km of Khormaksar from the Popular Committees of Mohammed Amzerba and Suleiman al Zamki. The uneven quality of the Resistance was fully on show in Khormaksar: Amzerba, the Abyan Salafi fighter, fought to the bitter end, dying in his neighborhood, while Zamki fled after having hidden the ammunition sent to his forces for later resale. The Khormaksar frontline was described in terms of the landmarks being won, lost and recovered in the fighting: the Ministry of Finance, the College of Arts, the Russian Consulate, the Aden houses of Hadi and Ali Mohsen, the Flamingo Roundabout and the Al Jumhuriya Teaching Hospital. As swollen corpses began to litter the wrecked streets, civilians found it too dangerous to recover the bodies for burial – a sign of how intense the fighting became, even at night.

The Houthis did not have it all their own way: accounts of the early April fighting suggest that the Resistance made at least two valiant efforts on 2 April to cut the Houthi line of supply with counterattacks. One targeted the airport, launched from the salt pans by the Popular Committees of Al Usaymie and the Saltworks, and its bloody failure foreshadowed the high casualties that Resistance forces would suffer in the future when assaulting the airport over open ground. Another costly effort was made further north, in the sparsely populated and open Al Areesh suburb, with a mix of military and Popular Committee fighters from Sheikh Uthman ambitiously trying to cut the coastal road by seizing the Al Alam roundabout. These two brave attempts resulted in the deaths of 30 resistance fighters, a huge number of fatalities for a couple of Popular Committees, each of which rarely numbered more than 60 fighters.

Probably by blind coincidence, the Houthi–Saleh forces committed their main reserves at precisely this moment of brittleness. The Houthis had captured six military bases in the Abyan area, and even with the abysmal state of Yemeni arsenals, this gave them access to scores of operational tanks, BMPs and heavy weapons. These forces had begun to flow down the coastal road by day and by night, and they were used to smash the Yemeni Resistance counterattack against Al Alam Roundabout, which ran headfirst into an armoured column of T-55 and T-62 tanks and BMPs.

## The Limitations of Air and Naval Bombardment

The fighting that followed would vindicate Mohammed bin Zayed's gut feeling that airpower could not save Aden on its own. Air power was necessary but not sufficient – it went without saying that the Resistance would have been far worse off without Coalition air support. In its first week, the Coalition air campaign had cleared the skies of Saleh-operated aircraft and bombed the few L-39 armed trainers still based at Al Anad. Coalition airpower had also done a valuable job of disrupting the air bridge between Sanaa's Al Daylami airbase and Al Anad, which Houthi–Saleh forces had briefly used to ferry troops to the south in United Yemen Air Force Illyushin IL-76 airlifters. So-called Battlefield Air Interdiction strikes were being undertaken daily against the bridges, roads, fuel bunkers and stopping points that the Houthi–Saleh forces were using to send military forces southwards to the Aden front. Egyptian and Saudi naval vessels were undertaking Naval Gunfire Support against the Aden-Abyan coastal highway, which was no more than 1.5 km from the shore at any point.

Nevertheless, no amount of firepower could hermetically seal off Aden from the north. Houthi–Saleh forces were getting through in sufficient numbers to overrun Resistance forces on the

vital Khormaksar isthmus. Once Houthi–Saleh forces got past
the open roads to the north of Aden city, they could seek cover
within the urban area, where collateral damage risks were higher,
and it became more difficult to find and target them. Already,
the Resistance-held territory between the Sheikh Uthman and
Greater Aden sides of Aden had been narrowed to a tenuous
500-metre-wide corridor between Regal Roundabout, named
after the nearby casino, and Labour Island (formerly Slave Island),
and thence to Caltex Roundabout, named after the old Caltex
fuel and diesel oil station. The newly arrived Houthi–Saleh tanks
were poised to force the entrances to Crater and the port areas. At
the south-western corner of Khormaksar, the road between the
Regal Roundabout and the port district of Mualla was squeezed
between the high fortress of the Jebel Hadid camp and the Inner
Harbour. At the south-eastern corner of Khormaksar, a similar
choke point lay between the old forts on Jebel Hadid and the
beaches by the Mercure Hotel. Both of these Thermopylae-like
defiles had been defended since ancient times, as evidenced by
the Ottoman and British fortifications above both choke points.
But, in April 2015, the defenders were lightly armed civilian volunteers, backed only by Coalition airpower and naval cannons.

There was no doubt that the Coalition could hit hard from
the air and the sea when the strike platforms were on scene. The
main strike aircraft used to hold back the Houthis at this time
was the Royal Saudi Air Force F-15SA, a twin-engine jet as long
as a semi-trailer and with a wingspan as wide as the Hollywood
sign. Known as the Strike Eagle, the US-built aircraft is a real
brawler in the air-to-ground fight. The Saudis tended to load
the aircraft sent to Aden with eight 500-lb GBU-12 Paveway II
laser-guided bombs, and thus each two-ship formation could
hit 16 targets. The F-15SA aircraft over Yemen were operated by
the most experienced Saudi Arabian squadrons – the 6th, 55th,

92nd squadrons plus the Weapons & Tactics School instructors. Since the sixth Houthi war in 2010, these squadrons had been intensively trained by US contractors and exercised in ground attack operations against the Houthis in anticipation of a new conflict. These F-15SA now pummelled the Houthi–Saleh forces north of the Mercure Hotel and on Jebel Hadid, but airpower had its limitations. Each F-15SA two-ship would make the hour-long flight down from Khamis Mushayt airbase in Saudi Arabia and would then only have enough fuel to loiter over Aden for an hour, during which it had to use its eight munitions. The invaders learned to time their short-range land grabs between such sorties.

Thus, the skies were empty when a Houthi–Saleh armoured column broke through to Crater and the Mashiq Palace on 2 April, and again when a similar thrust cleared the defile west of Jebel Hadid on 5 April, overrunning the Hamra Restaurant and Purple Aden water park. With just a handful of tanks and BMPs in each case, the Houthi–Saleh forces had punctured the Adenese defences. Desperation and panic began to grow. In Mualla and Tawahi, the jetties had been busy for days as Saudi, Chinese, Turkish and Indian warships evacuated foreign nationals and guest workers from the same ports at which the world's grandest ocean liners had once disembarked passengers. For the first time, Egyptian and Saudi warships came close enough to the outer harbour to engage in naval gunfire support against advancing Houthi–Saleh forces. Their high-explosive shells were landing just 4,500 metres from the disembarkation piers – close enough to feel as well as hear. Desperation was peaking: for the first time, UAE aircraft para-dropped ammunition and anti-tank rockets directly into the Tawahi area, on the western end of Greater Aden, using a GPS parachute system to achieve a safe and accurate delivery in the crowded area.

# VII

# BOOTS ON THE GROUND

In Abu Dhabi it was becoming clear that Greater Aden would shortly fall unless something changed quickly. Almost all the fixed targets in the Coalition's Joint Target List had been struck, often multiple times. Now it was all about what air campaign planners called 'dynamic' targets, which are targeting opportunities that emerge suddenly and for only a short time window. Dynamic targets – like tanks or a *chassis* carrying an anti-aircraft cannon – are often moving quickly, meaning that strike aircraft have to make snap decisions to release weapons or hold back. Engaging dynamic targets inside a city adds an additional layer of complication and risk due to the proximity and concentration of civilian targets, but this was the challenge that the Coalition had to master if it was to help the Adenese resistance survive the coming weeks.

MBZ tended to be one step ahead in his military thinking. He had a keen interest in military technology and tactics, and he was a pilot himself. UAE commanders understood that air power could only fully support the Resistance if JTACs were on the ground. In addition to getting a closer, ground-level look at terrain, civilian presence and the enemy, the JTAC was also trained to manage the airspace over a battlefield, allowing the optimisation of air cover around the clock. Putting boots on the ground was a big step, however, and the UAE had to be sure that the Yemenis would lead the fight.

The head of UAE Special Operations Command, Brigadier General Musallam R., visited President Hadi, who was now ensconced in a palace in Riyadh, having made his escape from Aden. The Yemeni leadership was ecstatic to hear that the UAE would be willing to deploy ground troops to Aden to help save the city. The UAE had only one condition: that the Yemeni president committed to personally leading his government back into Aden at the earliest possible moment, to minimise the time of being a government-in-exile and to quickly resume responsibility for Aden's administration. 'Of course,' he replied immediately. Late on 6 April, the UAE chain of command directed the immediate deployment of a clandestine special forces and JTAC team to Aden.

A new and untested command structure leapt into life when the UAE military leaders directed the beginning of clandestine special operations in Aden. The Presidential Guard (PG) had existed since 2011 and had taken part in numerous coalition operations, but this was different. The UAE was mounting the Aden campaign on its own. Presidential Guard commander MGM had been made the ground component commander for all UAE forces in Yemen by MBZ on 5 April, while the air component remained under the control of Major General Ibrahim A., the commander of the UAE Air Force and Air Defence. The PG's interim joint operations centre was activated on 7 April and MGM took up residence – quite literally, sleeping on a mattress in his office there during the hectic early days of operations. The new headquarters began to build its battle rhythm – the daily procedures and habits of military campaigning – starting with daily situation reports and intelligence summaries.

At this stage, destroying Al Qaeda was still the primary mission of the UAE in Yemen. The UAE Special Operations

Maritime lines of supply from the Horn of Africa and Eritrea

Command (SOC) was leading a Joint Task Force (numbered 291) in the east of Yemen, and had been instructed to build firm bases of tribal resistance wherever the Houthis were not present. These bases would resist not only any future Houthi advances but, more importantly, would prevent Al Qaeda from exploiting the collapse or redeployment of Yemeni army forces. In addition to the concurrent operations in Yemen, the air force shuffled new assets to sustain UAE involvement in the US-led anti-Islamic State campaign in Syria and Iraq. From now on, concurrent activity in at least three theatres would become the norm because the UAE chose to keep other counter-terrorism missions going alongside the heavy burden of marshalling the defence of Aden.

## Launchpad at Djibouti

The seed from which the Presidential Guard mission grew was the Combat Search and Rescue (CSAR, pronounced 'see-sar') capability that was quickly pulled together to support coalition pilots operating over southern Yemen. This was a deadly serious business: just months earlier on 3 January 2015, Royal Jordanian Air Force Captain Muath Safi Yousef al Kasasbeh had been captured by the Islamic State in Syria, and had been burned alive in a cage during a video-taped execution. In the opening days of Operation Decisive Storm, a Saudi F-15 had lost power south of Aden and the crew had been recovered by a US Navy helicopter after ejecting over the ocean. The UAE's Joint Task Force (JTF) set up bases in Saudi Arabia and Djibouti to cover possible contingencies in Aden, operating two CH-47 Chinook helicopters and a half-dozen propeller-driven AT-802i 'Air Tractor' surveillance and light-attack aircraft, plus Viking DHC-6-400 Twin Otter short take-off and landing aircraft. Twenty-six well-armed SOC 'operators' were assigned to the task force to handle the on-the-ground aspects of any rescue of downed pilots.

The first Aden team sent by the Presidential Guard would be led by Lieutenant Colonel Salem D., one of SOC's longer-serving officers and a Sandhurst graduate. The guidance given by MGM was barebones and straightforward: 'Find a forward base, do your intelligence preparation of the battlefield on the way and at the base. Get your team and the JTACs to Aden somehow. Don't make promises to the resistance you can't keep. This mission cannot fail.' At this point, there was really only one option for the forward base – the Republic of Djibouti, or DJ as it was known to SOC operators. A former French colony, Djibouti now hosted a French military base and a US Joint Special Operations Command outpost focused on Yemen and Somalia. As important, the UAE embassy there had excellent secure communications with Abu Dhabi. But DJ had a downside: unhelpfully, relations between the UAE and Djiboutian governments was at a low point in April 2015 due to disagreements over UAE investment in the Doraleh Container Terminal, the largest container port in Africa. The UAE's French hosts at Camp Lemonier did not want problems with the Djiboutians. This underlying tension would complicate everything that SOC tried to do from the Djibouti base.

The gathering of the team at Djibouti had all the elements of a classic heist movie like *The Usual Suspects* or *Ocean's Eleven*. An elite team of nine operators were gathered from all points of the globe. They were all veterans of Operation Winds of Goodness, the UAE effort in Afghanistan, and all were qualified combat medics. Alongside the commander, Salem D., was a team leader called Major Abdullah Y. A 36-year-old officer, Abdullah was one of the most popular and respected operators in SOC and an uncontroversial choice. Good-looking, fit, first to the finish line in races and swims, and strong like an ox, Abdullah's nickname was 'Abdullah Hammer'. To insert alongside Abdullah, a JTAC was called back from leave in Egypt and bundled onto private jets that took him from the Siwa oasis of Egypt's Western Desert to Dubai, Abu Dhabi, and straight back out to DJ. The team was hastily scraped together – just nine operators, not the doctrinal 12 or 14.

The facilities in DJ were very basic. When Salem D. arrived, he found a very hungry group of CH-47 pilots and ground crew. Though in the middle of the French base Camp Lemonier, their presence was meant to be secret so they were getting low on supplies. Salem D. and the TF 288 detachment commander made a classic deal between soldiers: Salem made sure to get them some food delivered, and TF 288 gave Salem's team a living and operating space. It helped that they knew each other from Afghanistan. The space given was half building, half tent, with huge 1:250,000 and 1:500,000 Tactical Pilotage Charts pinned to the walls. The kit was set up on folding card tables. It wasn't much, but it was home. And at least the team had a cool codename: Cobra.

Insertion of the team into Aden was no small hurdle. On a map, Djibouti looked to be a 240-km boat ride from Aden, but the going was more like 310 km (170 nautical miles) due to the strong currents and prevailing winds around the Bab el-Mandeb. Inquiries were made to the US Marine Corps – the key US training partner to the PG – about using the USS *Iwo Jima* (LHD-7), a Wasp-class amphibious assault ship, as a launch pad for Zodiacs, a kind of small assault boat. However, it became clear almost from the outset that this would be a complicated and lengthy process to approve, and the Emirates needed to move quickly. Other insertion options were considered: first, use of a Saudi warship and Saudi Zodiacs – a kind of small assault boat – or, second, a 'helocast', in which UAE CH-47s would drop UAE Zodiacs offshore. A third and dramatic option was a High-Altitude Low-Opening (HALO) parachute insertion, wherein the team would drop from 30,000 feet and freefall until they deployed their chutes as low as 800 feet above the sea. Above all, the insertion had to be clandestine and under Emirati control, to the greatest degree possible.

When other options began to look doubtful, the UAE decided to try it themselves with a direct approach using Rigid-Hulled Inflatable Boats (RHIBs, pronounced 'ribs'). The RHIBs set out from Djibouti on 11 April, but from the first moment the effort seemed marked by bad luck. The intent was to pilot two RHIBs all the way from DJ to Aden, calculated as a gruelling six-hour trip. As the mission prepared to launch from Djibouti, the local authorities took an interest in the RHIBs and tried to inspect them, resulting in a scuffle at the docks as a UAE operator did his duty and prevented the inspection. The RHIBs and the eight SOC operators (minus Salem D., managing the headquarters from DJ) got away at around 18:00 hours on 11 April but the going was tough. The 'sea state' – which measured wave heights and wind – was higher than expected, and by 00:40 hours on 12 April the RHIBs were less than halfway to Aden, around 110 km (60 nautical miles) out from Djibouti. The insertion was called off for the night, and the boats and their exhausted crews barely made it back to DJ by first light, around 05:00 hours.

Anxiety was growing within the team. All were veteran soldiers but they desperately wanted *this* mission: acting as the tip of the spear in the UAE's first real solo operation. A second effort to launch the RHIBs was stymied by withheld permissions from the Djiboutians and fear began to grow that the insertion and maybe the whole mission might be called off. All the PG commanders were frayed and ragged after a week of almost non-stop activity in Abu Dhabi and DJ. But the insertion on the night of 13 April would be different. The option chosen this time was 'helocast', in which two CH-47s would fly to a position about 15 nautical miles offshore and drop Zodiacs and men into the sea. So that the entire insertion could be self-contained, the SOC had trained themselves to serve as coxswains – naval language for those who pilot the boat. It was a rough-and-ready option: the CH-47s did not have a rail system to assist the safe and smooth delivery of Zodiacs off the back-ramp of the helicopters. Nor, annoyingly, did the Choppers have any armament: the deadly mini-guns usually mounted in side windows had not been brought to DJ. The team would have the call-sign Cobra 1-1. As they loaded onto a bus, they looked like footballers heading to an away game – right down to the goofy antics and the coach – in this case Major Abdullah Y. – undertaking a headcount.

At 19:37 hours on 13 April, the Djiboutian air traffic control made one last effort to block the mission but the choppers took off into the very dark and cloudy night. Salem D. recalled watching the Chinooks disappear: 'My adrenalin was peaking – we had been on edge for days. It was such a relief when they took off. No more of the administration and coordination problems of the last three days. Finally, we were in a world of military action; what we know, the kind of uncertainty we're trained for.' Salem and the remaining admin staff at DJ would have a long night, especially as communications proved spotty between the forward base and Abdullah's team. He wrangled with air controllers to keep F-16 cover for the insertion, even as it fell behind schedule. Salem manned the phones as headquarters staff back in Abu Dhabi called for updates, keeping a watch on either wrist

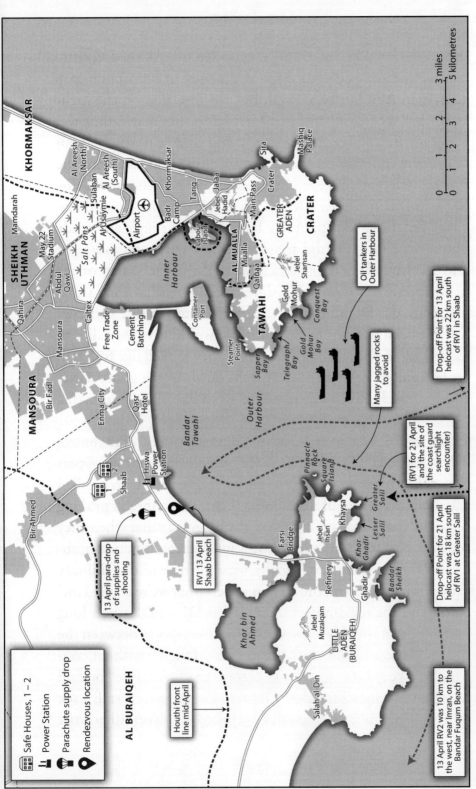

The insertion of UAE special forces, 13 and 20 April 2015

**Legend:**
- Safe Houses, 1–2
- Power Station
- Parachute supply drop
- Rendezvous location

**Labels on map:**

KHORMAKSAR
SHEIKH UTHMAN
MANSOURA
AL BURAIQEH
CRATER
GREATER ADEN
TAWAHI
AL MUALLA

Mamdarah
Al Areesh (North)
Sulaban
Al Areesh (South)
Al Usaymle
Badr Camp
Khormaksar
Tariq
Airport
Jebel Jalaa
Sira
Mashiq Palace
Crater
May 22 Stadium
Salt Pans
Jebel Hadid
Main Pass
Qahira
Abdul Qawi
Caltex
Inner Harbour
Labour Island
Mualla
Jebel Shamsan
Gold Mohur
Mansoura
Free Trade Zone
Cement Batching
Container Port
Qalbaa
Conquest Bay
Bir Fadl
Qasr Hotel
Steamer Point
Sapper Bay
Gold Mohur Bay
Telegraph Bay
Enma City
Bandar Tawahi
Outer Harbour
Oil tankers in Outer Harbour
Many jagged rocks to avoid
Bir Ahmed
Hiswa Power Station
Shaab
13 April para-drop of supplies and shooting
RV1 13 April Shaab beach
Pinnacle Rock
Square Island
Greater Saiil
Lesser Saiil
Farsi Bridge
Jebel Ihsan
Khaysa
Khor Ghadir
Refinery
Ghadir
Bandar Sheikh
Khor bin Ahmed
Jebel Muzalqam
LITTLE ADEN (BURAIQEH)
Salah al-Din
Houthi front line mid-April

Drop-off Point for 13 April helocast was 22 km south of RV1 in Shaab

(RV1 for 21 April and the site of the coast guard searchlight encounter)

Drop-off Point for 21 April helocast was 18 km south of RV1 at Greater Saiil

13 April RV2 was 10 km to the west, near Imran, on the Bandar Fuqum Beach

0   1   2   3 miles
0  1  2  3  4  5 kilometres

– one set to local time and one to 'Zulu' – the Coordinated Universal Time (UTC) that corresponds to Greenwich Mean Time, located at prime meridian: 0° (zero degrees) longitude – as a means to ensure precision when commanders may be operating in different time zones. Not usually a smoker, Salem needed a few puffs on a team member's pipe that night.

## Cobra 1-1: The First Team Ashore

The two CH-47s of the Joint Aviation Command (JAC) flew across the Gulf of Aden very close to the water, with the pilots and (gunless) gunners all peering through their night-vision gear. The outbound trip took a total of 78 minutes, arriving at the Drop-Off Point at 20:55 hours. In Aden, an air strike was going on, an idea supplied by the trusted agent (who cannot be named or described for security reasons) who would meet the team ashore. These explosions were intended to cause a distraction and cover the sounds of rotor blades. As soon as the Zodiacs crashed into the water and the SOC team jumped in, the Chinooks were gone. The SOC were not taking any chances. The Houthis were not operating coastal patrols but one of Ali Abdullah Saleh's old business partners owned many of the oil tankers that were still idling off Aden and there was a concern that the ships' radars or lookouts might detect the helicopters and Zodiacs. Using night-vision gear, the team scanned the surroundings, and then took GPS and compass bearings. They were 22 km (15 nautical miles) south of the Shaab neighbourhood, which lined the bay between Sheikh Uthman and the refinery at the peninsular known as 'Little Aden'. Due to the strong tides, it would be nearly 23:00 hours before they approached the main rendezvous point (RV1).

The beach at Shaab, RV1, had been selected by UAE

intelligence and the Yemeni agent because it was directly adjacent to the first team house (Safe House 1 or SH1), an anonymous villa 6 km inland that was donated by Salafi fighter. Overhead, a UAE F-16 was watching Shaab and reporting the scene back to Major Abdullah in the Zodiac. The plane was their link to the world as their Thuraya satellite equipment could not reach DJ or Abu Dhabi for some reason. Tracer fire was lazily arcing into the sky near the landing point. The Emiratis were told to expect two cars and five persons in the reception committee, but the pilot was reporting around 30 people shooting into the air. It later became clear that they were tribesmen trying to shoot down Saudi Arabian ammunition pallets that were being para-dropped to the resistance, hoping to cut short their drift so that they dropped in the militia's lap and could be seized, buried or sold. The JTAC and Major Abdullah looked at each other: one of them recalled, 'We were shocked. Here we are, all covert, on this fancy mission, and now this?' and then laughing: 'So that was a good start!'

The Zodiacs crawled across the outer harbour at a torturously slow rate, keeping their engine noise low, heading towards RV2, well to the west of the Little Aden peninsula, running a gauntlet of jagged rocks and small islands. It was 01:15 hours on 14 April when the SOC came ashore. They unloaded their kit and sank the Zodiacs in the shallows, then all the team members changed out of their tracksuits and shorts into Yemeni attire, using clothes provided by the agent. They were loaded into Landcruisers, and the agent told them their cover story; 'Pretend to be asleep, I'll tell the checkpoints you are fighters from the countryside coming to join us.' They reached the last checkpoint before Shaab, which was situated on the so-called Farsi Bridge, which linked Little Aden to the Sheikh Uthman side. The Popular Committee fighters at the bridge were agitated, stirred up on *qat*, and they startled the team by shooting into the air over the cars, a kind of welcome to the new 'volunteers'. It was 03:41 hours, almost dawn and nearly five hours behind schedule, when Cobra 1-1 arrived at the safe house and signalled their arrival to Salem in Djibouti and to Abu Dhabi. It was an anonymous brick villa south of Aden University's law school. In order that the safe house would have a nearby helicopter landing site, it was positioned on the northern edge of the urban sprawl, with wide fields of fire, but this meant the enemy was not that far away. From the roof of the two-storey villa, the SOC operators could see smoke from the tubes of enemy mortars just 4,000 metres to the north. 'Stealth and secrecy were our only defence,' one team member recalled.

## The Hammer Falls

Cobra 1-1 had barely settled in at SH1 when they were plunged unexpectedly into the fight. The team began to sense something was wrong, watching the anxious glances and whispered conversations of the Resistance fighters. SMS messages and calls were coming in non-stop, with each Yemeni working a lap-full of phones like an orchestra conductor. The agent had a grim look on his face and told them, 'I'm sorry to do this to you, as you have just arrived, but the Houthis are coming. Today they will take [Little Aden]. You should leave. We can't protect you.' Major Abdullah Y. wanted to know more. He needed 'eyes-on' the enemy but at this point there was no drone surveillance over Aden to tell where the Houthis were – or were not. The agent and other Yemenis pieced together the picture over Motorola radios: after seizing military arsenals at Taizz, the Houthi– Saleh forces had ferried numerous T-55 tanks and BMPs down the winding 170-km mountain highway to an assembly point, the Aden Steel Factory, just north of Imran. The Houthi–Saleh forces were seeking to emulate the same tactic that saw Ali Mohsen (then fighting on the opposite side of the south) crack open the defence of Aden in the 1994 civil war, using Imran and the Little Aden peninsula as a 'back door' into Sheikh Uthman.

Abdullah Y. could see that the situation in Aden was more precarious than anyone suspected. 'Tank fear' is a phrase that emerged in the First World War, when German forces first encountered British tanks and recoiled in shock because they could not harm the steel beasts. 'Tank fear' was setting in here as well. The resistance was getting perilously short of RPGs and all of the six immobile Resistance tanks had been emplaced on other fronts. The defenders could see around a dozen Houthi-operated tanks marshalling for a major attack on Imran and thereafter Salah al Din, the western entrance to Little Aden. But Abdullah had confidence: he had operated alongside JTACs in Afghanistan and knew what they could do.

He was clear in his mind that his commanders' intent was to fight, not to hide. The team's morale was high: one member compared their feeling to the national spirit when the UAE had hosted – and, against the odds, won – the Gulf Cup soccer tournament in 2006. 'We might not be seen as the strongest team,' the comparison continued, 'but we were going to win.' With no hesitation he told the amazed Yemenis: 'Don't worry. Let us deal with the situation.' They looked at Abdullah incredulously. What could he do? They were eight men and a radio.

Thus began the vital first 48 hours of non-stop combat for Abdullah and the JTAC, and their Yemeni helpers. When one imagines forward air controllers, it is easy to envisage soldiers at the frontline, 'lasing' targets with their laser designators, and calling down bombs within their visual arc. But, for Abdullah and his JTAC, the battle was entirely remote yet also strangely

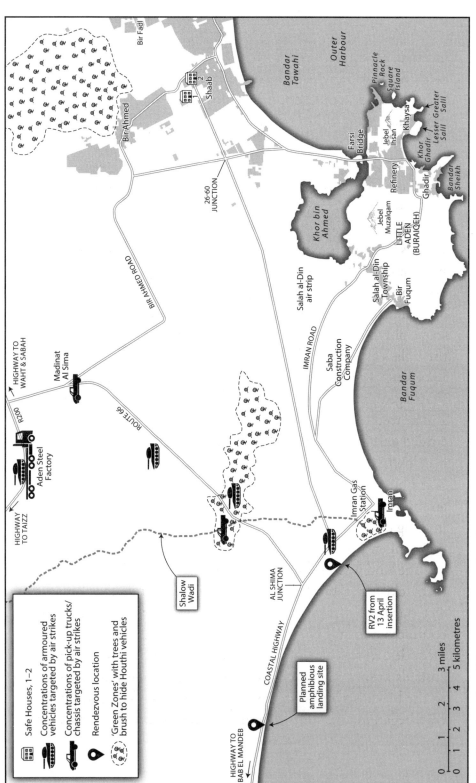

The first battle of Imran, 14–15 April 2015

intimate. They were clustered together under a billowing blue tarp on the roof, which the operators slashed in order that the blustery winds would not fill the tarp like a sail. Their hide was not visible from other houses due to the low wall around the roof. On the floor in front of Abdullah and the JTAC was a collection of communications devices: Samsungs and tablets drawing internet access from from the satellite internet router; a Thuraya satellite phone and dish; a Harris handheld radio; and the numerous Nokia flip phones of the Yemeni resistance agent and his friends. Power cords and chargers trailed back to extension leads that snaked up staircases and through windows. In the opening months of the battle, this is what a real special forces operations room looked like; there were no wide screens at this stage, only tiny ones – as often as not with spiderweb cracks in their glass faces.

Using Google Maps, as and when the internet allowed, the JTAC got a sense for the geography north of Imran. Abdullah and he were amazed to note that this was exactly where they had landed earlier that day, RV2. In fact, Houthis had overrun the beach where they had made landfall just two hours after they had landed there. Searching for para-dropped pallets of Saudi ammunition that might have fallen in the sea, the Houthis investigated dark shapes in the shallow waters and found the two sunken Zodiacs.

The land west of Little Aden was known as 'sabkha' (marshy or brackish coastal desert): salty low-lying lands that became wet during the rainy season or storms, but which dried out completely in full heat. The terrain was flat-looking but, like most desert, was actually undulating and cut by dried-out streambeds known as wadis. As a result, vehicle movement stuck to the blacktop highway, Route 66. UAE and Saudi strike aircraft began to take shifts covering the area – the pilots and their high-acuity sensor pods were the JTACs 'eyes in the sky'. There were no civilians around and the roads were empty. Following the highway north, the pilots began to report to the JTACs that enemy tanks, BMPs and *chassis* were dotted along the wadis and hidden under the trees of the 'green zones', areas where water allowed sparse vegetation to take root. At the top of the highway system was a large metalworks, the Aden Steel Manufactory Company, which seemed to be the main hub for Houthi–Saleh heavy equipment transporters bringing tanks and BMPs down from Taizz. With Yemeni eyes on the ground and strike aircraft overhead, the JTACs fused the picture together in their makeshift tent on their Google Maps applications.

The UAE aircraft above had no concerns about enemy fire, so they were able to maintain graceful orbits above. To ensure a permissive environment, all SA-2 and SA-3 surface-to-air missile sites in Aden had been targeted in the first days of the war, whether under Hadi control or not, and the Houthi–Saleh forces were no longer able to fly aircraft or helicopters due to the Coalition's combat air patrols. For the JTACs, pilots and air-to-air refuellers, the main challenge was maintaining coverage over the battlefront, which required the careful shuffling of aircraft, like cards in a deck. For Cobra 1-1 to stay in its hide site, the force protection rules stated that they also needed to have dedicated air cover over SH1, creating a further drain on resources. Yet, through careful husbanding of available air cover, the UAE strike aircraft were ready and waiting when the Houthi attack came.

The first airstrikes gutted the 500-metre-long steel factory and the truck park outside. Then the JTACs went after the 'dynamic targets'. They brought in three pairs of strike aircraft, back-to-back, to break the Houthi attack, which began at around 23:00 hours on 14 April. First a two-ship package of Mirage 2000-9 (known as 'dash-nines') took up station. Each

French-built Mirage carried six 500-lb laser-guided bombs and a Shehab laser targeting pod and infrared sight. Then a two-ship formation of US-made F-16s arrived, each, again, armed with six 500-lb bombs and a Sniper targeting and infrared pod. Finally, another two-ship of Mirages arrived to finish the fight. The Emirati pilots had undertaken strike missions in Afghanistan, Libya, Syria and during the frantic opening week of Operation Decisive Storm in Yemen, but this was different. They were protecting Emirati troops in contact with the enemy, in a solo UAE operation, drawing only on their own targeting intelligence, refuellers and logistics.

The enemy tanks, BMPs and *chassis* showed hot in the infrared sensor pods of the strike aircraft above. Over 90 minutes, 36 heavy detonations echoed around the desert north of Imran. Twenty destroyed vehicles were tallied – the attack had been completely smashed from the air by a couple of men under a tarp, 50 km away. The news of a great victory spread quickly among Aden's desperate defenders. Minarets began the chant of 'Allahu Akbar' – God is the greatest. Social media lit up, as did celebration gunfire, which dotted the skies over Aden. The Resistance offered amnesty to prisoners in Aden's jails if they volunteered for the Popular Committees to earn their freedom. But only a select few within the Resistance knew why Coalition airpower had suddenly become so effective and, for now, the SOC troopers would remain 'the grey men', hidden and unrecognised. Even the Houthis – despite having discovered the sunken Zodiacs on the Imran beach – had not put two and two together.

The Resistance liaison officers came to Abdullah's team with tears in their eyes, saying: 'You have saved our families.' Suddenly the young fresh-shaven UAE troopers looked older and more impressive to the Yemenis. 'You were eight, but we looked at you like you were eight thousand,' a Resistance commander recalled. When the wife of the most veteran Resistance commander, Hashim Sayyed, had their tenth child a few days later, the little girl was named Fatima, after the mother of Mohammed bin Zayed.

## Key Leader Engagement

As with all partner forces provided with modern air power, it took no time at all for the Resistance to get addicted to UAE airstrikes. Abdullah Y. and his JTAC entered a strange twilight world. They slept in their headsets, waking fully alert at the sound of the pilot's voice as he came on-station. The pilots and JTAC grew to know each other, by voice and by call-sign. Whether in a blacked-out room or on the roof at night, they lived in the dark, lit only by the green-grey light of screens and the headlamps that the JTAC wore. The static of radios filled the air with a strange discordant screech, punctuated by crazy bouts of loud talking and high-pressure calls for fire support coming to the Yemeni assistants through their banks of flip-phones.

Abdullah Y. was used to movement and action, but now he could not get away from the earphones and their endless calls for fire. Barefoot and in cut-off shorts, working in a dark, sweltering room, the youthful-looking Abdullah simply had no time to do the other part of special operations advising – so-called 'key leader engagement' (KLE) with the Resistance Council. Sitting at the other end of the Thuraya in Djibouti, Salem D. lobbied his bosses in Abu Dhabi for the chance to get into Aden to take over the KLE work. Desperate the get out of DJ and to the front, Salem tried every argument he could – including that he was a little older than Abdullah and already had a full-grown beard and so would look older to the Yemenis, while Abdullah and the others were still growing out stubble.

After three nerve-wracking days of aborted insertions, Salem got his authorisation to 'go forward' to Aden on the morning of 21 April, the same day that the Saudi-led Coalition headquarters announced the end of the war's opening air campaign, Operation Decisive Storm, and the beginning of a new phase, Operation Restore Hope. Salem would helocast into the Gulf of Aden with six other SOC operators that night. Years later, every detail of that night and all his feelings remain crystal-clear: 'Even after 20 years in the army, I was full of adrenalin. This mission was like a gift at the end of a military life. Not a Mickey Mouse mission. It was the best thing I can offer my country. Very important to the UAE. To SOC. To prove SOC's worth. To prove to the rest why we're special, and why all the investment was given by MBZ since 1991. All this lets you forget the danger that is right in front of you, lets you go to the land where the devils are.'

The final hours were nerve-wracking. This time both the Zodiacs were loaded into the same Chinook, which choppered away from Djibouti at 21:36 hours. At 22:53 hours the helicopter deposited Salem's command team at the Drop-Off Point. Both GPS units carried by the team failed to work, so Salem took a visual and compass bearing on the coastline and the boats quietly motored to tonight's RV1, a shoal of rocks called Greater Salil, just off Little Aden. It was a bright night with very clear stars and no cloud. At the RV, the team again tried to get a GPS reading and sought to make Thuraya contact with the local agent who would receive them on a fishing boat. Just then, a searchlight blinded them. There was a boat nearby. Salem told his men to hold fire and to quietly reverse their motors. They broke contact at 01:04 hours and headed for RV2, another small island off Little Aden, with the mystery boat combing the waters behind them with its searchlight. At 01:34 hours they reached the second RV and found the agent waiting in a big wooden fishing boat full of nets, fish guts and diesel-tinged water. After a suitable period of greeting hugs and kisses, the agent was mortified to hear about the team's searchlight encounter. He has forgotten to pay off the coast guard crew, who were still diligently patrolling the waters near the refinery and oil port.

A few minutes later, Salem's team splashed ashore at Little Aden under a bright moonlit sky and fluffy white clouds. He was met by a reception party of three bearded fighters, led by Abu Mohammed and Abu Anas, two moderate Salafis. Neither Salem nor his team relaxed with their new hosts, remaining wary of betrayal and scanning their assigned arcs of fire, and all using assumed names. They were taken by minibus to a new hide site in Shaab, Safe House 2 or SH2, which was owned by Resistance operations commander Hashim Sayyed, and which was only 380 metres from SH1. It was 02:49 hours when they arrived and began to set up covered communications and sniper positions on the roof.

No sooner were they in the house than the top Resistance Council commanders arrived to meet Salem. Hani bin Braykh, the Resistance's best orator and convener, brought with him the 20 top front commanders and his intelligence officer, Abdulrahman al-Muharrami, known as Abu Zaraa. It was immediately apparent that Salem had made the right call by deploying forward to Aden. These leaders needed engagement, and all was not well in the Resistance, who had just suffered another crushing blow when 40 fighters were killed in a single disastrous failed attack on the Houthi lines in Sheikh Uthman. Salem told them that he would bring them more support and lower their casualties, promising, 'I'll stop the bleeding of your fighters and bring you victory.'

He only had one condition: that they appoint a military leader to be Salem's counterpart and speak for the whole

Resistance Council on military matters. Almost unanimously, they chose the safe house's owner, the aforementioned Hashim Sayyed. Armed with the classic Arab-Afghan weapon – a short-barrel variant of the AK-74 known as the Krinkov – Hashim was an admired Salafi commander who had fought the Houthis in the six wars. He was also a colourful character who, in a former life, had been a Russian-trained acrobat. Give him two 23-mm cannons and some new tyres for his armoured car, Hashid confidently exclaimed, and they would be ready to retake Aden. Everyone was smiles: they were going to win.

All smiled except one man, that is. He was the quiet, fine-featured intelligence officer Abu Zaraa, another Salafi, who painted a different picture of a resistance effort that was close to collapse, even despite the heroic efforts of the Emiratis. At the time, Salem was keeping himself from crashing after days of sleep deprivation, staying awake largely through the assistance of multiple cans of 'Rani' – a sweet zesty orange drink that he drank as a child in the UAE and which was still a thing in Aden. He needed to hear positivity and confidence, while Abu Zaraa appeared negative and cynical. But, before too long, Salem would realise that Abu Zaraa was the shrewdest observer of the Resistance forces and their front commanders – a man who had an unrivalled thirst for detail and an elephant's memory. The victory at Imran and the mustering of militia leaders gave temporary respite and illusion that an easy victory was at hand. In fact, many of the Resistance fronts were living on borrowed time.

# VIII

# ENTER THE AL-FORSAN

It had been a huge relief when the first SOC team had made it ashore on 13 April but that night MBZ was already looking ahead to the next challenge. The operational commanders were piecing together the intervention on an hour-by-hour basis, while the UAE Deputy Supreme Commander could take a longer view, and he had a unique ability to make things happen. On the very night of Cobra 1-1's insertion, Mohammed bin Zayed had directed MGM and other commanders to make the arrangements to covertly bring ashore a G-6 self-propelled howitzer, a South African-made 155-mm artillery piece that could put precise and devastating fire down on any point of the Aden battlefield. In MBZ's view, the G-6 would be the perfect tool to harass and interdict the Houthi lines of supply into Aden. The kernel of this idea would spark an escalating series of preparations for amphibious landings. To safely operate the G-6 in Aden would require an engineering effort to bring it ashore, a force protection unit for the gun, a landing craft 5 km offshore in case the gun needed emergency extraction, plus the artillerists and maintainers. For the same reason, the option of forward-basing an Apache gunship – requiring even greater support and representing an even more attractive target – was rejected.

As the Djiboutian base was becoming less tenable by the day, MBZ pulled out his iPad and suggested an alternative he had kept up his sleeve for just such an occasion. The remote and practically unused harbour he had in mind was called Assab, in the reclusive Red Sea nation of Eritrea. The founding father of the UAE, Sheikh Zayed, had built a relationship with Eritrea's long-term president, Isaias Afwerki; the UAE had recently negotiated the leasing of the base for military use for 99 years. Assab was not much further away from Aden than Djibouti and the UAE could count on having almost complete freedom to come and go unhindered. Not for the first or the last time, Mohammed bin Zayed injected an option that no one had considered. As MGM recalled: 'His Highness was always thinking out of the box. He constantly surprised his military commanders, especially in those opening days of Aden. You see, he can make the impossible possible.'

The UAE military was keen to get on the offensive and there were soon signs from Aden that the Resistance was in desperate need of a win – not merely the destruction of enemy forces from the air but a visible success in Aden city. The sudden end of Operation Decisive Storm on 21 April had confused the Resistance – and indeed the Emirati soldiers who had newly landed in Aden. The bombing campaign was said by Coalition headquarters in Riyadh to have 'achieved its military goals' and there was an immediate hiatus in new airstrikes. To the Resistance in Aden, the future was suddenly uncertain – did this mean an end to the Coalition intervention? What about Houthi–Saleh forces still in Aden? On the ground, Salem D. could sense the need to keep up momentum. From MBZ, the guidance to the PG commander was clear:

We must motivate the resistance to retake Aden. We are to lead, fight and mentor. This will be the UAE's first major solo operation, and it will be historic, and therefore we must win.

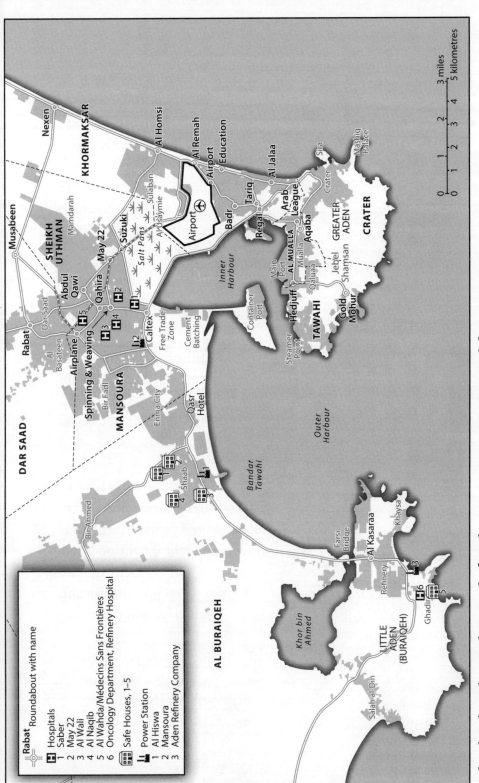

**Aden landmarks used to guide familiarization, orientation and fire support**

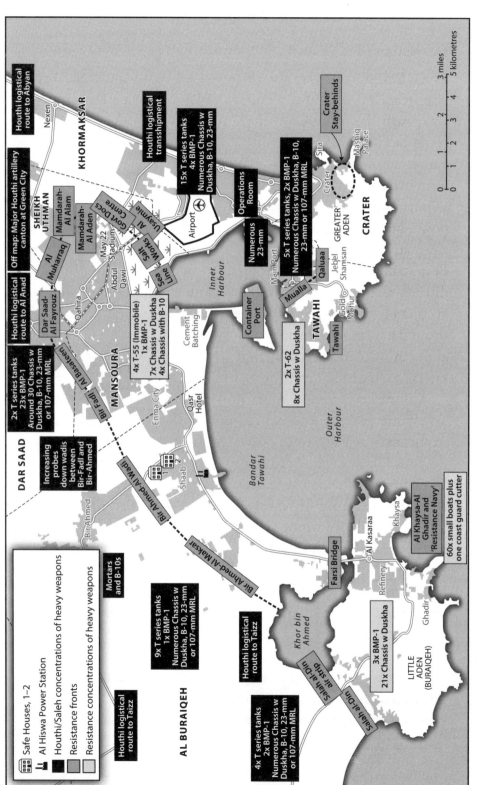

The Resistance defensive pocket and Houthi-Saleh dispositions in late April 2015

## Designing the Liberation Operation

Every Emirati plan for the liberation of Aden identified the airport at Khormaksar as the enemy centre of gravity. The airport was clearly the windpipe of the Houthi effort to take Aden. If it could be closed off, the enemy would choke. The question was: *how* to seize the open, fire-swept ground of the airport? There were two basic options. The first was a Resistance assault on the airport, supported by clandestine UAE special forces and fire-power but without visible Emirati presence on the ground. The alternative was the amphibious insertion of a larger, more visible Emirati mechanised battlegroup that would march on Aden and directly seize the airport. A desire to maintain a light and low-visibility footprint, but also to retain the option of 'going heavy', drove the UAE to develop the forward base at Assab, as it would allow an amphibious battlegroup to assemble in secrecy just 330 km (180 nautical miles) away from Aden.

Conditions at Assab were far worse than Djibouti. Imagine a volcanic plain, constantly scoured by howling winds from dawn until the late afternoon. All the trees are dead and there is no grass. There is only dust, scorpions, rats, snakes and hyenas. The leftovers of British and Israeli military ports lay all around: a rusty forklift, out-of-service oil tanks, pot-holed dirt roads, a sun-cracked 3,500-foot airstrip and a small natural harbour, but no fresh water, no electricity and no cellphone service. The P-6 coastal highway ran right through the base and there was no perimeter, just some Eritrean observation posts on nearby mountains. The small local population, who lived in primitive huts of volcanic rocks with palm frond roofs, wandered through the base and grazed their cattle there.

The Emiratis only had tiny two-man tents that could not stand up to the wind. 'You would sleep on any visiting ship when-ever you could, but they came and went,' one former resident remembered: 'We changed sleeping places every night. If you could find a good place, even in an old hangar, you felt like you were a VIP.' The days were non-stop wind and dust, making it impossible to be outside without sunglasses and head coverings. The nights were punctuated by the gruesome sounds of hyenas noisily killing their prey and fighting over the scraps. 'This was a place for ghosts, not for humans,' one UAE sailor remembered.

As the war passed from days- to weeks-long, a realisation dawned that Assab might need to be developed as a long-term operations hub. The men could not live in small tents and eat ration packs forever, and it would be impossible to source adequate amounts of fresh food and water from the tiny local markets. The men at Assab queued for over an hour each morning to use one of the three portable toilets. The deeply pot-holed road from the airstrip to the tiny port was a 25-minute, bone-jarring ride.

The man brought in to fix this was Major Hamid K., an ace logistician for the Presidential Guard. With C-17 aircraft allocated fully to four waves of combat forces due to arrive between 23 and 26 April, Hamid K. used leased Ilyushin and Antonov aircraft to rush in construction equipment and camp-building materials. He selected a site for the UAE base that was close to the airstrip, to allow rapid offloading and storing of equipment, consumables and ammunition. Three or four huge cargo aircraft arrived each day to bring generators, large tents and fridges.

Next, he reached out to the local Eritrean villages and hired every available working-age man. They proved to be hard-working and Hamid K. earned their trust by providing pay, medical care and small treats for their families as well as the workers. To assure alignment across the beginning, middle and end of the logistics route, Hamid K. emplaced liaison officers at Abu Dhabi and on the *Al-Quwaisat* (A81) Landing Ship Tank

(LST), which would become the command ship for the Assab-based amphibious task group. Hamid K. also handled the tricky negotiations with the Eritrean authorities, who initially refused entry at the port to civilian ships carrying UAE logistics, on the grounds that only military vessels were permitted by the lease. The entire base structure had been built from scratch in just ten days, from MBZ's order on 13 April to completion of the main life-support facilities on April 23.

With liveable quarters, the newest inhabitants of Assab had quickly begun to assemble. The massive C-17s formed a continuous air bridge between Abu Dhabi and Assab. From 17–20 April, the UAE presence at Assab built to 331 troops, including 31 PG Al-Forsan commandos, 86 logistics specialists drawn from across the UAE armed forces, and 88 UAE sailors. Shelters were hastily constructed for drones. Electronic warfare and intelligence units arrived. By 26 April, all UAE helicopter forces and a Sabr rotor-wing drone were pulled out of Djibouti and shifted across to Assab. As May began, the UAE personnel at Assab numbered 819, including a 200-man mechanised infantry company of the PG Khalifa bin Zayed Mechanised Brigade mounted in 12 RG-31 Nyala Mine-Resistant Ambush-Protected (MRAP) vehicles and eight BMP-3s, the modernised version with a powerful 100-mm cannon. A G-6 155-mm howitzer and two Agrab 120-mm mortar carriers gave the force its own organic artillery support. The battlegroup would become known as the Amphibious Task Force.

In command was Colonel Ali A., who had just completed his tenure as the commander of the Al-Forsan battalion, with the UAE Navy's Colonel Sayyed Z. as his deputy in charge of naval operations. Ali A. was known as a tough commander who could take units to a new level of capability, and he had transformed the UAE's small marine force into the Al-Forsan battalion, a very capable direct-action special forces unit akin to the US Rangers. The Special Operations Command was Ali A.'s second home. As a young SOC operator, he had landed in Somalia the day before the infamous Battle of Mogadishu in 1993 – memorialised in the book and film *Black Hawk Down* – and later fought in Afghanistan. Given command of the Presidential Guard Marine battalion in 2011, he had participated in multiple Presidential Guard training cycles at the US Marine Corps' 29 Palms training base in California and helped turn the UAE marines into an air, land and sea assault force. Ali A. was a SOC success story: a man who had earned his promotions by superb service to his country and the men under his command. Ali A. was delighted and relieved when given the command of the Amphibious Task Force. He had been packing his bags for a stint at the US Marine Corps War College at Quantico, Virginia. 'This is great!' Ali A. told his superiors. 'I'll take the war, you keep the college!'

Ali A. threw the task force into an intensive series of amphibious warfare drills, both in the waters off Abu Dhabi (where they drilled at landing the G-6 and armoured vehicles) and in Assab (where the Al-Forsan practised company-sized marine commando landings). The naval task force included *Das* (P162), a Muray Jib-class UAE guided missile corvette with an on-board Puma helicopter, the aforementioned *Al-Quwaisat* (A81) Landing Ship Tank (LST), and two 64-metre Landing Craft Utility (LCU): *Al-Bahya* (L62) and *Zarkoh* (L67). The plan was to be ready to land the whole force on Qawah Bay, just west of Imran. The assault would be undertaken in four waves: first two pathfinder platoons of Al-Forsan in ten Zodiacs with a heavy complement of anti-armour weapons would secure the beach. Then the MRAPs, trucks and the G-6 would arrive in the second wave, and the fuel and ammunition in the third. Finally, the BMP-3s and Agrabs would land. The force would drive 70 km to the Sheikh Uthman area, establish an artillery gun-line and logistics hub, and then directly assault the airport.

Getting ashore was a big challenge. The UAE had not envisaged having to do a complex 400-troop, 100-vehicle landing on their own. The landing might be a disaster if the sand could not take the ground pressure of 48-tonne G-6 howitzers, or if the beach proved too shallow for landing craft to approach. Back in Abu Dhabi, the Presidential Guard commander MGM hit the books, downloading and reading the USMC amphibious warfare doctrine on a Kindle. In order to optimise the choice of the exact landing point, the SOC operators at Assab undertook a clandestine beach reconnaissance on the night of 22–23 April. The mission was commanded by Major Hamid M., who controlled the operation from the corvette *Das*, and Lieutenant Mohammed J., who went forward with the divers and a three-man reserve. Twelve nautical miles offshore, the ship released two Zodiacs at 20:00 hours, each carrying a diver and a navy coxswain. The divers entered the warm water 5 nautical miles offshore. They had seven hours to gather depth, gradient and sand density readings at five sites. The JTAC carefully watched over a Houthi coastal observation post at Qawah and a large Houthi camp close to the beach. At 03:00 hours the divers were ordered to 'exfiltrate' ahead of the dawn, with three sites surveyed. It had been a superb test of the UAE's ability to improvise and learn a new skill in the midst of an operation. And it had been worth it: the initial site chosen for the landing would, indeed, have been a disaster and a safer alternative was found.

Ultimately, however, the amphibious landing was not to be. The Americans were signalling strong reservations and other Coalition members were considering taking part, injecting new complexity and potential delays into the planning process.

There was clearly some hidden reticence towards such an overt demonstration of military power by the UAE. The decision was made in Abu Dhabi: remain ready to land the Amphibious Task Force but let the Resistance and Cobra 1-1 take the first swipe at the airport.

## The First Airport Battle

Salem D. had high hopes for the attack, which was scheduled for 25 April. The Resistance Council's senior leaders appeared eager to see what the combination of Yemeni ground forces and UAE fire support could achieve. Hashim Sayyed, the newly appointed resistance major-domo, sat alongside Salem as he meticulously planned the upcoming battle. The Yemeni part was simplicity itself: a force of 600 former military personnel under a retired general, Fadhil Baysh, would storm the airport from the north, over the causeway that traced the line of the old British-built aqueduct that brought water from the ancient storage tanks in Crater to the oasis at Sheikh Uthman. A second front, made up of Popular Committee fighters under former army colonel Saleh Nokhbi, would advance from its forming-up point at the May 22 school, moving down the 'Sea Line' causeway to Labour Island and assaulting the airport from the west. Salem's main challenge was setting up the carefully orchestrated fire plan, which was designed to dump a devastating number of airstrikes on key targets around the airport at 04:00 hours and suddenly lift at 04:10 as the resistance attacks went in, hot on the heels of the bombardment.

Salem found it hard to sleep in the hours before the assault. He was too excited and presumed the Yemenis would probably be equally keyed-up for the big attack. He expected to see the first Popular Committee militiamen assembling at 02:00, in plenty of time, but kept himself occupied by checking and re-checking

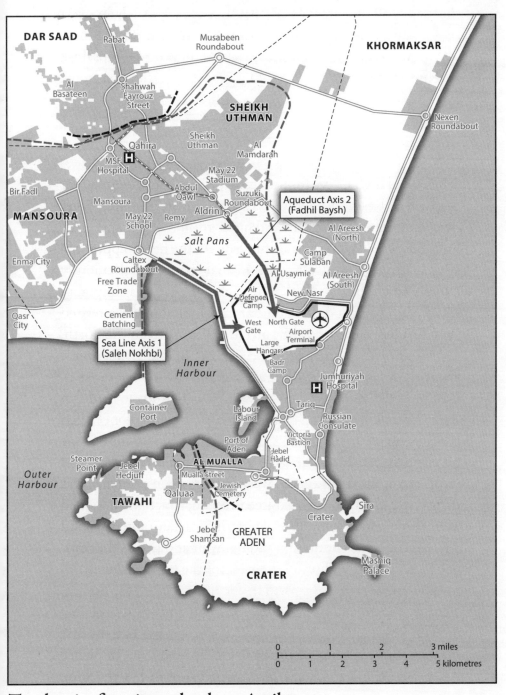

The abortive first airport battle, 25 April 2015

the maps and preparations. By 03:00 no one had arrived: Salem thought they were cutting it close. Minutes before the 04:00 beginning of the fire plan there were still no troops to be seen. Perhaps understandably, the complete no-show of the attack force was not a contingency that Salem had planned for. He considered calling off the fire support but it was too late, with strike aircraft inbound and almost over Aden. He watched the strikes go in and listened to the calm back-and-forth between pilots and JTACs: 'Weapons release ... 20 seconds ... 10 seconds ... splash ... good effect'. Nine large 'K-Span' prefabricated British hangars were destroyed at the southern edge of the airport and in Badr camp. A number of identified tanks and 23-mm anti-aircraft cannons were also struck at the airport and on nearby Labour Island, which flanked the Sea Line axis. On the Abyan Road, six Houthi–Saleh armoured vehicles were attacked to prevent them reinforcing the airport.

As all civilians had been driven out of the airport by the Houthis, most of the bombs dropped were large 2,000-lb GBU-10s delivered by a mixture of Saudi Arabian and UAE strike aircraft. The 2,000-pounder makes a 15-metre-wide crater at the point of impact and leaves almost no one alive in a radius twice the size of the crater. Even 40-tonne main battle tanks may be picked up and thrown, or pulverised into unrecognisable fragments by direct hits. Such explosions can clearly be heard and felt as tremors, tens of kilometres away, and on this night, there were almost too many to count in the intense ten-minute 'fire strike'.

The 04:10 H-Hour for the attack passed and Salem waited for the Yemenis to arrive. In Salem's words, 'The Houthis died, went to heaven, ate some apples, and still had time to get back to their posts before we attacked.' At 05:00 hours he sent for Hashim Sayyed, who – to Salem's shock – was in a deep sleep. After visiting Salem on the blue-tarped roof of SH-2, Hashim

Sayyed hit the road to find out where the troops were. By 10:00 some began to turn up at the assembly area. Of Fadhil Baysh's promised 600, only 60 came. Saleh Nokhbi's Popular Committee leaders were full of excuses. Some said they had not eaten for over 24 hours, and others complained merely that they had not had breakfast yet. Some said they did not know the plan, or that their troops had run away. Some had too much *qat* and slept through the attack entirely. Some troops said they had no ammunition and it turned out that their commanders had indeed pocketed the provided arms and ammunition so that they could sell them later. The former military members of the Resistance had been particularly weak, which Salem had expected, but the Popular Committees had failed just as dramatically. Salem began to look at the cynical intelligence officer Abu Zaraa with new respect: his scepticism had been proven exactly right. The attack was called off at 11:00 hours. Salem was determined to learn the lesson: 'You told yourself a nice story and you believed myself too much,' he recalled thinking.

## Send in the Al-Forsan

The abortive first airport attack caused some rethinking in Abu Dhabi. Salem D. and his 20-member SOC team had done a great job of shoring up the defensive pockets in Sheikh Uthman, Little Aden, and the Tawahi peninsula, but more Emirati support would be needed if the Resistance were to retake and hold terrain. One option was the landing of the Amphibious Task Force and there were favourable tides for a landing on 30 April. MBZ would have to give a green light on the evening of 28 April to set in motion the complex preparations and movements. But the effort was still undermined by serious doubts. Most of these were in the form of subtle, and sometimes not so subtle, recommendations from the US military and from other Coalition partners. The US was afraid that the Emirates might fail badly. On the night of 28 April, the UAE chain of command paused the amphibious plan and instead directed that 21 more UAE operators would be inserted into Little Aden and the Sheikh Uthman pocket. This would freshen up the team in Aden, allowing the relief of the eight original SOC troopers and boosting the overall remaining number to 31 Presidential Guard operators, bringing the Al-Forsan firmly to the forefront of the operation.

Eighteen of the newly inserted 21 men would be drawn from the Al-Forsan, the four-company assault battalion that Ali A. had previously commanded. The young men were mostly – though not uniformly – veterans of Afghanistan and other conflicts. Presidential Special Guard (PSG) snipers were also sent in with the Al-Forsan. These PSG shooters were the counter-snipers who would watch over Emirati senior leaders at public events, akin to the US Secret Service snipers.

Many had served with SOC overseas and were good to go after quick military refresher training. Earlier in April, the 21 were told they were joining a secret mission and they bade farewell to their families under the cover story of a training exercise. Since then, they had been on the move constantly – to Assab, sleeping on the ground with the bugs and nearly no food; then the crowded *Al Uwaisat* command ship, where the waiting never seemed to end, and the choppy seas were nauseating. Al-Forsan are like US Rangers: young men, the average being 24 years old, and full of energy and fight. Waiting was agonising and they were raring to go ashore. Tension rises when that many young fighters are cooped up in the tight confines of a hot ship, with limited food and not much chance of exercise. Competition to be among the 21 was fierce. Like brothers, they fought and complained and appealed to their superiors; anything to get on the mission.

When it deployed, the team was 'loaded for bear', to use the US military phrase, referring to how American huntsmen had to double-load their muskets with gunpowder to give them enough stopping power to kill a bear. The commander was a 24-year-old Major called Seghayyar N., and he was supported by two other majors as his team leaders. The Al-Forsan brought a JTAC, a communications specialist, and 16 other shooters. There were two PSG sniper teams among the group, each with a shooter and a spotter, and they carried both 7.62-mm and 12.7-mm or 14.5-mm sniper rifles in shoulder-strapped camouflage gun bags and plastic crates. The group had an unusually large complement of heavy weapons – two Javelin anti-armour firing posts plus missiles, a whopping 24 RPG-27 disposable anti-tank rockets, RG-6 six-shot, revolver-type 40-mm grenade launchers, plus two hefty General Purpose Machine Guns and two M-249 Minimi Squad Automatic Weapons. With the personal weapons and advanced sights of the remaining Al-Forsan, plus the airpower available via the JTACs, the UAE could now throw a small army's worth of firepower at the enemy.

Insertion of the new team was simpler than previous helo-cast operations, in part because confidence had been built between the UAE and the main Resistance commander in Little Aden, a brave boat operator called Abdullah al Reyni, who would bring the team ashore. The UAE corvette *Das* left Assab at 11:44 hours on 29 April and brought the 21 men to a point 9 km south of al Reyni's anchorage at Al Khaysa. At 21:32 hours, the Al-Forsan tensely loaded their arsenal onto al Reyni's fishing boat after the rendezvous at sea. By 22:30 hours they had landed at Al Khaysa and were received by Salem D. The landing was kept very secret and the Al-Forsan wore Yemeni attire and carried AKs, while their distinctive foreign equipment was all stowed away in kit bags. By 01:00 hours on 30 April, they were settling in at SH2, the house where Salem had been living for a week. The SH1 safe house was closed down as Abdullah Hammer and Cobra 1-1 headed back to the UAE for a well-deserved rest.

Ali A. made very clear what he expected from the UAE commanders in Aden. Salem D. remained in place at SH2 with his two JTACs, and he was instructed to focus his efforts on key leader engagement with the Resistance Council. Major Seghayyar N. was given the immediate objective of quickly shoring up Resistance confidence with tactical wins, and also the longer-term mission of assessing what the Resistance needed to win and then to train them how to attack without incurring demoralising casualties. Though the JTACs had ventured out beyond the safehouses on a number of occasions, these had been clandestine outings in tiny numbers. Never before had Emirati troops been told to go to the frontline in small but noticeable numbers, but this was the Al-Forsan way – to get straight into the attack. Efforts were still made to keep a low profile. Hani bin Braykh took a disguised Seghayyar N. to the markets where they bought everything on the shelves to stock up SH2, notionally to feed a local militia. The men tried to conceal their Ops-Core helmets below headscarves, and they uncomfortably wore their Blackhawk body armour under their Yemeni clothes. Contact with the Resistance was initially minimised. But all these efforts quickly became unfeasible because the mission required the Al-Forsan to 'super-charge' the next Resistance effort to take the airport. And that meant being visible.

## The Second Airport Battle

The next attack on the airport was planned to unfold on the night of 2–3 May, just a couple of days after the Al-Forsan had landed. The plan was a little more complex than the first battle and would set the basic shape of every airport assault to follow. A heavy fire plan would begin at 18:00 hours, involving both air strikes and (for the first time) direct support fire by Al-Forsan machine-guns, grenade launchers, snipers and Javelin missiles. This firepower would be provided from two 'bases of fire' – the Container Port and Cement Batching Plant about 2,500 metres to the west across the Inner Harbour, and the Sea Line causeway, just over 2,000 metres north-west of the runway. Blocking positions would be seized by the Popular Committees to the north-east of the airport along the coastal road at the Al Areesh Roundabout and airpower and naval gunfire would interdict enemy reserves on the outskirts of Aden city. Inactive Resistance fronts in Little Aden, Sheikh Uthman and Mualla would brace for Houthi–Saleh counter strokes and have airpower on-call to break up enemy tank attacks. Offshore, the Amphibious Task Force would be postured to reinforce success by landing at the eastern end of the runway, on the broad strand of beach east of the Al Remah Roundabout. As ever, the plan sounded awesome, on paper.

In reality, the Resistance remained difficult to muster. The second airport assault was postponed for three consecutive days due to low cloud cover that would disrupt the air support, but also due to growing Resistance fatigue. This was not like sitting back and letting UAE airpower eviscerate the enemy at Imran, and nor was this the skirmishing between buildings that the Popular Committees were used to. The Resistance rightfully feared assaulting over the open ground at the airport, which they referred to as 'walking into an ambush'. From the Resistance

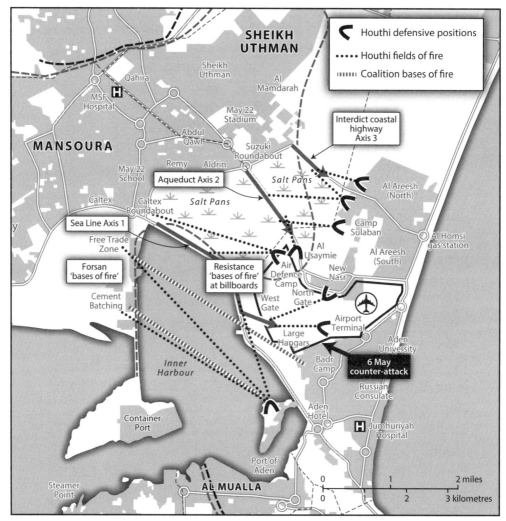

The second airport battle, 2–3 May 2015, showing lines of fire over the open terrain

jump-off points in Sheikh Uthman, the airport looked intimidating. The wall around the airport's northern side was, in reality, less than the height of a man but that was not apparent from the north, from where it looked tall and solid. On the eastern side, the distinctive Air Traffic Control tower, terminal and a scattering of taller buildings peered over the wall menacingly. At the western end, the Aden and Coral hotels looked down on the airport approaches, and the low, dangerous profile of Labour Island bristled with 23-mm anti-aircraft guns, like a crocodile lying in the blood-warm cyan water of the harbour.

In order to infuse the Resistance with more confidence, the Al-Forsan began to accompany the Popular Committees to the front line and to provide rudimentary training to the Resistance. The Al-Forsan could clearly see for the first time that the Resistance was almost entirely composed of untrained civilians, city people with almost no tradition of fighting. On occasion, the experience of 'advising and assisting' could be bizarre, verging on comical. As a Al-Forsan trooper would 'take a knee' or lie prone whenever he was stationary – to make the job of Houthi snipers less easy – bemused Yemeni fighters would stand around the UAE soldier and watch. They could not understand why he was lying down on the dirty ground, which was often littered with rotting trash, hessian sacks, plastic bags used to carry *qat*, rags, cardboard, water bottles, broken glass and rubble. By standing around the troopers, the Yemenis would draw fire to the Al-Forsan, but they didn't seem to notice, instead peppering the newcomers with curious questions such as: *'Why are you here? This is not your home. You could be in Abu Dhabi having fun.'*

Operating in daylight, it was inevitable that the Al-Forsan would be detected by the enemy and by the international media. Piecing various media reports together with war diaries and interviews, it seems that a foreign special forces presence was detected by the Houthis on about 1 May, approximately 36 hours after the Al-Forsan arrived, and by the international media on 4 May. Arab media presumed that the unidentified special forces were Egyptian or Saudi Marines. This was in line with what the Emiratis were hoping, and their efforts to disguise the Al-Forsan were limited to blurring the exact identity and composition of the force, not their foreign nature. Nonetheless, a clock started ticking on 1 May, with the Houthis becoming aware of the coalition presence and starting the hunt for enemy commandos.

On 4 and 5 May, the UAE ground forces came under aimed fire for the first time in Yemen. Caltex Roundabout, the Cement Batching Plant and the Sea Line are all very open areas with little natural cover, dense dark brown earth and rocky landfill where foxholes could not be dug. There were long lines of observation and sniping and the Al-Forsan began to experience the unsettling accuracy of Houthi mortar fire. For some of the younger Al-Forsan, this was their first real battle experience and they felt the gnawing, grating fear of being bombarded but having no way to return fire or even find good cover.

On 5 May, as the Al-Forsan held the Sea Line from which the Yemenis would assault the airport, an Al Jazeera camera team recorded footage of professional-looking Arab special forces working alongside Yemeni guides. They wore blue T-shirts and cut-off shorts, carried heavily modified US small arms, and they had modern body armour and Ops-Core tactical ballistic helmets. But most striking, they had the cutting-edge Javelin missile, which meant they were troops from one of America's closest partners. The Presidential Guard's only friend – surprise and secrecy – had now deserted them. Among the UAE leadership, the television images from Yemen were a source of secret pride but also concern. The Al-Forsan were told to stay out of sight during the day to reduce their vulnerability to mortar fire.

Only the PSG snipers and JTACs would directly observe the coming battle, from the cranes of the Container Port or the roof of the May 22 stadium, covering each of the two main axes.

Once again, things started unravelling quickly once the second airport battle commenced at 14:27 hours on 5 May. Low cloud prevented a lot of Coalition aircraft from participating because their rules of engagement prevented them from operating below 16,000 feet, and that meant bombing through the clouds.

The JTACs now numbered four: a mixture of two newly arrived Al-Forsan, navy and air force airstrike controllers, plus Salem D. and his initial two JTACs, who stayed on even as the other SOC operators were sent home. After over two weeks of consecutive operations, the longest-deployed JTACs were heavily bearded and bone tired, but they were also at the top of their professional game of providing urban fire support. They had a sixth sense when parsing real strike opportunities from unnecessary calls for fire from panicked Resistance forces. They knew Aden like they knew their own hometowns, learning the many roundabouts by heart and splitting the city up into sectors of responsibility. They knew all the Houthi hiding places and tricks, and they were expert at using angles of attack and local human sources to reduce the risk of collateral damage and stay within an increasingly complex set of rules of engagement.

The JTACs were also finally getting out and about. This allowed them to use their Long Range Thermal Video (LRTV) system, which was about the size and weight of a heavy set of naval binoculars, and which included a cooled thermal imager, colour video camera, integrated laser rangefinder, digital magnetic compass, GPS and laser designator. Operating from the cranes of the Container Port or the roofs of tall buildings such as the May 22 stadium, the JTACs could now directly 'lase' targets with the designators, projecting a dot that was visible to the sensors of the aircraft above. In complicated urban terrain, this greatly simplified some strikes, obviating the need to painstakingly 'talk' a pilot onto one identical-looking building instead of another.

By taking the battle into the third dimension, that of the rooftops of Aden, the UAE forces were also able to unleash their snipers for the first time. In the initial two days of offensive UAE sniper operations at the end of April, the Emirati snipers racked up 15 confirmed daylight kills – their single-most prolific hunting period, Aden's skyline was a sniper's paradise: masses of undifferentiated four-storey white and grey buildings with empty, cavernous windows. The Houthis tended to have already taken up residence in the small number of eight- to ten-storey buildings – including Jumhuriyah Hospital, the Good Mosque, the Aden Hotel and the Al Arab Mall. Nonetheless, that left a good number of five-, six- or seven-storey buildings that were mostly half-built and perfect for 360-degree lines of sight and easy relocation between multiple firing positions. But the work felt dangerous, for there were no real front lines and the Houthi patrols and snipers could be anywhere. Houthi spies were known to be all around, and the UAE forces felt like anyone could sell out their positions at any moment.

Now, heading into the new airport battle, the JTACs' main focus was the Badr camp just south of the runway. Reflecting the many twists and turns and hidden corners of the base, the JTACs described Badr camp as 'the Crystal Maze', after the 1990s British television show that was re-run on Dubai Channel 33 and even had its own indoor theme park at the Wafi Mall in Dubai. Over 20 individual aim points inside the Crystal Maze were targeted for destruction, largely with the heavyweight 2,000-lb GBU-12. The camp was so thoroughly gutted that the

33. A fateful 5 March 2015 picture of a port tugboat leaving Tawahi with fleeing civilians onboard. The same tug was sunk on a subsequent trip by Houthi 23mm cannons, heavy machine guns, and mortars, with at least 40 men, women and children known to have been killed and possibly as many as a hundred never accounted for according to an investigation by *Médecins Sans Frontières*. The Houthis publicly celebrated the massacre.

34. Refugees fleeing the Arabian Peninsula for the Horn of Africa. For the previous 30 years, hundreds of thousands of economic migrants had sailed across the Gulf of Oman to enter the Arabian Peninsula via southern Yemen. In an amazing role reversal, Yemenis began to flee to Somalia, Puntland, Somaliland and Djibouti in 2015. Here a Puntland soldier carries a Yemeni child from a ship which has arrived at the port of Bosasso in Somalia's Puntland on 16 April 2015.

35. An Al Forsan fighting patrol out and about in the Al Usaymie neighbourhood, north of the airport. The area was a kind of no-man's land: spookily quiet and only episodically visited by the forces of either side. The UAE troops tried to blend in, but looking fully Yemeni was a true art form. Yememi kids hanging out on street corners were typically not fooled by the muscular and fashionably attired Al Forsan.

36. Conditions in the field. The Al Forsan raiding teams spent about 6-7 hours a day holed up in their sniper hides and observation posts. It was hot and humid. By early afternoon many Yemenis were settling down to begin their qat chews and the battlefield quieted. The Al Forsan had to consciously learn how to slow down, rest, synchronize with Yemeni patterns of life, and settle in for the long game. Note the trooper has his sidearm prepped for use, and his M4 carbine stowed muzzle-down inside his armour, keeping it relatively clean and ready for use.

37. A UAE sniper's perch. Snipers of both sides used pallets, beds and stacked-up furniture to make horizontal shooting positions at the level aligned with the window or shell hole that they employed as their firing aperture. In this image, a 7.62mm DSR-Precision DSR-1 sniper rifle is prepared for use, and a huge NTW-14.5 anti-materiel rifle is placed on the floor, unloaded, for potential use, with a 3-round box magazine alongside. A spotter's scope tripod is seen on the left, next to an improvised stool made out of concrete blocks.

38. A Kornet Interdiction Team (KIT) in action. The long lines of fire and lack of tall buildings suggest this team is in action on the Musabeen front, where a single Kornet team could use the weapon's long range (2.5 to 4 kilometres) to deny an entire flank of the Sheikh Uthman area to the enemy. The firing position could quickly be shifted with the tripod and firing posts splitting and being cartable by each team member. One rocket has recently been fired, as evidenced by the expended tube on the floor, with its rear cap popped off just before the launch. A fresh canister is being quickly mated with the firing post while the gunner maintains his watch, perhaps tracking a new target. The scattering of rifle cartridges suggests this small sangar of plastic feed bags had previously been used by a sniper. Note the Chinese Aokly battery in the foreground, for recharging the Kornet firing post. The gunner's seat is a concrete block.

39. The martyr Sergeant Saif Youssef Ahmed al Falasi hard at work in the kitchen of the Salah bin Fareed safe house. Saif made the coffee ahead of each Iftar fast-breaking for the first 26 days in Ramadan. He was a good comrade who used his off-hours and his spare moments in combat to help others. In 41°C heat and 68 per cent humidity he was shuttling 60lb Kornet tubes up to the sixth floor of a half-completed tower when he was mortally wounded by falling debris.

40. The Saleh bin Fareed house was the first truly secure and restful environment the Emiratis had experienced in Aden. It was surrounded by mountains and faced a beautiful ocean bay. Every previous safe house might easily have been overrun if the Houthis had discovered that UAE troops were present. At Saleh bin Fareed's house, for the first time, the Al Forsan could cook at the scale needed to feed scores of hungry men. First though, they disinfected the kitchen thoroughly: so much so, that Yemenis said the house had begun to smell like a hospital.

41. The view from a balcony in the Saleh bin Fareed house, looking towards Blue Beach Mountain. Note the Kornet thermal scope, set up to ensure night-time surveillance of the bay. The Kornet's day and night scope was considered superior to that of the Javelin in terms of range and night performance. Even when the Kornet missiles were not being employed, the scopes provided a way to observe and call fire upon the enemy at night and over long distances.

42. The apron space at Assab, the Eritrean base leased by the UAE. This photograph shows the base when the UAE's whole Mirage 2000-9 force had deployed to Assab. Unlike the F-16s, the Mirage proved hardy enough to work out of the windy and gritty Assab, a volcanic plain where the afternoon and evening winds were merciless. Placing the Mirage in Assab meant that it could carry more munitions or stay aloft over Aden for longer. Aircrew on cockpit alert slept in the aircraft, with ground crew underneath the planes. Three sleek-looking Air Tractor AC-802i ground attack aircraft are also on the runway. These slow but long-endurance turboprop aircraft could employ a variety of guided bombs, missiles, rockets and guns.

43. The mighty G-6 howitzer, photographed at a UAE military parade. This 155mm self-propelled gun looks like a steel lizard or a crocodile when it is moving, and can strike out nearly 40 kilometres with deadly precision. Once the first G-6 was ashore at Al-Ghadir in early June, the UAE could range any point in Aden no matter the weather, cloud cover, or flying conditions. The UAE Deputy Supreme Commander told his commanders to use the G-6 until the barrel melted, which they almost did, necessitating additional howitzers to be landed to allow one gun to rest while the others were active. The Yemenis called the G-6 the 'Shaiba' – the grumpy old man – and his grumbling was used not only to harass the Houthis night and day, but also to signal to the Adenese that the Emiratis were still with them.

44. Another form of fire support came later in the battle in the form of the Agrab 120mm mortar carrier. The Agrab was mounted on the chassis of a modifier RG-31 mine-resistance ambush-protected vehicle. It could get 15 rounds in the air within 90 seconds, meaning that by the time the first heavy mortar rounds impacted 8 km away, there would already be half a dozen more in the air following it and no time to find cover. The picture shows the Agrab in Aden, fully loaded with 46 bombs ready for use.

45. Where the magic happens: the joint fires cell at Saleh bin Fareed house. As the battle progressed, the joint fires room was equipped with larger and larger wide-screen TVs, but at this point the JTACs and joint fires officer are working off laptops. Hardcopy maps covered most of the walls, with the rough outlines of the Houthi and Resistance frontlines visible on the JTACs' wall map. In Aden, the UAE learned how to run an increasingly powerful joint fires cell purely using its own intelligence, surveillance and reconnaissance (ISR) assets – with no assistance from the United States.

46. The UAE -produced Al Sabr (pronounced Sep-r) S-100. The Sabr is a rotary-wing drone, meaning that it essentially looks like a small, unmanned helicopter, 3 metres long and shaped like a sturdy fish. Indeed, as soon as the Sabr began to fly over Aden, the Houthis mistakenly started reporting sighting of 'Apache' helicopter gunships. Quiet, able to hover and boasting a six-hour endurance over Aden, the Sabr allowed persistent surveillance of the Houthis wherever the 'main effort' was focused. It also allowed the performance and location of friendly forces to be monitored.

47. A 20 July 2015 image showing a destroyed Houthi multiple rocket-launcher. This is a 122mm rocket launcher with six barrels. It has been mounted on a *chassis* – the ubiquitous pick-up trucks – so that it can be very rapidly brought out of overhead cover to a pre-surveyed launch point, oriented towards the target, fired and then returned to a new concealed site for reloading. In this case, not quick enough.

Saleh bin
Fareed house

Ghadir

July 10, 2015 image
showing SH5 before the
later destruction of the
main house by an Al Qaeda
car bomb

Aden Refining
Company Beach
Club

Jetty

Bandar Sheikh

Blue Beach
Resort

Blue Beach
Mountain

Al Ghadir
Fish Farms

July 10, 2015 image
showing landed
Oshkosh hidden behind
shipping containers

Bermed G6
fire base

July 10, 2015
image
showing landed
Oshkosh

Jebel
Al Ghadir
Fort

July 10, 2015
image
showing ramp

48. Satellite imagery from
Google Earth taken on July 10,
2015 showing the key areas of
Little Aden used by the UAE
forces. In the west, the Saleh
bin Fareed house is shown. To
the east, there are two beaches
used for concealing UAE
vehicles and the G-6 battery.
UAE Navy Colonel Sayyed's
ramp is shown clearly in
the imagery. The 'terrain
masking' opportunities of the
Ghadir bays and mountains
now seem quaint since
the advent of ubiquitous
surveillance drones: in 2015,
the UAE could hide its
build-up from the Houthis
merely because there was no
direct line of sight to Houthi-
held areas. Such conditions
may not come again.

49. The majestic C-17A Globemaster III – a warehouse with wings. In early 2015, the UAE had just brought into service all of the eight C-17s that it recently purchased. The UAE's equipment – from airlift to aerial refuelling tankers to naval corvettes to Egab mortar boats – was almost all brand new as the war began, meaning it had little wear and tear but had nonetheless been fully tested and incorporated. With the C-17, the UAE could get vehicles to Assab in three hours, as opposed to 96 hours by sea.

50. Colonel Sayyed's ramp at Khor Ghadir. The Aden Refinery Company power station and Ghadir fish market are in the background. The ship is the *Khazna* (L61), a 64-m landing craft servicing the Assab to Aden route. All the vehicles required to seize Aden airport passed over this tiny – but vital – manmade jetty.

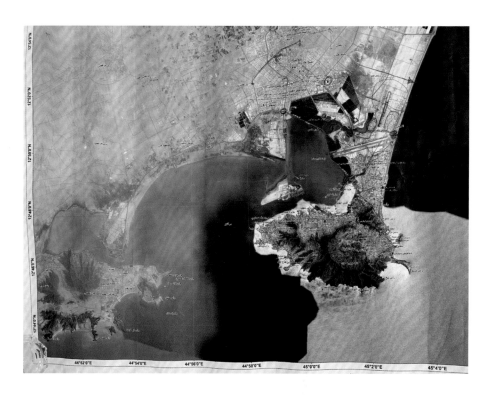

51. The original paper map used by the Amphibious Task Force commander to plan and track the final assault on Aden International Airport. In pen, the key features are marked: the line of departure at Caltex; the bases of fire at the Container Port and Saltworks; the axes of advance; and the identified risk of a Houthi counter-attack from the northeast. On 22 June the UAE Armed Forces were given the resources they needed but also had a hard deadline: liberate Aden by the end of Ramadan, which was just 25 days away.

Houthi–Saleh forces quickly began to avoid it after the second airport attack, viewing its hangars and sunshades as death-traps.

As with the first airport battle, the fire plan went off smoothly but the Popular Committees did not show up on time or in the necessary numbers on 5 May. Instead of an 18:30 hours assault, after four hours of booming fire preparation, a couple of undersized Resistance groups began their advance only at around 21:00 hours. A Resistance *chassis* with a 106-mm recoilless rifle was brought forward to directly support the assault and the Resistance gained a good hull-down position behind the concrete base of the Sea Line billboards. A tiny lodgement was briefly held at the western end of the runway, about 1,500 metres off the Sea Line, with the outermost hangar seized but then lost when the Houthi–Saleh forces counter-attacked under the cover of a heavy 120-mm mortar barrage. The attack was formally called off at 02:44 hours on 6 May.

Valuable lessons were learned. It was simply unrealistic to expect the Resistance to make a night assault because most of their fighters were deep into their *qat* chews by dusk. The only window that would work was a productive attacking period between 09:00 and 12:00 hours – the typical Yemeni working day. And the most dependable fighters were the Salafis, who did not chew. But beyond these general lessons, the UAE commanders began to sense just how tired and demoralised the Yemenis were. To a Resistance fighter, the airport was beginning to look like an impregnable fortress: encircled for most of its perimeter by a tall, ominous dark grey concrete wall and guard towers, and backed by low rows of apartment buildings with endless dark windows and cavernous deep rooms for snipers to shoot from. An attack over open ground against an entrenched enemy was simply too much to ask of these untrained civilians after two months of daily struggle. As Hashim Sayyed recalled:

They felt like their lives were being thrown away. They hated attacking the open land of the airport. They were not soldiers and were emotionally and physically worn out. They were defending their kids and families but that was a worry too – we had faced death every moment and our families were with us. So, we were really all *done* with it. The Resistance would shatter if they got hit one more time.

That shattering blow would come within hours of the untidy end of the second airport battle.

# IX

# THE FALL OF TAWAHI

To understand a battle, one must not only speak to many participants to work out what never made it into the records *and* peruse the records that contain the things that humans forget, but also make the closest map study of the terrain and then walk the ground. Only by getting on the ground can one really appreciate the extreme topography of Greater Aden. The township of Crater is quite literally a deep volcanic caldera, where the ground collapsed into the volcano's emptied magma chamber around 16,000 years ago, leaving up to a thousand feet of cliffs looking down on the ancient trading post. Crater was thus a natural fortress, practically unassailable on three sides.

Meanwhile, Mualla and Qaluaa were the towns that clung to the northern face of the volcano and its small coastal plain, wherein the twentieth-century port of Aden was built on reclaimed land. Tawahi lay further west, the 2-km-square tip of Greater Aden in which the famed Steamer Point and much of Britain's colonial administration had been concentrated. Mualla, Qaluaa and Tawahi were bounded on their landward sides by ominous dark volcanic slopes up to 700-feet high. Where these slopes came close to the shore, they formed narrow 150-metre defiles, choke points where the road ran practically along the sea front. Qaluaa was linked to the Tawahi side's Gold

Mohur beach resort by a 350-metre tunnel burrowed deep into the porous volcanic rock of the mountain.

These features made Mualla, Qaluaa and Tawahi claustrophobic, but they had also slowed the Houthi–Saleh advance into these crowded areas. The first defensive stand had been made on 2 April in the restaurants and waterparks that separated the Regal Roundabout from Mualla, but this narrow defile had been outflanked by Houthis moving over the Jebel Hadid. By 6 April, the Popular Committees were trying to hold a 500-metre front running between the mountains and the Inner Harbour, anchored on strongpoints such as the Abdullah Azzam Mosque and the Jewish Cemetery – an unlikely pair if ever there was one – and, later, the Aden governorate building and the Trade Union Congress (TUC) headquarters.

In the weeks that followed, the Houthis demonstrated their instinct for manoeuvre and mountain warfare by outflanking multiple defensive lines via the sparsely settled slopes above Mualla, even manhandling artillery pieces like 23-mm anti-aircraft cannons along the ridges to shoot down into the town. The Houthi strategy was to bypass the densely populated urban canyon of Mualla Street, with its British apartment blocks, skirting along the shanties and slopes of Qaluaa before hooking back northwards to the port facilities at the western edge of Mualla. By the end of April, most of Mualla and Qaluaa had fallen, with civilians fleeing westwards into the last defensive pocket at Tawahi. Though skirmishing continued east of this line, the real defence was based on the Jebel Hedjuff, the mountain overlooking the next defile on the coastal road, where the key landmarks were the Ministry of Fisheries, various oil tanks and the British cemetery in Mualla. To the south, a particularly tough group of Resistance fighters held the Qaluaa Tunnel and the hills above it. Coalition airstrikes pounded the ridges encircling Mualla

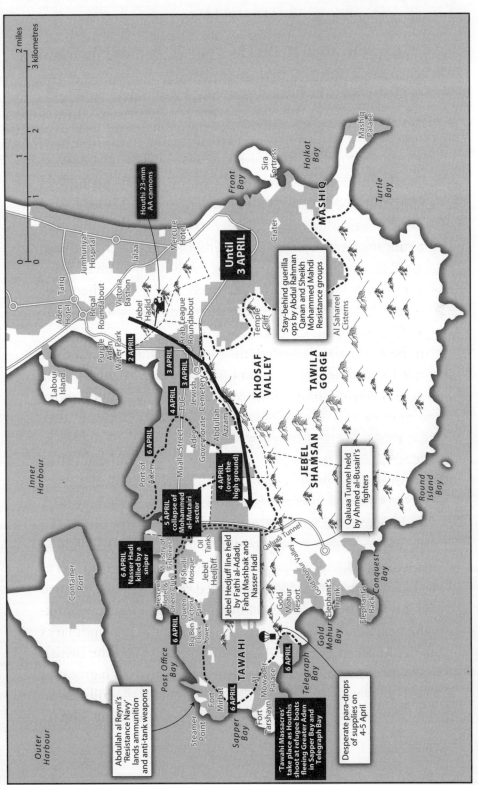

The fall of Tawahi and Gold Mohur, 6–7 May 2015

Houthi 23-mm AA cannons

Until 3 APRIL

2 APRIL

3 APRIL

3 APRIL

4 APRIL

6 APRIL

4 APRIL (over the high ground)

5 APRIL collapse of Mohammed al-Mutairi sector

6 APRIL Nasser Hadi killed by a sniper

6 APRIL

6 APRIL

6 APRIL

Stay-behind guerilla ops by Abdul Rahman Qanan and Sheikh Mohammed Mahdi Resistance groups

Qaluaa Tunnel held by Ahmed al-Busairi's fighters

Jebel Hedjuff line held by Fatthi al-Adadi, Fahd Mashbak and Nasser Hadi

Abdullah al Reyni's 'Resistance Navy' lands ammunition and anti-tank weapons

'Tawahi Massacres' take place as Houthis shoot at refugee boats fleeing Greater Aden in Sapper Bay and Telegraph Bay

Desperate para-drops of supplies on 4–5 April

Outer Harbour

Inner Harbour

Container Port

Labour Island

Port of Aden

Post Office Bay

Steamer Point

Sapper Bay

Fort Mirpat

Fort Tarshayn

Al Mowader Palace

TAWAHI

Queen Victoria Park

Big Ben Clock Tower

Crescent Hotel & Orient Club

Ministry of Fisheries

Al Shadili Mosque

Jebel Hedjuff

Oil Tanks

Mualla Street

Adep Governorate

Jewish Cemetery

Abdullah Azzam

KHOSAF VALLEY

TAWILA GORGE

JEBEL SHAMSAN

Al Sahareel Cisterns

Temple Cliff

Crater

Gold Mohur Resort

Gold Mohur Bay

Telegraph Bay

Gold Mohur Valley

Qaluaa Tunnel

Elephant's Trunk

Elephant's Back

Conquest Bay

Round Island Bay

Jumhuriyah Hospital

Aden Tariq Hotel

Regal Roundabout

Purple Aden Water Park

Victoria Bastion

Jebel Hadid

Mercure Hotel

Jalaa

Arab League Roundabout

Front Bay

Sira Fortress

Holkat Bay

MASHIQ

Mashiq Palace

Turtle Bay

2 miles
3 kilometres

0   1   2

0   1   2   3

and Qaluaa, preventing Houthi foot patrols from orienteering over the defence line. Foreign navies had evacuated hundreds of non-Yemenis weeks beforehand, but Tawahi and the Gold Mohur beach resorts were still full of thousands of Yemeni refugees from Mualla and Crater. This was truly a line of no further retreat: once Hedjuff was passed, there was not much of Greater Aden left to conquer. The tiny headland was packed with refugees and their backs were to the sea. There was no longer any room for error.

There were no UAE forces in the Tawahi defensive pocket, but they had a frontline view from the white cranes of the Container Port 1500 metres across the Inner Harbour. Through a network of Motorola and boat radios that the Emiratis (and the Houthis) were monitoring, the Resistance fighters exchanged messages about their situation in coded language. A couple of 'stay-behind' guerrilla groups were still hitting and running in Crater, on the other side of the giant volcanic slope, under leaders Abdul Rahman Qanan and Sheikh Mohammed Mahdi. At the western edge of Mualla, three Popular Committees had toeholds outside the Tawahi pocket: Fathi al-Adadi, Fahd Mashbak, and a Muslim Brotherhood fighter called Mohammed al-Mutairi, a former bodyguard of Islah cleric and US-designated terrorist Sheikh Abdul Majid al Zindani. The 30 or so tunnel defenders were led by Sheikh Ahmed al-Busairi. But holding all these strings of resistance together was an energetic former air force officer called Brigadier General Pilot Ali Nasser Hadi, a former fighter pilot who led the Aden-based 4th Military Region Command in early 2015.

As even a small number of tanks could puncture Resistance blocking positions, the UAE began working more closely with Ali Nasser Hadi to firm up the anti-armour arsenal of the Tawahi pocket. One option was the practice of air-dropping weapons but this was a desperate measure, used only if all other options were blocked. As the first UAE special operators had seen for themselves on 13 April, pallets of arms parachuted freefall often fell in Houthi areas, resupplying the enemy, and still others were seized by tribesmen and buried for later resale or even cheekily sold back to the Coalition just days after they landed. It was an inefficient way to arm up the defenders and the tiniest crosswind sent such pallets crashing through house roofs.

Instead, the UAE Navy worked closely with the hard-working and honest Resistance 'navy' commander, Abdullah al Reyni, who ferried shipments of anti-tank rockets from Assab to the sea off Aden using the corvette *Das*, which was much faster than a landing craft. The arms would be transferred from the *Das* to al Reyni's boats and thence smuggled into the Tawahi pocket under cover of darkness. Three hundred UAE-supplied M72 Light Anti-Tank Weapons (LAW) were provided in the last days of April, and the defenders of Tawahi could be seen in news footage with the single-use unguided 66-mm rockets on their shoulders. Using Yemeni ro-ro ferries (roll-on, roll-off cargo ships), the Resistance even brought two fully functioning T-62 tanks and a 23-mm anti-aircraft cannon (bearing the name 'The Bride of War') over from Sheikh Uthman into the Tawahi pocket. It was Ali Nasser Hadi who ensured these arms were divided fairly between the sectors.

The fatal blow fell in Greater Aden in the early hours of 6 May, just as the Resistance was winding down its latest assault on the airport. Mohammed al-Mutairi, the main Resistance leader in western Mualla, was wounded in the head by a sniper and his Islahi fighters fell back, rushing him to a boat, to begin his medical evacuation to the Gulf. Al-Mutairi's Muslim Brotherhood fighters began to collapse in the vicinity of the British Cemetery and nearby landmarks such as the faculty of engineering in the

Hafoun area of Mualla. The Houthi–Saleh forces seemed to be gearing up for something. Unusually, Katyushas were being fired towards Tawahi, along with tank and 23-mm cannon fire, suggesting a preliminary bombardment to soften the defenders up for an assault. To ensure the rigidity of the front, Ali Nasser Hadi went forward to a post near the Al Shadli Mosque by the coastal choke point at Jebel Hedjuff. At around 03:00 hours on 6 May, a Houthi sniper spotted Ali Nasser Hadi and killed him with a shot through the body. Houthi night-sniping was so rare that conspiracy theories would quickly grow that Ali Nasser Hadi had been betrayed and lured to a particular spot where a sniper was waiting for him.

The word spread like wildfire. Panic took hold. Tawahi began to fall to Houthi probes that quickly penetrated along the coastal avenue as far as Queen Victoria Park, overrunning once-iconic landmarks of the British Empire like the Crescent Hotel, the Orient Club and the parade ground, now home to the Unknown Soldier monument. UAE JTACs tried to stem the inflow of enemy forces by directing naval gunfire onto the road lining the Inner Harbour. So-called 'final defensive fire' – the last salvoes possible, almost called down on top of friendly troops to stop them being overrun – crashed down into Hedjuff's Ministry of Fisheries complex and as close as 80 metres from the northern entrance to the Qaluaa Tunnel. Three Houthi–Saleh armoured vehicles were knocked out, but the damage was done. Houthi troops in fast-moving *chassis* sloshed around the coastal road in Tawahi like floodwater. The defence shattered. Tawahi was falling, and even the tunnel defenders were retreating further inside the mountain, taking the fight for Qaluaa underground for the first time. They would be the last to surrender.

An exodus of civilians now began at every jetty and beach. As dawn broke on 6 May, the sea front was a mass of fishing boats, tugs and ferries, all crammed with men, women and children headed for Little Aden, the Resistance-held oil port directly across the harbour from Tawahi. The Houthis showed no mercy. *Chassis* with twin 23-mm cannons opened up, followed by heavy machine guns, mortars and even RPGs. From the high ground of Fort Mirbat, the Houthis raked the ships fleeing from Sapper Bay, while anti-aircraft cannon at the Al Mowadar Palace opened fire on a tugboat full of refugees in Telegraph Bay. The tug sank under heavy fire, with at least 40 persons known to have been killed and possibly as many as a hundred according to an investigation by Médecins Sans Frontières. In a Tweet on 7 May, the Houthi spokesman in Sanaa, Mohammed Abdal-salam, described the massacre at Tawahi as the killing of 'agents and traitors'. This moderate-seeming spokesman would later become the Muscat-based interlocutor between the Houthis and journalists and think-tankers.

The brutality of the Houthis had been on show for weeks, with men dragged from their homes in Khormaksar and Crater, and summarily executed on the street under suspicion of being guerrillas. Widespread looting of homes and businesses was also undertaken by the Houthis, including determined (but unsuccessful) efforts to blow the doors off the sturdy British-made bank vaults across Mualla and Crater. Civilians could be killed by Houthi snipers for leaving their houses at prescribed times or for crossing certain roads that were set as no-go zones by Houthis with loudspeakers.

'In this war they were different,' recalled one Resistance leader who had fought the Houthis in the six northern wars, 'there was no customary law of war or tribal rules. They just killed, even women and children.' It was becoming clear that the Saleh forces were no longer the main enemy in Aden and that the Houthis were now running the show. Real hatred was building towards the enemy; the Resistance spoke of the Houthis as 'gangs coming from the cave', or 'illiterate messengers of Iran'. For the first time, helplessly watching the Tawahi massacres via drone coverage, the UAE soldiers began to feel the hate too.

# X

# COMING BACK FROM THE BRINK

The double blow of the failed second airport attack and the fall of Tawahi created a dangerous moment in the UAE-Resistance relationship. Never that cohesive to begin with, the Resistance Council was particularly splintered by early May. The Shaab Popular Committees, holding the vital supply line between Little Aden and Sheikh Uthman, were arguing over land disputes, returning to their traditional subject to fight over, now that para-dropped supplies were no longer landing in the area.

The loss of Tawahi set the Islahis, Salafis and Al Qaeda fighters against each other, with accusations of cowardice and betrayal. Salafi clerics under Houthi control in the northern Yemeni district of Kitaf were being used by the enemy to send entreaties to Aden Salafis to cooperate with the invasion. Islahis were likewise being tempted to quit the fight, receiving word from Muslim Brotherhood contacts in other countries that they would be made comfortable in Djibouti if they deserted. Some former army leaders in the Resistance were exploring the handover of their fronts to Saleh forces – though not to the Houthis. These negotiations would be the last substantive involvement of Ali Abdullah Saleh's forces in the Aden battle, for he was growing tired of the war of attrition and was slowly withdrawing his best forces back to the north. From this point on, taking Aden would increasingly be a Houthi fight.

Right after Tawahi fell, the Resistance was rife with internal suspicions and recriminations. Even worse, the UAE was being openly criticised. The new attack on the airport was condemned by some Popular Committee commanders as a wrong-headed approach as each commander felt his front was more deserving of support and should be made the main effort. Resistance fighters vented their frustration, complaining that they were doing just fine on their own before the UAE arrived and started running things. Attacking the open ground of the airport seemed like madness. In the heat of one such debate, held early on 6 May, a junior Resistance commander called Basheer, no doubt high on *qat*, publicly blew the cover of the UAE troops: 'Foreign forces are here in Aden controlling airstrikes,' he had blurted out, 'they could have saved Tawahi.' When asked, by curious Yemenis what foreign forces, he said: 'The Emiratis.' The hunt for the UAE operators had begun.

At 03:00 hours on 6 May, Salem D. got word that all of Aden was now talking about the UAE troops, and that the mood within the Resistance was volatile. 'You need to leave. If someone gives you away, we can't protect you,' he was told by the Resistance Council. To minimize the risk of discovery, Salem was ordered to move the team to a new safe house in Bir Ahmed, SH3, which belonged to a martyred (i.e., killed in action) Resistance commander called Aymen al-Aqrabi. The new house, like all the others, was close to open helicopter landing sites in case a quick extraction was needed. Salem was rightfully paranoid. One spy had been caught by the Resistance marking the locations of UAE Al-Forsan for Houthi mortarmen. The Houthis would also greatly value a UAE hostage to parade and use for leverage. Capture was the worst fear of all the UAE operators, due to the humiliation and cost it might incur on the Emirates to recover hostages. The Al-Forsan team had been given

200,000 Saudi Riyals and $30,000 (in US dollars) to buy safe harbour and ease their passage back to friendly lines if need be. Pairs of operators had also made draconian plans to die fighting and not allow each other to fall into enemy hands alive. Now, as dawn came on 6 May, surveillance flights showed numerous parties of Yemenis turning up at the recently evacuated SH2. It was impossible to tell if they were checking to see if the Emiratis had really left or if they were there to trap and sell them.

Salem and his team temporarily withdrew to a UAE ship in the Gulf of Aden that night. At 20:30 hours, a convoy of Hiluxes came to SH3 and drove the UAE troops along the Shaab waterfront to Little Aden. At 21:45 hours, the team began to load their gear onto a coastguard cutter that had been donated by the UAE to Yemen's government years earlier. 'I know this boat,' Salem told the captain, recalling the ship that had hunted his two Zodiacs with its searchlight over a month earlier. 'Of course you do, it's the only one we've got!' replied the skipper.

At 23:34 hours, the cutter chugged out into the Gulf of Aden, threading between Katyushas fired from the Houthis' new positions in Tawahi. Just under 10 km (5 nautical miles) due south, they met up with a UAE Navy Baynunah-class corvette, *Al Hesen* (P172), one of the powerful new guided-missile ships that came into service in 2012. From the *Al Hesen*, the troops were ferried out to the *Al Uwaisat* (A81) command ship, further out in international waters. It was 07:05 hours on 7 May when Salem reached the ship's command centre, made his report to Ali A., and then trudged down to his assigned cabin. He was weary after weeks of non-stop operations but furious too. He slammed the metal bulkhead door shut and then kicked it. This felt like failure. And then, after venting his anger, he crashed onto the bunk and fell into a deep and long-overdue sleep.

## Continuing the Fight from the Ship

As Salem finally got the sleep that he had deprived himself of in Djibouti and Aden, the command staff in Abu Dhabi and on the *Al Uwaisat* were busy discussing the UAE's next move. Salem need not have feared the end of the mission: there was determination, from MBZ to MGM to Ali A., to keep going. They had all accepted the real risk of UAE fatalities when the mission first began. 'This is no picnic,' Ali A. said on a video-teleconference that night. 'We will kill them, and they will kill us'.

To ensure that the remaining defenders of Sheikh Uthman and Little Aden did not lose heart, the *Al Uwaisat* – 'the ship' in PG parlance – would become the new safe house. All the joint fires – airpower, naval gunfire, and even shipboard operation of the Sabr drone – would be brought onboard the *Al Uwaisat*. Four Resistance intelligence officers also came to the ship to be a link to the land-based Resistance Council and to continue processing and aiding requests for fire support. Salem D. and the 34 Al-Forsan and SOC operators would join Ali A. on the ship, getting reacquainted with its slower pace, cramped quarters and constant motion. Salem had lost 26 lb of weight in Aden during his weeks at the safe houses: now the food was plentiful again and there was even time to relax, which Salem used to teach himself to fish off the side of the boat.

To restore the bonds of trust between the UAE task force and the Popular Committees, the Resistance Council would be regularly brought out to the ship, which would become a hub for the distribution of arms, ammunition, medicine and money to the Resistance. On the odd occasion that the ship was visible from the coast, it was almost always rocketed – surprisingly accurately – so it never stopped moving, both for security and because it was needed in so many places to do so many vital tasks.

Aside from the maintenance of JTAC support to the

Resistance pockets, the next most urgent task was firming up the cohesion of the Resistance Council and their relationship with the UAE forces. The exodus from Tawahi had concentrated all the Resistance Council leaders in the Sheikh Uthman side of Aden now. The Resistance Council Operations Room was collocated with the municipal council at the May 22 school in the heart of the Sheikh Uthman region. A sharp young tribal politician, Naif al-Bakri al-Yafaei, was the senior civilian, having served as deputy governor since October 2013, and acting governor since the governor Abdel-Aziz bin Habtour fled Aden in late April 2015. The Resistance Council required all members to renounce their ties to the Muslim Brotherhood, so Naif al-Bakri had nominally resigned from Islah in April 2015, but he was known to have ties to foreign backers of the Brotherhood. The acting governor and political leader of the Resistance Council was very ambitious, canny and took his media advisor everywhere with him. Ahead of the second airport battle, Naif al-Bakri's triumphal entry to the liberated airport had been one of the better planned parts of the operation, but, alas, his victory parade was not to be. The UAE's military liaison to the Resistance Council was still Hashim Sayyed but a new figure was emerging in the form of President Hadi's appointment to replace the martyred head of the 4th Military Regional Command, Ali Nasser Hadi. The new commander was Brigadier General Ahmed Saif Mohsen al-Yafaei, who had served as the head of the Marib-based 3rd Military Regional Command since 2013. He was popular with the UAE commanders because, unlike most Yemeni leaders, he was clear about how little control he had over the Popular Committee fighters, which was refreshingly honest.

The overall UAE task force commander Colonel Ali A. was well suited to grip the situation and get UAE-Resistance relations back on the right track. Ali A. was a 'natural' with his troops and with the Yemenis, somehow managing to be both humble yet authoritative. Indeed, until you knew he was the commander, you might not have been able to pick him out from the crowd, so well did he blend in with his men in their mixture of football and Formula 1 shirts, track suits and shorts.

Ali A. recalled: 'We never show off in front of the Resistance. When people watch us [and the Resistance] together, they think we are family. The key is respect. They admire the UAE. There is no need to lord it over them.' But Ali A. was also clear in his mind that he was there to do a job and the UAE was in Aden to help the Yemenis win, reminding his command staff after one early meeting with Resistance leaders, 'I'm not coming to build friendships for the sake of it. I'm coming to finish the fight.'

Ali A. understood that respect had to be two-way, and that meant mixing the stick and the carrot. 'I shake their hand, I hug them, we eat together, I help them, but if I need to, I take their eyes,' he explained, using the old Arabic metaphor denoting 'toughness'. Though he could change his mind when justified – for instance, recognising that the former military officers were less reliable than the Salafis – Ali A. had strong instincts about how to manage the more problematic elements of the Resistance. No one was cut off entirely, as that would only give room for the Houthis to splinter the Resistance, and logistical, medical and humanitarian support would actually increase to rebuild trust. But the Emirates would distribute the support – not power-hungry officials like Naif al-Bakri. In an example of Ali A.'s approach to key leader engagement, Naif al-Bakri was shown deference and patiently listened to, and was gifted food-stuffs to distribute plus two new Hiluxes, but he was also cut off, from that moment, from being allowed to communicate with anyone but Ali A. There was only one address to get the things he wanted: Ali A.

## Humanitarian Assistance in the Aden Battle

From the very beginning of the Aden operation, the UAE leadership had been thinking hard about the role of Civil-Military Cooperation (CIMIC). In Yemen, as in Afghanistan and other theatres, there would be close cooperation between the UAE National Security Council, the General Headquarters of the Armed Forces, the Ministry of Foreign Affairs, the intelligence services and the Emirates Red Crescent foundation. The already crowded Sheikh Uthman side of Aden was now swollen with tens of thousands of new refugees from the Tawahi evacuation, who had been housed in schools and in newer, unfinished stages of the Enma housing projects – a sprawling multi-phase development of identical light, cream-coloured homes.

The population was packed together inside during the day to reduce civilian casualties. The Houthis cut off the traditional source of fresh water to Sheikh Uthman, the British aqueduct fed from the ancient cisterns in Crater. The electricity grid was failing for most of each day and fuel was in short supply for neighbourhood generators. Malnutrition was becoming more widespread, as was the build-up of rotting trash and stagnant water, worsening the ever-present threat from mosquito-based tropical diseases like dengue fever and malaria. For over a month, the Red Crescent had warned of a 'catastrophic humanitarian situation' unfolding. Whereas, for decades, economic migrants from the Horn of Africa had been making their way to Aden, the flow had reversed. In Djibouti, one refugee told reporters: 'Aden is a broken place, full of death. It's become like Syria. We cannot go back.'

The first steps taken by the UAE were immediate life-saving measures. Thanks to Hamid K.'s work in Assab with the Eritreans, a large Emirates Red Crescent ship was allowed to dock at Assab on 11 May, packed full of food parcels, each intended to give a family two weeks' worth of staples such as rice, sugar and powdered milk. Thus commenced a mammoth logistical undertaking, unloading the massive ship with a crane, Hamid K.'s hundreds of Eritrean labourers, and the single, rusty fork-lift left behind by the British or the Israelis. By now, the UAE Navy had four 64-metre landing craft servicing the Assab to Aden route – *Al Bahya*, *Zarkoh*, *Al Shareeah* and the *Khazna* (L61). These ships delivered cargo after cargo to waiting dhows off Aden, the first humanitarian assistance to reach the city since 2.5 tonnes of aid had been landed by Médecins Sans Frontières and the International Committee of the Red Cross on 8 April, more than a month earlier.

From 16 May onwards, the UAE Navy began receiving wounded Resistance fighters and civilians on board their ships. Each night, 20–30 badly wounded or sick persons were shuttled to the *Al Uwaisat* and the medical ship *Al Shareeah* (L71). The shuttling in and out of medical supplies and patients was obviously not a workable long-term solution to Aden's growing health and electricity crisis. The UAE needed to quickly rebuild capacity in Aden's hospitals and power plants, and that meant putting professionals in direct contact with Adenese health and electricity workers to survey local needs.

A UAE military Medical Service Corps doctor called Ayesha D. would become the centre of this effort. She had worked alongside the Presidential Guard in Kosovo and Afghanistan and was drawn from her duties at the Zayed Military Hospital to meet the PG commander MGM in the early days of the Aden intervention. She accepted the highly classified mission without seeking further details and was quickly drawn into the planning group and the daily briefings for the Yemen war. Strong direction was given by MGM, at the direction of MBZ, on the issue of humanitarian assistance, which was considered vital both to strengthen the willingness of Yemenis to protect the UAE advisors and to build the morale of the Resistance. Dr Ayesha suggested a first step would be for herself and a civil engineer to visit the *Al Uwaisat* to confer with local Yemenis, and this was quickly actioned. On the ship, they met with representatives of the Aden health and electricity directorates and received lists of hospitals and power stations that needed upgrading.

Back in Abu Dhabi, cross-checking of these documents showed that they were non-prioritised wish-lists and could not be used as a basis for planning. Some of the hospitals slated for immediate assistance were even in Houthi-controlled parts of Aden! Dr Ayesha began working on another, even more ambitious plan, to covertly visit the city of Aden with the engineer, where they could move hospital by hospital, and to every power station, to get the real ground truth. When Ayesha proposed this to MBZ, MGM and Ali A., they could all tell she was steelily determined to make it happen. 'No hesitation?' MGM had asked. 'None', Ayesha replied. 'Confident?' he pushed. 'Yes', she confirmed. Ayesha recalled afterwards that they all seemed pleased with her answers. They had all wanted and needed her to go on the ground but could not order her to do it. She had to come up with the idea herself and volunteer. Ali A. would later say: 'She's more of a man than most men', meant as a high compliment. Ayesha and her two nurse assistants were going to Aden.

## Back in Aden Until the Job Is Done

By 21 May, the Emiratis were headed back ashore. The Camp David peace talks to resolve the Yemen conflict had ended inconclusively and it would no longer go against the spirit of those US-brokered talks if the UAE reinforced its presence in

Aden. It had been two weeks since the UAE extracted its men, and in that time a lot of goodwill had been rebuilt with provision of medical support, food supplies and arms shipments, even including the first body armour and uniforms for the Resistance. They would return to tip the balance: to train and arm the Resistance, and to target the enemy more thoroughly than ever before.

A new safe house, SH4, was identified, again in Bir Ahmed. A two-man reconnaissance was undertaken on 21 May, followed by the reinsertion of Salem D. and eight others on 22 May. By 25 May, there were 21 UAE operators dressed in civilian attire at SH4. These comprised Salem D., his communications officer, two JTACs, four snipers and two other operators. The two-bedroom safe house was getting crowded, but the site was never more than a stopover, especially due to mounting security concerns. A Yemeni fiddling with wiring in a BMP-1 near the house accidentally set it firing, causing it to shoot off all its precious magazine of cannon rounds before anyone could stop it. Houthi Katyushas began landing nearby, and a Houthi tank was seen moving in the distance north of Bir Ahmed. Salem moved quickly, relocating the team to Little Aden in the early hours of 26 May.

It was there that they found their favourite base used during their campaign in Aden – the Saleh bin Fareed house, or SH5. The magnificent house was owned by Saleh bin Fareed al-Awlaki, the sheikh of sheikhs from Shabwah governorate and a Sandhurst graduate, now living in Abu Dhabi. Abu Zaraa, the intelligence officer, had found the house after being directed to secure a safer location near the coast in Little Aden. Saleh bin Fareed turned the house over to the UAE military without hesitation. The site had a lot to recommend it. It was a solid five-storey mansion with thick walls and was perfectly sheltered from Katyusha fire by the surrounding mountains. The house had a jetty, a lookout tower and a wonderful view of the bay, Bandar Sheikh, and the island opposite, Blue Beach Mountain. It smelled of the sea, of paint drying on fishing boats, and of diesel fuel. There were almost always some distant battle sounds – including the reassuring boom of the G-6's outbound fire – but, just as often, it was celebration fire from elsewhere in Little Aden – a family mourning a martyr, or celebrating the safe return of a fighter or a prisoner swap that would bring their loved one home.

Compared to all previous safe houses, this was heaven. SH5 could easily fit over a hundred guests in comfort, or three times that number on mattresses. It had ornate wooden doors and archways, and high ceilings. The large kitchen was thoroughly scrubbed and sanitised by the Emiratis until the Yemenis complained that it 'smelt like a pharmacy'. For Dr Ayesha, the Saleh bin Fareed house was a place of happy memories from the start. She arrived on the prow of a banana boat, channelling her inner Kate Winslet and feeling 'like I was in the movie *Titanic*'. Ayesha got the best room in the house, the top-floor master suite with a wonderful balcony overlooking the bay. But this was still a war zone. One day she found herself flying down the stairs from the top floor to the basement, a blur of movement she could hardly remember afterwards, with Katyushas flying close over the house and splashing into the bay. The struggle in Aden was flaring up again, and June would witness the most intense exchange of firepower in the battle so far.

# XI

# A WAR OF ATTRITION

On 23 May, with the UAE forces back ashore in Aden, the decision was made in Abu Dhabi to finally shelve the amphibious operation due to a lack of support from the US and the broader Coalition. Instead, the clandestine force in Aden would become the main effort and would be reinforced by Colonel Ali A. from the current 36 troops to nearly 80 UAE personnel on the ground. Troops from Al-Forsan and select Land Forces units would build out the base in Little Aden until it was strong enough to support the successful liberation of Aden airport, which would cut off the coastal line of supply used by the Houthi forces in Greater Aden. Thus began the deadliest phase of the war in Aden, a month-long slugfest during which the UAE and the Houthis competed to 'win the firefight', bringing heavier and heavier firepower to bear.

## The ISR Surge

The JTACs sent ashore prior to the 6 May extraction had done a fine job holding back the Houthi attacks but they had mostly been reactive, prioritising defensive calls for fire from the Resistance. Aboard the ship in mid-May an effort was made to prepare for more proactive, offensive uses of so-called 'joint fires', the combination of all kinds of fire support into a deliberate and measured effort that could support decisive operations to seize terrain. The new joint fires programme was coordinated by a specialist, an air force officer called Major Mohammed M., who was designated the Joint Fires Officer. A quietly spoken Mirage pilot, Mohammed M. would ensure that much more air support would be overhead at all times to support the Aden operation and he would professionalise the system of close air support, breaking Aden up into so-called 'kill-boxes' where pilots were either allowed to free-hunt or operate only in conjunction with JTACs.

Another of Mohammed M.'s first tasks was to fully integrate all the UAE's Intelligence, Surveillance and Reconnaissance (ISR) capabilities into one system. This would be a joint effort by the UAE Signals Intelligence Agency, the National Intelligence Service, the Directorate of Military Intelligence and the Presidential Guard's intelligence section. From the Sniper pods on UAE strike aircraft to signals intelligence collection undertaken from the ship or the safe house, to the human sources operated by the Resistance and the devices used to mark the Resistance front lines, all sources of intelligence would be fused together to make one continuously updated 'common intelligence picture'.

First on the *Al Uwaisat* and then at the Saleh bin Fareed house, it would all come together. The joint fires room was a hall with a huge, panelled roof and boarded-up windows, brightly lit and with a blue neon fly zapper. Whole walls were covered in mammoth colour satellite images with intricately colour-coded sticky notes all over them. Seated on pillows and couches, Salem D. and Mohammed M. would stare at the wide-screen television showing full motion video from the Sabr drones. All around them, gathered like a watchful family of meerkats, were one or more JTACs, the source-handlers from the Resistance and the UAE National Intelligence Service, plus a representative from the Directorate of Military Intelligence and the Presidential Guard's intelligence section.

Of all the sensors employed in this effort, one would stand out as especially valuable – the UAE-produced Al Sabr S-100 drone. The Sabr is a rotary-wing drone, meaning that it essentially looks like a small, unmanned helicopter, 3 metres long and shaped like a sturdy fish. Perhaps unsurprisingly, its introduction over Aden coincided with a rash of inaccurate Houthi reports that Apache helicopters were flying around the city. The UAE's own drone design proved to be its most effective drone system. The Sabr was quieter than other drones and other UAE ISR platforms like the AT-802i Air Tractors, and it could hover at low altitudes, making it a stealthy watcher. The Sabr allowed both the enemy to be catalogued and also friendly forces to be observed – a useful verification tool to learn whether a Resistance commander might only be pretending to attack or to have used up his ammunition. The Sabr was even so intuitive to fly that it could be 'taken over' briefly by JTACs or intelligence officers to get exactly the right view of a target.

Initially operated from the *Al Uwaisat* due to its vertical take-off capability, by late May, it was getting dangerous to operate the Sabr from the ship in daylight. Due to range constraints, this required the *Al Uwaisat* to come close to the shore, whereupon it had two close shaves when targeted by a D-30 122-mm artillery piece that the Houthis were firing from the mouth of the Qaluaa Tunnel. Indeed, one such six-round salvo landed just as Ali A. and his command team were on the daily video call with Presidential Guard headquarters and Assab. With rounds bracketing the ship 50 metres to either side, everyone suddenly disappeared from the screen for a number of minutes as they scrambled for cover. In a trap, suggested by MBZ himself, the *Al Uwaisat* was sent back in to show itself on the horizon

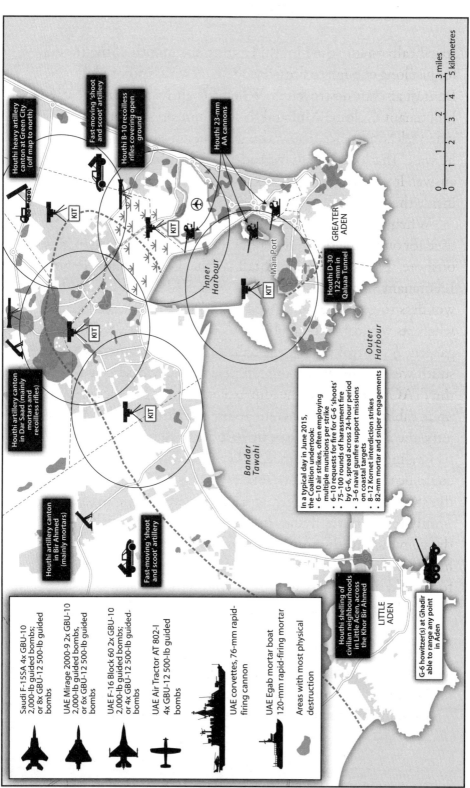

Firepower in the attritional fighting in June and July 2015

Legend (bottom left box):

Saudi F-15SA 4x GBU-10 2,000-lb guided bombs; or 8x GBU-12 500-lb guided bombs

UAE Mirage 2000-9 2x GBU-10 2,000-lb guided bombs, or 6x GBU-12 500-lb guided bombs

UAE F-16 Block 60 2x GBU-10 2,000-lb guided bombs; or 4x GBU-12 500-lb guided bombs

UAE Air Tractor AT 802-I 4x GBU-12 500-lb guided bombs

UAE corvettes, 76-mm rapid-firing cannon

UAE Egab mortar boat 120-mm rapid-firing mortar

Areas with most physical destruction

Labels on map:

Houthi heavy artillery canton at Green City (off map to north)

Fast-moving 'shoot and scoot' artillery

Houthi B-10 recoilless rifles covering open ground

Houthi 23-mm AA cannons

Houthi artillery canton in Dar Saad (mainly mortars and recoilless rifles)

Houthi artillery canton in Bir Ahmed (mainly mortars)

Fast-moving 'shoot and scoot' artillery

Houthi D-30 122-mm in Qaluaa Tunnel

GREATER ADEN

Inner Harbour

Main Port

Outer Harbour

Bandar Tawahi

LITTLE ADEN

Houthi shelling of civilian neighbourhoods in Little Aden, across the Khor Bir Ahmed

G-6 howitzer(s) at Ghadir able to range any point in Aden

KIT

In a typical day in June 2015, the Coalition undertook:
• 6–10 air strikes, often employing multiple munitions per strike
• 6–10 requests for fire for G-6 'shoots'
• 75–100 rounds of harassment fire by G-6, spread across 24-hour period
• 3–6 naval gunfire support missions on coastal targets
• 8–12 Kornet interdiction strikes
• 82-mm mortar and sniper engagements

0 1 2 3 miles
0 1 2 3 4 5 kilometres

specifically to lure the Houthi D-30 to the mouth of the tunnel for just long enough to fire a few shells, at which point a loitering Emirati aircraft destroyed it. When the air force representative Lieutenant Colonel Mubarak N. was not present on the daily video teleconference to give this good news, MGM asked where he was. 'That was him flying today, he's not back yet,' came the answer. It was Lt Col. Mubarak who had put the bomb precisely inside the tunnel and took out the pesky howitzer.

When the UAE leadership noticed that the Sabr was being used for only a fraction of its endurance each sortie, it was moved onshore. Deputy Chief of Staff of the UAE Armed Forces, Lieutenant General Issa Saif bin Ablan Al Mazrouei worked wonders to get the Sabr moved to the Saleh bin Fareed house, where its vertical take-off ability allowed it to operate from the garden. A control van for the Sabr was placed 40 metres to the south-west of the main house, linked to the widescreen TVs in the JTAC's room in the headquarters by thick bundles of fibre-optic cabling. Without a crane to unload the control van at the jetty, the 2-tonne trailer was stevedored by Yemenis and Emiratis hauling on old-fashioned pulleys and ropes. Now the Sabr could be used to its fullest capacity, always in range, not forcing the ship to sail into danger, and faster to reach the battlefront – only ten minutes flying time out and ten back (half that of the commute to the ship), reserving anything from two to five hours' endurance over Aden, depending on how long the operators could maintain focus.

The Sabr was a game-changer, recalled Salem D.:

It made a huge difference and helped every weapon to achieve its potential: air, artillery, mortars, naval gunfire. When air was up above 16,000 feet, it could spot from close up. We used it to guide and confirm all strikes and gather [battle damage assessment] data. It was a decisive weapon that changed the whole battle. The enemy really started to suffer. From the arrival of the Sabr, it was basically like PlayStation.

Indeed, it was like playing way too many hours of PlayStation. Videos from the time of the joint fires cell show Salem D., the joint fires chief Mohammed M. and the JTACs and intelligence officers looking increasingly weary but obsessed. The constant watching of the enemy – a sense of hunting without moving – becomes addictive and something of an obsession. No sooner had one target been destroyed than another interesting hunt began. Such slow-motion remote killing is hard to look away from. Every so often a weapon would be released: 'Twenty-five seconds ... ten seconds ...' A soundless black explosion and a few claps from the crowd. Human targets were scattering: some were dead men running, still not feeling blood loss while 'the hit was hot' but then dropping. Others would lead the strike cell to new targets and it would all start over again. They now lived in a strange and ghastly twilight zone. After the war, one UAE JTAC remembered: 'Our strike operations are not to kill somebody, they are to secure somebody.' This was the thought that kept him going.

## The Enemy's 'Pattern of Life'

In intelligence terminology, 'pattern of life' refers to a method of surveillance specifically used for documenting or understanding a target's habits. The overlapping ISR systems watching and listening to the Houthis began to build just such an intimate picture of the enemy for the first time. In a sense, the Houthis had been a mystery for much of the battle. Though Salafi fighters like Hashim Sayyed had fought the Houthis for years, that was up in the mountainous north, in the Houthis' own back yard, and that was before the Houthis received intensive training and equipment from Saleh's Republican Guard, Iran and Lebanese Hezbollah. The UAE went into the Yemen conflict assuming that any capabilities fielded by the Saleh military were now in Houthi hands but knowing nothing more about the enemy. Basic details, such as the Houthi 'order of battle' or ORBAT, were completely absent, in part because they did not organise like a conventional army, and they were highly secretive. What the UAE learned about the Houthis would entirely be the product of closely watching them fight, move, hide and resupply.

They were a fascinating enemy – both impressive and repugnant at the same time. They fought to the death and often showed great bravery, and they were ingenious at deception and urban combat, yet they were also needlessly cruel to the civilian population and ruthless with their troops' lives, in part because they recruited endless cadres of the poorest Yemeni men and child soldiers. As noted earlier, it was clear by the end of May that the Houthi part of the Houthi–Saleh partnership was in the ascendant. The enemy simply looked and acted differently. As one UAE intelligence officer remembered:

> Initially most of the enemy attacks in April and May looked like a military force and you could see the Ali Abdullah Saleh Republican Guard. They used radio like a military force, and they let tanks and artillery do a lot of the fighting for them, like Saleh forces. By June, they were different. They didn't use tanks as much and their style was different. Fewer wore uniforms. They were the real Houthis – very thin and really fit and they moved in small groups. They didn't use normal military radio procedure anymore but

they used a lot more codes, just like the Houthis did in the north.

The Emiratis studied the Houthis as a target system, like a hunter learning the ways of his quarry. The highest payoff targets were clearly command, control and communications headquarters but the Houthi system was rudimentary and difficult to map. The Houthis didn't have real battalions, companies and platoons, like a normal army. They seemed to be organised geographically into fronts, one per neighbourhood. An operations room existed in Aden, but it gave off few signatures. Exploitation after the battle would show that the Khormaksar-based operations room was in the basement of the Aden Hotel, but it transmitted no signals. It only undertook passive monitoring of Resistance Motorola messages using radio scanners and it issued orders via couriers on foot and on trail bikes. These messengers then linked up with mobile retransmission nodes that used low-power, handheld radios to communicate with the Houthi sector commanders, known as supervisors. Each supervisor was a 'Houthi Houthi', meaning a trusted Houthi fighter from the Houthi home province of Saada, and their sectors roughly matched up with Aden's districts – such as Dar Saad, Khormaksar, Al Areesh, Crater and Mualla. Communications with the Houthi leaders in Sanaa were minimal and the war in Aden largely ran itself. Later it transpired that, because the Houthis controlled cellular phone and internet networks from Sanaa, they used encrypted messaging applications like Telegram to transmit orders to Aden and to relay intercepted Resistance cell phone messages captured at the cell-phone companies in Sanaa. Wherever had these mountain men learned to do that? The fingerprints of Iran and Lebanese Hezbollah were present everywhere.

The Houthi lines of supply were much easier to find and would constitute one of their greatest weaknesses. Evidently the Houthi–Saleh forces had expected an easy victory in Aden, akin to their almost bloodless successes in Sanaa, Hodeida, Ibb and Taizz. This victory did not come, and the challenge of taking Aden was further complicated by the gradual ebbing away of many of Ali Abdullah Saleh's Republican Guard troops as the battle wore on into May. As a result, reinforcing Aden from the north became vital to the success of the invasion and that meant relying on three well-known lines of supply: the route via Taizz to the steel factory north of Imran, the highway from Al Anad and, most importantly, the coastal highway from Abyan. In addition to a dwindling stream of tanks and BMPs from nearby captured bases, the Houthis surged troop reinforcements from northern Yemen down this coastal road in mid-May, taking advantage of a supposed ceasefire that coincided with peace talks and a US–Gulf summit at Camp David. The Houthi system of logistics was laid bare by 24-hour aerial surveillance. It relied on a spread-out relay of *chassis* that sprinted along the open highway at high speed, via the Al Alam and Nexen roundabouts. These vehicles would then get under cover in warehouses in Al Areesh to split up their cargoes for further distribution.

Houthi artillery was also reasonably easy to find when it was firing, but their rocket launchers and howitzers stayed highly mobile. They mostly used cubes of 107-mm rocket tubes, and medium mortars or twin-barrel 23-mm cannons, all mounted on *chassis*. These vehicles dashed out of overhead cover, fired a few shots and then relocated at speed. The Houthis also made effective use of decoy guns – either scrap metal arranged to look like a gun or actual destroyed guns left in the open. They also seemed to be able to get 23-mm anti-aircraft cannons into remarkable places – on top of flat-roofed buildings, inside unfinished high rises, and buried deep within destroyed structures. When they did use less mobile, static artillery pieces or larger multiple rocket-launch trucks, these were kept hidden under overhead cover and rarely fired more than one or two shots before disappearing.

These shots were often disconcertingly accurate, giving Houthi artillery fire the characteristic of 'heavy sniping'. Many buildings appeared to have been pre-registered with ranging shots, which allowed for accurate nocturnal shooting simply by taking the artillery piece to the right spot and aligning it correctly. The Houthis even had a somewhat comical method of correcting fire, which arrested spies described to their captors: they sent young agents to carry sheep on their shoulders and watched them with binoculars. The spy then watched the fall of shot and twisted his body left, right, forwards and backwards to signal the adjustment needed.

Watching the Houthis every day, the Emirati ISR operators learned just how difficult it was to get a clear look at the Houthi foot soldiers for more than a few seconds at a time. As one UAE intelligence officer noted: 'They adapted to our air support by fighting invisibly, moving in very small groups in-between covered positions and hide sites.' They 'mouse-holed' the dividing walls between apartment complexes to allow themselves to move from one building to another under cover. The Houthis did most of their movement at night or when exploiting hazy visibility and low cloud. They seemed to intuit which buildings the Coalition was not allowed to strike – the so-called 'no-strike list' – and they exploited this by mingling with civilians at hospitals, mosques, malls and markets, and generally by emulating the 'signature' of civilians whenever possible – moving between positions unarmed whenever possible. To make their sniper positions harder to locate, they would knock a small loophole high in a wall or use an existing shell hole away from an obvious window, then raise a bedframe on top of a stack of furniture inside the room to create a comfortable laying position at just the right height so that a sniper could stay still for days on end. Dead Houthi snipers and 23-mm gunners would sometimes be discovered with intravenous drips (IVs) in their arms, presumably to stay hydrated while they lay unmoving for days.

A cocktail of drugs and religious zeal was also a big part of the Houthi soldier's life. When not high on *qat* and Captagon amphetamines, they used tablets designed to treat heavy menstrual bleeding in women to slow blood-loss from their wounds. 'They had one pill to stop bleeding and one to make them crazy,' Salem D. recalled, adding 'we were fighting a man in a foxhole, high on drugs. They would fight till they die. You could hit a building with a 2,000-lb bomb and it would burn for a day, and they would pop up again and keep fighting.' The Houthis always fought hard – but never more so than on Fridays after receiving sermons from their supervisors. Foot-soldiers wore nickel-plated Yale-type 'keys to heaven' around their necks, an Iranian custom from the Iran–Iraq War that was said to protect the user from bullets.

As formidable as they were, the Houthi system in Aden began to succumb to 'pattern of life' analysis as their ways became known and even predictable, which is a deadly vulnerability in modern warfare. The UAE engaged in what is known to ISR professionals as 'deep soaks', wherein the enemy would be patiently watched for days on end. This is maddening work, for it often ends with no result and it requires great self-restraint to watch an enemy without attacking them at the first opportunity or the second, or the third even. But the approach pays off. By following Houthi motorbike couriers, the command posts used by supervisors were mapped and then all attacked at the same time, including the basement of the Aden Hotel, which was dug out by a 2,000-lb bomb delivered at just the right steep angle to drill through into the areas below the ground floor. Likewise, by following the daily *qat* deliveries among the Houthi positions, the bunkers and foxholes were catalogued on a daily basis.

Patterns began to emerge in how the Houthis moved and fired their artillery, allowing known firing positions to be monitored and struck quickly. When the Houthis flaunted their exploitation of 'no-strike list' locations too openly, the rules could suddenly change. This is what happened one day when the airport's badly damaged Air Traffic Control tower, VIP lounge and a presidential Boeing 747 suddenly went from being untouchable safe havens to death-traps for the scores of Houthis inside, who thought they were safe. Fingertip feel for the enemy, built with ISR 'soaks', backed by knowledge of the local environment provided by Abu Zaraa's human source network, was a deadly combination.

## Joint Fires from Air, Land and Sea

In June, the 'joint fires' capability in Aden expanded greatly to service the growing list of Houthi tactical targets. Air power remained an important source of supporting fires and the UAE ensured that its Mirage and F-16 pilots could remain patiently overhead through the provision of air-to-air refuelling via the new UAE Airbus A330 Multi Role Tanker Transports flying orbits over the Red Sea. The sensor pods used by F-16 and Mirage had sufficient acuity to track specific vehicles and differentiate their colour from safe altitudes. Turboprop aircraft like the Air Tractor AT-802i – which the Yemenis called 'the bicycle' because it was so slow – proved invaluable, covering the night hours due to their long endurance and advanced forward-looking infrared (FLIR) sensors. Indeed, the main problem in the skies over Aden was warning off nosy US surveillance drones that moved in and out of the airspace without forewarning and risked mid-air collisions with UAE aircraft.

The JTACs were very sharp after months of operations. Even after taking all necessary precautions, collateral damage incidents are inevitable in any air campaign, particularly urban battles where the enemy looks just like the friendlies and deliberately impersonates civilians. In some cases, accidental collateral damage incidents were undoubtedly real but, in others, even the international media swallowed Houthi propaganda. For instance, in early July, a large group of men – possibly including a hundred persons – was struck by a Mirage two-ship in the town of Waht, just north of Aden. To the world, the strike looked like the tragic misidentification of a goat market as a Houthi gathering. But there was no goat market on the day and time in question: at 6 a.m. during Ramadan. Local Resistance intelligence contacts could quickly check whether the market was open, which it was not. A motorbike followed from a Houthi command node had led the UAE straight to a Houthi tactical assembly area for an attack that morning.

As the joint fires campaign dragged on, the rules of engagement got tighter and tighter as JTACs were being increasingly asked to provide 'danger close' air cover for Resistance troops operating right next to the targeted Houthi positions. With great care, the JTACs struck such sites and then waited with bated breath for the Resistance to answer after each strike in order to confirm they were unharmed. The JTACs had even mastered their game to the extent that they could be a lot more discerning with Resistance 'calls for fire', balancing the genuine needs of their partner forces against other considerations. 'A GBU-12 costs 18,000 UAE dirham [around £4,000] and will destroy a house. For a sniper? No,' remembered one JTAC.

Available UAE naval gunfire support had been built up during the interregnum after the UAE extraction in early May, in part as a way to 'do something' at that low point in the intervention and to show the Houthis that the UAE was still in the fight. In addition to the corvettes *Das* (P162) and *Al Hesen* (P172), the flotilla was sometimes reinforced by another modern Baynunah-class corvette, *Al Hili* (P176). These ships normally operated about 37 km (20 nautical miles) offshore, but they would dash in closer, to around 15–20 km (8–11 nautical miles), to bombard key Houthi logistical hubs on the Abyan coastal highway. The 76-mm rapid-fire cannons arming these corvettes were used to undertake high-explosive 'area fire' on Houthi-controlled camps at Al Kawd, Jaar and Zinjibar, and also key roundabouts at Al Alam, Nexen and Musabeen. The idea of this 'area fire' was simply to fill a space with explosive effects and deadly fragmentation as a convoy ran the gauntlet.

Alongside the corvettes, the Navy introduced two Egab coastal artillery boats (P203 and P206), which were Ghanna-tha-class 24-metre amphibious transport boats, armed with a rapid-firing 120-mm mortar system. The Ghannatha was armed with a 120-mm automatic mortar and was developed by Abu Dhabi Ship Building (ADSB) specifically for littoral warfare in shallow coastal waters. The genius of the Egab was that it could quickly get into position within 8–10 km of the coast due to its high speed of 38-knots (70km/h) and its shallow draught. The automatic mortar could execute a 15-round bombardment of a camp or junction within 90 seconds and then the Egab could speed away. With a crew of three and representing a small target, the Egab allowed fire missions anywhere along the coastal road without risking a corvette with 35–45 sailors onboard. To really appreciate the deadly nature of a fast-firing 120 mm mortar, the weapon will have four to six rounds in the air before the first one lands, and then they will keep coming every 15 seconds. On some days in June, the Egab made multiple 'gun-runs' into the shallows, firing off their entire onboard ammunition load of 60 rounds.

The final component of the new joint fires effort was land-based 'tube artillery' – howitzers that are capable of firing at very high trajectories so they can lob shells over intervening vertical obstacles. After over a month of preparation, MBZ had directed on 27 May that a G-6 155-mm howitzer should be clandestinely inserted into Little Aden, from where it could range any target in Aden city or its rural outskirts. The insertion was handled by the Navy's Colonel Sayyed Z., who reconnoitred the landing spot at Ghadir beach during a hazardous 28 May ground visit in which he and Abdullah al Reyni were nearly shot by overzealous Resistance sentries. Ghadir was the perfect place for the G-6 because it was sheltered on all sides, with no line of sight from any Houthi-held areas. The downside was that Ghadir beach had no jetty, so Colonel Sayyed took matters into his own hands and had one built by 31 May, within 48 hours. Demonstrating the agility and ingenuity that the UAE often showed, Sayyed quickly spent 230,000 Saudi Riyals (nearly £50,000) to rent the land, sink a shipping container into the surf, and build it up as a ramp with sand and rocks. This little jetty would become the single disembarkation point for over 200 vehicles in the coming month, making a unique contribution to the success of the operation.

At 20:00 hours on 1 June, the Al Shareeah (L71) sailed out of Assab and into choppy seas, personally piloted by Colonel Sayyed and naval lieutenant Abdullah S. By 02:00 hours on 2 June, the ship approached Ghadir, the first time a UAE vessel had come so close to shore. Sayyed went aground wearing an infrared strobe that was being monitored by UAE aircraft overhead. Ali A. joined to survey the security arrangements. A

13-man artillery crew led by Captain Khalifa J. built a berm as a firing position and surveyed the gun's exact position for pinpoint-accurate fire over long ranges. At 10:34 hours on 2 June the G-6 fired its first barrage; a counter-battery 'shoot' against a Houthi D-30 122-mm piece spotted by the Sabr. Yemenis in Little Aden. Even the Al-Forsan at SH5 thought it was a new enemy gun, as friendly artillery fire had never been heard in Aden until then. The Yemenis would come to know the G-6 as the Shaiba – the grumpy old man. His voice would be a comfort to them, and they would complain to the Emiratis if they did not hear it enough times in a day.

Initially the problem would be the opposite – overuse of the single gun. The G-6 could reach so many known targets and it was so quick to operate in any weather that it immediately became the 'go-to' fire support tool in Aden. For the first time, the Resistance could count on fire support no matter the weather nor the hour. On day one, the G-6 fired 70 rounds against enemy lines of supply and strongpoints. Captain Khalifa J. had to tell the JTACs to slow down and adopt a more deliberate rate of fire: 'You will break the gun. We need time to clean the barrel' – which quickly became fouled with explosive residues. Indeed, the G-6 *did* break after another intense 72-round bombardment of Houthi assembly areas north of Dar Saad, earning another warning, this time from UAE General Headquarters, that 'the G-6 is not a machine-gun'. In Little Aden, the gun now had to be taken apart. This should not have been possible outside of factory workshop conditions, but the G-6 crew carried out the maintenance right there in their makeshift Ghadir beach field workshop. When they test-fired the gun after reassembly, they made sure to trigger the firing pin by pulling a very long rope ... just in case. In a short period of time another G-6 was added for redundancy, to allow one to be maintained while the other was in use. As the senior sniper, Captain

Hamdan N., noted sagely: 'If you have two guns, you'll always have one ... Two is one, one is none'.

After that, the G-6 became an everyday fixture, with its sound being used to signal evening prayer and the breaking of the fast in Ramadan. The 'old man' kept up a lively commentary right the way through to the end of the battle. Harassment fire was maintained on the Houthis round the clock, with three or four shots fired at known enemy strong points each hour during the night, to deny the enemy sleep and wear them down. But, as important, it became the UAE's way to signal to the Yemenis all over Aden that they had not gone anywhere and that they were still supporting the Resistance all around the clock.

## The Al-Forsan Interdiction Teams

Alongside these remote fires, the reinserted and expanded Al-Forsan teams and PG snipers would also bring their direct fire capabilities to bear. In addition to training Resistance forces on use of the LAW anti-tank rocket, the Al-Forsan would try to teach the Resistance basic force protection skills – such as taking cover when under fire! In parallel, the Al-Forsan would embark on a programme of aggressive fighting patrols intended to wear down and overmatch the Houthis on the ground – classic behaviour for an aggressive, ranger-type elite infantry unit. These tactics fit both Ali A.'s experience of urban fighting in Afghanistan, and also his aggressive personality.

Split into six-man teams of JTACs, snipers, Kornet operators and mortarmen, each Al-Forsan team would cover an eight-hour shift. They would travel 12–15 km out from SH5 to various points on the battlefield where there was a high concentration of Houthi targets or where the Resistance needed bolstering. The teams self-sustained in the field, each team carrying a generous 5,000 Saudi Riyals (over £1,000) for food, water and well-paid drivers. To reduce the risk of being targeted and to keep up pressure on multiple fronts, the Al-Forsan switched areas constantly. They would not be spotted wearing their Ops-Core helmets again; the posture was fully clandestine, with the teams moving around in beaten-up-looking Yemeni trucks and wearing Yemeni headscarves and fouta (skirts).

They were busy days but good days. The Saleh bin Fareed house was full of life and laughter as the Al-Forsan shifts came and went. The place was always full of drying clothes, as the operators were short of spare gear and had to hand-wash their kit each day and dry it before their next sortie. Each shift made their own breakfast of coffee, eggs, cheese and honey. Delicious oven-hot bread came from Little Aden bakeries three times a day for the teams. A family in Khaysa cooked three dinners a day for the returning shifts of Al-Forsan, often freshly caught fish. A big metal urn of *karak* – black loose tea leaves, crushed cardamom, saffron and lots of evaporated milk and sugar – was kept filled and hot on a bed of charcoal.

The most important weapon brought on these fighting patrols was the Russian-made AT-14 Kornet anti-tank guided missile (ATGM), a laser beam-riding missile that had proved its worth in conflicts in Syria, Iraq and Libya. Three tripod-mounted Kornet firing posts had been brought into Aden on 5 June. The Al-Forsan and SOC soldiers had always had RPG-27 and Javelin anti-armour missiles; these were mainly for emergency self-defence, but the Kornet brought a new level of offensive long-range capability. UAE operators knew there was no better anti-armour weapon in the world than the US-built Javelin – as Ukrainian soldiers showed against Russian forces in 2022 – but its effective range, under Aden battlefield conditions, was really around 1,600 metres, while a Houthi sniper could target the recognisable Javelin firing post at well beyond that distance with their 12.7-mm AM-50 anti-materiel rifles. The Kornet was much more useful for interdiction of Houthi armour and lines of supply at a safe distance from the enemy, and it had a longer-ranged thermal sight that gave the teams a powerful tool for watching the enemy at night. At $26,000, a Kornet missile was also a tenth of the cost of a Javelin, so they could be expended in large numbers. Like the G-6, and unlike air support, the Kornet could also operate no matter the weather.

Sometimes these Kornet-armed fighting patrols were defensive, moving to block dangerous enemy probes that would lance down the wadis from the northern outskirts. These attacks never stopped until the last days of the Aden campaign, and often it was the Al-Forsan who closed up any breaches. In neighbourhoods like Basateen, Bir Fadl and even Memdara (to the east of the Sheikh Uthman side), the Al-Forsan would sally forth and set up positions to block the enemy approaches 'by fire'. This meant sniping and Kornet fire typically, including 'heavy sniping' of personnel targets with the Kornet – for which there were no anti-personnel warheads but which a skilled gunner could, nonetheless, use to great effect on soft targets by exploding the round on the pavement in front of groups of enemy fighters. These engagements also saw some of the only Javelin use in the battle of Aden. There were four firing posts active, and up to two were allowed to go forward at any time. Usually, the patrols just used the excellent thermal scope to acquire targets for other means of attack, but occasionally the Javelin was unleashed against a troublesome bunker or anti-aircraft gun hidden under overhead cover.

More often, the patrols were out proactively dominating no-man's land and causing mounting attrition among enemy forces. The so-called Kornet Interdiction Team (KIT) would take one or two Kornet firing posts with them, and a pickup truck full of missiles (usually between 10 and 20 tubes). They would select an elevated building five to seven storeys high with good lines of fire onto the enemy concentration area. Once the building was chosen and searched, multiple rooms would be prepared for use, creating improvised sangars from breeze blocks and clearing the space behind the firing position to vent the dangerous back-blast from this recoilless weapon. Then the teams would lug the 80-lb firing posts and a number of 60-lb missiles up multiple flights of stairs. In a couple of minutes, the firing post and missile would be mated, and the gunner would begin working the archaic-looking metal dials and focusing rings, so different from the solid-state electronics of the Javelin.

Upon finding a target, the gunner would check behind him, warn everyone that he was firing, and send the missile off at about 200 metres per second. Depending on the range, he would need to keep his laser beam on the target for 10–30 seconds. This was a real art form when the target was a fast-moving, jinking *chassis*, or even a tank, moving from cover to cover. To slow down the *chassis*, the KITs called for air strikes to crater the coastal highway and many stretches where the enemy had to slow down. Stationary tanks, vehicles, bunkers and snipers were as good as dead – even at night. To ensure that civilians were not targeted, the Resistance set up a system whereby local people could pre-inform Abu Zaraa's network that they were planning a shopping run at a certain time in a certain car and would be back within an agreed time window. Kornet gunners could always ask their Resistance liaison 'Is that grey Hilux by the water tank a friendly?' and their default position was not to shoot if there was any doubt.

Over time, many of the Al-Forsan troopers taught themselves to operate the Kornet, to give the gunners' eyes a rest, and many became very capable at 'heavy sniping' with the Kornet. Firing between 10 and 20 missiles a day, and with a high hit rate, the Kornet started to dominate the Houthi lines of supply along the coastal highway and could quickly and reliably break up Houthi tank attacks on the Sheikh Uthman pocket. 'Kornet was an awesome weapon. Decisive,' Salem D. enthused. 'It was an anti-tank battle, and we could tell we were winning.' The Houthis could tell it too, resulting in increasingly determined efforts by the enemy to find and kill the KITs. The very visible back blast of the Kornet meant that the KITs were sure to be located as soon as they fired. By the end of June, Houthi multiple rocket launchers were firing whole 'mattresses' of one or two dozen 107-mm and 122-mm rockets at the KITs from firing positions in Green City, to the north-east. Enemy tanks also took terrifying high-velocity pot-shots at the Kornet posts.

The other main concern for the Kornet teams was enemy snipers. The Presidential Security Group and SOC snipers were the antidote. They treated the Houthi snipers with respect, recognising that the enemy was quite capable of identifying commanders, JTACs and radio operators by their antennae, and that they could be good marksmen. Indeed, the Al-Forsan and snipers were sometimes hesitant to wear their Ops-Core helmets as it would mark them out as Emiratis and quickly draw the attention of enemy snipers. Alongside counter-sniping, the UAE snipers in the KITs also provided vital extra eyes on the enemy, performing the under-appreciated role of snipers: that of information gatherers, locating enemy heavy weapons and usefully correcting the fall of shot from a different, shallow angle than the joint fires room back at SH5, looking down steeply through the sensors of drones and aircraft.

All that being said, the UAE snipers also performed the classic role of stalking, suppressing, and sometimes killing enemy soldiers. This was particularly the case around the airport, where one of the main fears of the Resistance was being picked off as they advanced over the open ground. Suppressing and wearing down the defenders of the airport was a vital part of the UAE mission, and minimising avoidable damage to the airport was an important consideration. For this reason, multiple UAE sniper teams were allocated to the Usaymie front, recognisable by the distinctive J-shaped creek north-west of the airport. This front was run by four Popular Committee leaders: Abdalrahman al-Lahji, Adnan bin Braykh, Riyadh al-Sabihi, and Mohsen al-Waili. The area covered the wetlands and salt pans between the airport and Sheikh Uthman – a super-humid, salty environment that was vital terrain in the forthcoming assaults on the airport. The snipers' aim was to neutralise and pin down the Houthis, both between and during airport assaults.

UAE snipers were cautious to get positive identification of Houthi fighters – usually comprising two factors such as carrying a gun or binoculars *and* wearing tell-tale items like the 'keys to heaven'. At the airport, this was less of a concern as the Houthis had turned the walled complex into a no-go zone for civilians. Depending on the exact firing site chosen, the snipers tended to work at between 400–1,600-metre range, which gave them reach into the airport's southern edge. They used a mixture of 7.62-mm and 12.7-mm rifles, using the latter for longer-range shots or to disable vehicles. Early morning was the best time to stalk targets, with crisp visibility and no heat shimmer. Kills could be clearly and gruesomely confirmed during the daylight hours and the sniper group counted 42 kills, mostly in June and July.

At night, results could not be confirmed but another 48 probable kills were recorded. Night-shooting required a tighter focus on specific target locations ranged during the day, such as bunker entrances or doorways. The enemy tended to get careless at night, even their snipers, who lacked night scopes and had little to do after dark. At the very least, Emirati sniping stopped the enemy from relaxing and moving around in the cool evening air, but often the results were deadly. Off-guard after chewing *qat* and feeling safe in the dark, multiple Houthis were killed at certain choke points, with bodies piled up as man after man came to investigate the sounds of shooting.

## Attrition Is Not Enough

The Houthis were undoubtedly suffering from attrition by the opening days of Ramadan, which started on 17 June. By most metrics, they were breaking down as a military force; their known command posts had been regularly struck and their radio traffic had reduced. According to a tally of UAE daily reporting backed up by full-motion video, almost 400 of their vehicles had been destroyed and they were making less and less frequent use of armour. Their bombardments were slackening due to an apparent lack of ammunition resupply, and they had taken to ransoming civilians in exchange for small containers of fuel, pointing to severe shortages.

Battle damage assessment claims, based on full-motion video before, during and after strikes, suggest that every day in June the Houthis were losing an average of: 25 fighters killed; half a dozen vehicles hit; another half-dozen fortified sites destroyed; and three rocket or mortar teams struck. Houthi attacks on the Sheikh Uthman and Little Aden pockets never stopped but they did grow weaker, with air and artillery support stopping probes dead at the western side of Little Aden, on the creek separating Bir Ahmed and Enma city, and in Dar Saad. The UAE's onshore team of 64 combat operators plus the 13 artillerists had undoubtedly wreaked havoc upon their enemy.

But in one vital metric – the most important one – there had been no real breakthrough. The Resistance was still unable to seize and hold terrain, specifically the enemy's centre of gravity at the airport. This was clearly illustrated in the way that the third, fourth and fifth airport attacks unfolded in May and June.

After eight days of delays, the third airport battle had unfolded on 25 May. The concept was firepower – more of it than ever before – to shock the defenders and 'shoot' the Resistance forces right onto their target. The attack would have a complex fire plan, including the interdiction of the coastal highway by Egab mortar boats, and heavy airstrikes on 28 targets in the vicinity of the airport. The operation also had a more complex scheme of manoeuvre that envisaged Resistance attacks towards the coast north-east of the airport and from the Sea Line west of the runway, with these two pincers converging on the coast road east of the runway. A tiny lodgement was seized at the western end of the airport and held, but the northern axis completely failed to make advances. Saleh al-Nokhbi, the serially unsuccessful Resistance northern axis commander, gave up being a leader and fell in with the normal fighters for the rest of the Aden campaign.

The fighting was getting tougher and drawing in more UAE troops into frontline operations. Four members of an Al-Forsan mortar crew were wounded by accurate enemy mortar fire. UAE Javelins and Kornets were taking a heavy toll on Houthi vehicles, with 45 daylight vehicle kills confirmed. The battle dragged on for almost five days in worsening weather conditions, especially at night. The only aircraft to fully participate were UAE Mirages, which impressed the JTACs by ducking under the cloud, lasing their targets, lobbing their laser-guided bombs at short range, and then arcing back upwards through the clouds

after executing their graceful shallow dive. The Al-Forsan had
seen the brutal conditions at Assab, where the Mirages were
now operating from, and this was pretty fancy flying for pilots
who were sleeping in their cockpits to get away from the scorpions and mosquitos.

The Resistance was clearly still too shaky to advance in the
face of firepower. 'Some ran at the first bullet. Others stuck
around till midday but only to collect their *qat*', recalled one
Al-Forsan advisor. 'If they even got one mortar round, they ran.
We asked ourselves if we were pushing these civilians too far.
We realised we must fight in front of them, not behind.' Ali
A. brought in his deputy commander at Al-Forsan, Lieutenant Colonel Mohammed K., to orchestrate the next attempt.
This effort began on 10 June. This fourth airport battle mis-
fired due to rough sea states, which disrupted naval support,
but also failed due to an unwillingness by Resistance infantry
to assault across the open ground of the airport. Some kinks
were also being ironed out in the Yemeni Resistance chain of
command. An octogenarian tribal leader called Saif al-Bukri
al-Dhalei disrupted the battle plans by inciting young tribesmen to surround the Saleh bin Fareed house because he wanted
to become the sole distributor of UAE aid. With an Al Hur
drone overhead and Abu Dhabi nervously watching the scene,
the solution came in the form of Mubarak N. – the hotshot
Mirage pilot who had put his bomb directly onto the Houthi
howitzer inside the Qaluaa Tunnel. Guided in by a JTAC, he
was cleared to break regulations and swoop down below the
16,000 foot minimum. 'Roger, wait out ...' he calmly answered,
and then proceeded to scatter the mob with repeated deafen-
ing low-level passes at high sub-sonic speeds. A week later, Saif
al-Bukri decided to leave Aden and enjoy the quiet life in the
Emirates.

In the dying days of June, the fifth airport assault was also a failure. The date for the attack was 20 June. Tremendous supporting fires were laid on and the starting hour for the assault was a generous 09:00 hours, to give plenty of time for the Resistance to wake up and assemble. With only a minimum of begging and pleading by the Emiratis, the Resistance attacked down the Sea Line and across the aqueduct causeway through the Usaymie front. The attack bogged down as soon as the Popular Committees reached the airport's perimeter, whereupon Houthi mortar fire, Dushkas and anti-aircraft cannons sent the attackers to ground and there they stayed. The senior Resistance commander Hashim Sayyed of the Sea Line axis returned sweaty, dirty, and crying in frustration.

Something had to change. No matter how much firepower was added and no matter how weak the Houthis were, the formula was not working. Every battle had shown improvements in planning and execution but at the end of each battle day, the Houthis held the airport. The struggle for Aden was not a game you could win on points because the Houthis would never run short of cannon fodder – it required a knockout. The Resistance attack force had to be strengthened.

# XII

# BREAKING THE DEADLOCK

One of the greatest attributes of Ali A. was that he stayed on target. In an operation like Aden, it was a big temptation to move the goalposts and point to the many things that were going *right*, instead of the one big thing that was going *wrong*. Yes, the defence of the Resistance pocket had been put on a sound footing and the enemy had suffered heavy attrition. Every effort to seize the airport was drawing out more enemy reserves and destroying them. Well over 200 credible claims of vehicle kills had been logged, usually supported by full-motion video or multiple corroborating witnesses. The tactical fight was going extremely well, with massive losses inflicted on the enemy and no UAE fatalities or serious casualties. But Ali A.'s mission was to liberate Aden, and that meant taking and holding terrain – lots of it, including, most importantly, the airport. Ali A. was not the least bit comfortable with the stalemate that was developing. 'We have nothing! Attrition is nothing!' he fumed at his team. 'If the war ends now, the Houthis have won.'

At the strategic level back in Abu Dhabi, frustration was steadily building. The UAE would welcome peace via the talks in Geneva, but there was a danger that – unless Aden could be liberated – a ceasefire might actually freeze the war, with the Houthis controlling much of Aden and all of the Bab el-Mandeb and the Red Sea coast. The Houthis would see the invasion of the south as well worthwhile if they could secure these gains at the cost of a few thousand of their foot-soldiers killed and wounded in Aden. The enemy would indeed have won and the UAE intervention would have achieved little, except to create a pocket of resistance that would need external protection in perpetuity or would need to be abandoned, at great cost to the UAE's credibility. In early June, MBZ had signalled that the Resistance needed to be made to understand that the UAE would not stay indefinitely in Aden. The Emirates would never give up on the Adenese Resistance, and indeed planning had commenced for Coalition support to 'stay-behind' guerrilla cells, which would remain even if the city was lost. But if they wanted to end the conflict in their city, the Resistance had to act with greater unity and stop wasting opportunities to liberate the airport.

Salem D. had come back to Abu Dhabi, as Ramadan began, for a long-overdue week of leave. For months, UAE leaders and their staff had been brainstorming the factors that might get the Resistance forces on a winning streak, able to take ground and hold it. The headquarters was under increasing pressure to find 'the key' to empower and encourage the Resistance. MBZ wanted more innovative ways to enable the airport liberation. Salem's presence in the UAE from 15 June was helpful in these deliberations as no one knew the Resistance or the ground in Aden better than he did.

By now, the UAE operators knew this partner force inside-out: they knew that 20 per cent of funds would always go to *qat* and that 20 per cent of ammunition would always be wasted in celebration fire; they knew that there was no point scheduling an attack before mid-morning; and they knew that there was no way the Resistance would consolidate positions after they were taken. And they also now knew that making the Houthis weaker only mattered if the Resistance could exploit this weakness by attacking. Many of the potential solutions had been tried already: the leadership of the Resistance had been unified and rotated periodically; provision of fire support, arms and training had been consistently upped. Being brothers to the Resistance had not succeeded and nor had 'tough love', threats and shaming tactics. This was not what they taught at the academies of Sandhurst, St Cyr, West Point or Duntroon and this was not the way wars were supposed to work. But this was the reality of battle in the early twenty-first century.

The team at PG Headquarters went back to basics and reviewed the previous assaults to see where they had gone wrong. Fire support and isolation of the battlefield from enemy reinforcement was consistently good. Seizing and holding terrain was clearly the weakness and, specifically, assaulting across open terrain. Most of the airport attacks had ground to a halt when Resistance troops began taking casualties from Houthi snipers, Dushkas and anti-aircraft cannons. The enemy was in cover and the Resistance was on foot in the open. Ergo, the Resistance needed 'protected mobility', which meant armoured vehicles.

A second insight related to tactical leadership. The Resistance simply did not have the young, capable platoon and squad leaders required to press the assault, correctly assess the situation, accurately call for fire support and defend newly won terrain (instead of leaving to go and chew *qat*). Ali A. believed that the UAE could no longer 'lead from behind' but instead needed to be 'shoulder to shoulder' with the Yemenis. UAE soldiers would need to accompany the attack at the sharp end and ensure the consolidation of gains. Drawing on Australian doctrine used by NATO in Afghanistan, the headquarters sketched out how the UAE might deploy small Operational Mentor and Liaison Teams (OMLTs, pronounced 'omelettes') within and across the whole airport assault force and, specifically, as vehicle commanders.

## An Audience with MBZ

At this inflection point, the UAE's command system experienced one of its finest moments, bringing together the strategic leaders who could make anything happen with the operational commanders who knew what had to be done. The venue was MBZ's villa on the night of 22 June, right after the disappointment of the fifth airport battle. It was the sixth night of Ramadan and PG commander MGM and Salem D. were invited to a gathering with Mohamed bin Zayed to discuss ways to break the deadlock. It was about 22:30 hours when they arrived and saw that some of MBZ's brothers were also present – including Sheikhs Tahnoun, Abdullah and Nahyan. Salem was shocked at the warmth with which he was greeted. MBZ embraced him and touched noses as they shook hands, an act of friendship and respect from Abu Dhabi's (then) crown prince and the UAE's (then) Deputy Supreme Commander. Salem was stunned to be so warmly received in this company.

Mohammed bin Zayed wanted to hear the 'ground-truth' from the battlefield. At moments like this, MBZ always impresses visitors with his listening skills. He patiently devotes all of his attention to the speaker and is genuinely interested in hearing a new point of view; this is a discipline and a great trait in a leader. The UAE Deputy Supreme Commander displayed a firm grasp of many details of the battle, and he showed interest in ensuring that all the weapons provided were being pushed to their limits. If the Sabr had endurance for six hours, keep it airborne for the full six. Don't spare the barrels of the G-6: use it as much as is needed, let the barrels melt if need be, and start using the laser-guided rounds, no matter the expense. 'Do the maximum,' he cautioned, 'always think outside the box.' It was becoming clearer to Salem where some of the recent battlefield innovations were coming from: MBZ had always been there in the background, putting tools in the right hands.

Soon the meeting settled down to the main matter at hand: 'What is stopping us from liberating Aden?' MBZ asked Salem with his typical precision and directness. 'Why does the Resistance not press the attack?' The answer had been uncovered in the preceding months and days by MGM and Ali A., and Salem found himself ready to answer. The Resistance needed armoured vehicles. 'Where are the Oshkosh?' MBZ asked his aides. He was referring to the hundreds of US-built Oshkosh Mine-Resistant Ambush-Protected (MRAP) vehicles that the UAE had ordered after seeing the type in service in Afghanistan. They had mostly not been fielded yet with UAE forces and were still in storage, without their radios or weapons installed.

'How many do you need to liberate Aden airport?' MBZ asked Salem.

'Twenty would mount the assault force,' Salem replied.

'Take a hundred Oshkosh. And 30 BMPs,' offered MBZ, referring to heavily armed tracked infantry fighting vehicles. Then an English joke: 'You can't be just a little bit pregnant.'

Ever practical, he then asked: 'Do you have somewhere in Aden to keep them hidden?'

'Yes, sir,' answered MGM and Salem, thinking of the sheltered bay in Ghadir, Little Aden, where the first G-6 had recently been landed.

'Then move them to Aden and make sure they have cages on them,' the commander-in-chief ordered.

This was classic MBZ: no one in the military had anticipated such a decisive step. With a hundred Oshkosh, Salem thought, he could take the whole city. 'It had never entered our minds that he might send them *our* vehicles. But the boss didn't hesitate,' MGM reflected. He also didn't miss a trick. To best protect the troops, the MRAPs needed to be sheathed in slatted steel armour designed to catch and pre-detonate RPGs at a safe distance from the vehicle hull. After this meeting, fire support would also be further strengthened with laser-guided 155-mm munitions, the doubling of the number of G-6s (to allow three to work while one was rested). The Deputy Supreme Commander also ordered the despatch of two Agrab 120-mm mortar carriers mounted on RG-31 MRAPs, providing rapid-fire automatic mortar systems similar to those mounted on the Egab mortar boats.

But there was a condition too: 'We need to liberate Aden before Eid,' MBZ directed. That was 25 days away, with Eid starting on 17 July. Twenty-five days would have been a tall order under any circumstances, but these exact 25 days constituted practically the entire month of Ramadan. For almost everyone else in the Muslim world, life had slowed down as it always did during the long days of fasting in Ramadan and the long nights of fast-breaking and celebration. For the UAE Armed Forces, the pace was about to jump to light speed. 'Pressure is building. Much to do in little time,' MGM noted in a late-June war diary entry. The clock was ticking.

## Getting the Oshkosh to Aden

The Oshkosh Corporation had made trucks since trucks were made. The American company was founded in 1917 in the town of Oshkosh, Wisconsin, which was named after a Native American chief of the Menominee nation called Oshkosh (meaning 'claw'). Over its 100-year history, the company started by pioneering the four-wheel-drive truck and eventually built the toughest armoured vehicles to protect US troops in Iraq and Afghanistan.

It was in Afghanistan that the UAE forces saw the Oshkosh M-ATV (Mine-Resistant Ambush-Protected All-Terrain

Vehicle) in action. The 16-tonne M-ATV was designed for a 2008 US government competition to build a vehicle to Mine-Resistant Ambush-Protected standards of protection but which was lighter and thus able to move off-road and across tough terrain. The M-ATV had the high off-the-ground, V-shaped hull that diverts explosions away from the vehicle, as well as other features that allowed it to drive out of trouble, even with two flat tyres and a busted radiator. The truck could carry a driver, commander, gunner and four troops. Oshkosh had impressed the world by providing 8,722 M-ATVs to hard-pressed US forces in just under six months, and the UAE had placed its own order for 750 M-ATVs in July 2012, receiving them all by August 2013. Most of these UAE Oshkosh's were still factory-fresh and in air-conditioned storage, without weapons, radios or anti-RPG cages. Now they had found their purpose.

The task of moving 130 armoured vehicles to Aden would require a whole-of-government effort, spanning many civilian as well as military agencies. To aid the effort, the UAE Joint Operations Command (JOC) swung into action. Led by UAE Land Forces commander Major General Saleh A., JOC was set up to give the war fighters – in this case the Presidential Guard headquarters – everything they needed to get the job done. The JOC moved into high gear on 23 June, just hours after the UAE made its decision to extend 'protected mobility' to the Resistance in Aden. The effort would be run out of JOC's underground headquarters in Abu Dhabi in support of a forward-based Joint Logistics Team in Assab. The JOC had an underground headquarters in Abu Dhabi and a forward-based Joint Logistics Team in Assab

The first leg of the line of supply to Aden was the air bridge between the UAE and Assab. It would take well over a week to move heavy equipment by sea all the way from the UAE, which would eat up too much valuable time. Instead, every Oshkosh would be air-lifted to Assab on C-17s operated by the 4th Aviation Group of the UAE Air Force and Air Defence. Like a lot of the equipment that would be vital to the mission in Aden, the C-17A Globemaster III had been delivered years before they were needed, and just months before in the case of the newest airframes. An initial order for four C-17s – which became an eventual total order for eight – was signed in 2010. Six of these were in UAE service by June 2012 and two more arrived in the first half of 2015.

By anyone's standards, the C-17 is a giant with long legs. The aircraft is 53 metres long and has a similar wingspan. Stood on its wingtip, it is about as tall as Nelson's Column in London or the Arc de Triomphe in Paris. The huge cargo compartment inside is like a warehouse: 27 metres long, 6 metres wide and nearly 4 metres tall. It has an 85-tonne carrying capacity and was designed to transport two US M1A1 main battle tanks across the Atlantic to fight the Soviet threat in 1980s Europe. It could just about carry four to six M-ATVs on the 1,800-km trip from Abu Dhabi to Assab, and fly back, all without refuelling. The first Oshkoshes touched down in Assab on 25 June, just three days after MBZ directed their deployment. Four days later there were 30 Oshkoshes in Assab, and the first ten vehicles were sent forward by boat to Aden. The pilots, co-pilots and loadmasters of the C-17 fleet had done more operational sorties in two weeks than most strategic air-lifters do in a year.

The UAE Navy then took up the challenge of getting the vehicle ashore in Aden under conditions of absolute secrecy. Part of the plan for liberating the airport was exploitation of the shock effect of so many armoured vehicles suddenly appearing on the battlefield in Aden. This meant a covert insertion, as Ahmed al Issi's oil tankers were still out there in Aden's Outer

Harbour and other spies might be watching. To avoid the build-up of vehicles being seen by any spies or gossips, the local UAE logistician, Captain Mohammed M., purchased 50 40-foot United Arab Shipping Company containers from the Container Port and placed them on the two beaches that lay beneath Jebel Ghadir, the G-6 beach and another small beach next to the Al Ghadir fish farms. These blue, green and red containers were stacked to make enclosures that would shield the vehicles from prying eyes.

Between 10 and 20 vehicles would be landed in a short window each night between 02:00 and 03:00 hours. Each 64-metre landing craft would be loaded at Assab with 9 to 12 vehicles, which would be tightly secured in case the seas got rough. They took a deliberately long route, hugging the Eritrean coast and staying far away from the Houthi-controlled islands at the Bab el-Mandeb. The 13- or 14-hour inbound trips were a test of endurance and guts. The sea state was usually three or four, known as a moderate swell, with wave heights and dips of 1–2 metres. The wind was typically pushing the landing craft from behind as they headed to Aden, which is known as a favourable 'following sea' that carries a heavily loaded ship along. But if the winds picked up in the Bab el-Mandeb, the trip could become a dangerous nightmare, especially on the return, when some landing craft experienced monsoon-like sea states as high as nine or ten and could not get back into the port at Assab, bobbing around for days like corks floating on the sea.

At the Yemeni end, the landings occurred on 'no moon' nights, to reduce the risk of discovery by Houthi lookouts on the mountains of Greater Aden. The ships were fully darkened on these pitch-black nights, with the elimination of any type of light. They were also quiet, keeping their engines at a low idle. From shore it was astounding how invisible the ships were. They were only tens of metres offshore yet could not be seen without night-vision equipment. Yemenis on the Jebel Ghadir, a mountaintop observation post, provided low-visibility red lights to guide the landings. On 29 June, the first vehicles were landed at Little Aden, and all of them were ashore by 10 July. Like the air force, the navy had come through magnificently. It had been just 19 days since the order had come to send the Oshkosh to Assab. In that time, they had been flown 1,800 km, fitted with weapons, radios and anti-RPG cages, then sailed 290 km (155 nautical miles) and landed. Now they were all in place and their entry had not been observed by the enemy.

Crews were deployed to Aden in parallel to the arrival of the vehicles. The OMLT concept presented to the UAE chain of command on 30 June would require the insertion of 80 additional UAE personnel on the ground, a doubling of the current UAE presence. These UAE soldiers would serve as vehicle commanders on most of the Oshkoshes delivered to the Resistance. Each four-man OMLT could advise a whole platoon of Yemeni-crewed Oshkoshes. A search was quickly undertaken for the best and brightest junior combat officers and sergeants and first corporals from the PG and Land Forces, with a focus on talented commanders and proficient communicators. In MGM's words: 'We looked for good leaders – resourceful, aggressive, and tactically astute – the best of the best.'

Alongside these UAE troops, 224 Yemenis were secretly sent to train as operators and turret machine-gunners on the Oshkoshes. These were also the hand-picked best fighters of the Popular Committees, selected by the Resistance Council. They were volunteers and tended to be the most robust of the Resistance troops. Most of them were Salafis, which had the added advantage that they did not chew *qat* – which would serve them well as the Emiratis allowed no *qat* at the training site. To pass his trained eye over them, and to focus them on their jobs, Ali A. stayed with them for the first three days of their ten-day training. The UAE commenced unit training with the Oshkoshes, bringing together the Emirati commanders and Yemeni crewmen, and undertaking realistic live-fire exercises. The Yemeni gunners were almost uniformly good shots with the 12.7-mm machine-guns and the Mk 19 automatic grenade launchers that equipped one in four Oshkoshes. For the *qat* chewers, the training was especially tough as they had no leaf during their whole stay and had to survive by chain-smoking Indian *bidi* hand-rolled cigarettes. When they deployed back into Little Aden to link up with their vehicles on 10 July, the Yemenis and the Emiratis looked like one unit, almost indistinguishable, with each wearing T-shirts, cut-off camouflage trousers and Emirati Ops-Core helmets. Now all that was needed was a plan and the signal to attack.

# XIII

# THE SIXTH AIRPORT BATTLE

The man charged with writing the plan for the sixth airport battle was Ali A. He took his responsibility very seriously. During a visit to Assab in May, two senior dignitaries had reminded Ali A., 'You are not just fighting for the UAE but for the whole Coalition and the world.' Ali A. recalled feeling a sense of crushing expectation: 'I felt pressure, I must not lose us the battle.'

At the end of June, Ali A. took part in a short commander's conference in Abu Dhabi, his few days outside the theatre of war between 25 April and his eventual departure from the front on 6 August. Deputy Chief of Staff of the UAE Armed Forces Major General Issa was briefing the senior leadership on the after-action report of the fifth airport battle. Ever the careful listener, MBZ asked Ali A. the same question he had asked Salem D.: 'Why have we not taken the airport? What's missing?' Ali A. confirmed the broad concept put forward by MGM and Salem a week earlier.

'We have to be shoulder-to-shoulder with them,' he argued, referencing the OMLT concept of accompanying the Resistance right up to the front line.

'What else do you need?' MBZ asked.

'Just the vehicles.'

'You will get 130 of them. What else?' pushed MBZ.

'Nothing,' said Ali A.

Sheikh Hazza prompted: 'And then what will happen?'

'We will take the airport,' Ali A. confirmed.

MBZ nodded, stood up and left. The pledges had been made by the commander-in-chief and the commander on the ground. What more was there to say?

When it came to plans, Ali A.'s rule was triple redundancy. He always had three plans, so that even if two failed, the third would succeed. As he put it, 'I wanted to leave no way to lose.' This was ingrained in his nature, which was to fight and to win. This is what made Ali A. so trusted – he was a self-made man, a tireless worker and he got the job done, no matter what. One of his maxims was: 'Be clear and direct in your purpose.' In this battle, his purpose was to seize and hold the airport and he now had tools at his disposal that could finally make it happen.

The previous airport attack plans had not been conceptually flawed, they just lacked a protected and well-led assault force. This meant that many of the staples of prior plans could be incorporated into the new blueprint. The plan was first sketched out on a large map laid on a bed and on pieces of paper stuck to the walls of Ali A.'s house in Abu Dhabi. Each axis would be led by one of Ali A.'s hand-picked junior commanders from the 51 Al-Forsan who had been on the ground since late May. These axis commanders were mostly Al-Forsan lieutenants, much younger men than the captains and majors that the US or UK would have thrown at such tasks, but Ali A. had con- fidence in them. There would be 94 UAE soldiers at the tip of the spear with the Yemenis and a further 188 Emiratis would be onshore in support roles. In the back of each Oshkosh would be a handful of willing Yemeni Resistance fighters, often friends of the Yemeni driver and gunners serving in that vehicle. At least 600 Resistance fighters were expected to participate – assuming they showed up, of course.

## The Axes of Attack

In previous airport battles, the Houthis had always relieved pressure on the airport by launching strong diversionary attacks from Al Anad into Dar Saad and most recently down the wadis and electricity transmission corridors into Bir Ahmed. Thus, Ali A. made his first effort, Axis 1, a screen of 24 Oshkoshes, JTACs, 81-mm mortars and Kornets that would be ready to blunt any Houthi counter strike into the city from the north. This axis was comprised of Al-Forsan senior, non-commissioned officers and their job was to hold the line and watch Ali A.'s back.

With his flank and rear secure, Ali A.'s next move, Axis 2, would drive east from Caltex down the Sea Line with only a rise of high ground north of the Air Defence Camp that looked over the airport wall and had a clear field of fire into the northern and western ends of the airport complex. This axis comprised ten Oshkoshes and was led by a skinny young-looking officer called Lieutenant Nasser K. Inside the Oshkoshes were 12 Emiratis (i.e. three OMLT teams), including a Kornet firing post, an 82-mm mortar and a sniper team. The axis would use its 12.7-mm machine-guns, Mk 19 grenade launcher, Kornet and mortar to suppress enemy firing positions with overwatch of the airport and Sea Line. Three kilometres to the north, two newly arrived Agrab 120-mm rapid-firing mortars would create a base of fire at the Saltworks.

Next, Ali A. imagined three axes fanning out from the line of departure at Caltex at approximately the same time. Axis 3 would hook around the north on the salt pans on the wide Ghazi Alwan Road that led straight to the coastal highway junction at the Al Homsi gas station. This group of 17 Oshkoshes carrying 134 Yemenis would block the coastal road and create a defensive line on the Ghazi Alwan road to protect the Emirati flank from counterattacks. Axis 4, under Lieutenant Salem D., would also hook north of the L-shaped creek but would cut south-east to clear Camp Sulaban and create a thick skirmish line of 18 Oshkoshes and 144 Yemenis, facing the presumed enemy strongpoint of the southern Al Areesh neighbourhoods along the seafront. If these two axes stayed abreast of each other, they could provide mutual support and could count on at least one secure flank.

Axis 5 was planned to drive down the Sea Line causeway from Caltex Roundabout, past the flamingos of the Swan Lake preserve and the western end of the runway. This force would prevent any interference from this direction, either a flank attack up the sea line or heavy weapons fire from Labour Island. The seven Oshkoshes and 54 Yemenis in this axis were led by Major Seghayyar N. and the remaining three Emiratis from his OMLT team. To aid this axis, two Kornet posts would be set up in the Container Port and cement batching plant to enfilade any Houthi guns or vehicles laying in ambush.

With the airport isolated from reinforcement or support-ing fires from the north and the west, Axis 6 would then drive down the Sea Line and mount the main assault on the airport and the adjacent Camp Badr. This was the largest force, with 24 Oshkoshes, 200 Yemenis and a heavy complement of 32 Emira-tis – or eight OMLT teams. This axis was led by the Al-Forsan deputy commander Lieutenant Colonel Mohammed K., who had the tough job of clearing out the den of rats that was Camp Badr and the large structures that lined the southern edge of the runway. He planned a controlled sweeping movement in which his 17 Oshkoshes would move deliberately, using probing fire with their turret guns to identify strongpoints that could then be destroyed with joint fires.

The final offensive axis (Axis 7) would follow Major Moham-med K.'s movement down the Sea Line but would charge

52. Council of War. The last-minute plans for the sixth battle were confirmed at Saleh bin Fareed house. The Resistance Council were not fully informed about the influx of armoured Oshkosh vehicles until the last moment, to ensure secrecy was maintained. Notebooks and cellphones are the key battle management tools. Note the Kalashnikov on the table in the foreground, which has thoughtfully been unloaded.

53. The 'forming up point' at Little Aden, where the column of over a hundred Oshkosh were revealed. To ensure the UAE-trained drivers and gunners did not disappear before the launch of the attack, they were made to sleep beside their vehicles the night before. The Emiratis had learned a few tricks by now, after numerous 'no-shows' by the Resistance in previous attacks. A leisurely 9:00 hours start-time was planned.

54. A Resistance fighter at the point of release for the attack column in Little Aden. As the column got rolling, the mood changed and a powerful energy began to build in the attacking force – a 1,500-metre-long column of over a hundred brand-new armoured vehicles bearing the flags of the Southern Movement. This vehicle is probably the lead Oshkosh of an axis, which carried the UAE flag as a recognition symbol to guard against friendly fire.

55. As this wonderful Saleh al Obaidi photo shows, by the time the column had reached Caltex, wild excitement began to grow. Tribal women were ululating – making high-pitched warbling sounds with their tongues. Running alongside the vehicles were young Yemeni men lacking even guns and carrying only sticks or knives. Others were just desperate to snap pictures and videos with their phones. A huge crowd began to follow the attack force towards the enemy fire.

56. The wide open approach of the Sea Line, imaged just hours after the airport was seized. At this time, the air was still crackling with distant gunfire and smelled of fires and explosives. It is easy to see why the Resistance feared assaulting over the raised Sea Line causeway in the face of Houthi snipers, 23mm cannons and mortars.

57. Reserve forces drive down the runway towards the eastern end of the airport Note the mirage effect on the runway. To Lieutenant Colonel Salem D., the special operations officer in Aden since April 21, the Oshkosh looked impossibly tall due to the effect of air rising off the hot runway. To him, it looked almost like they were flying across the airport.

58. Oshkosh from Axis 7 are consolidated on the eastern end of the airfield. As the Yemeni troops went home after the battle, to break Iftar with their families and tell war stories, each UAE vehicle commander was left on his own to step into the gun turret and consolidate the gains. After fighting for a full day, the Emiratis had to stand watch all night, alert to Houthi counter-attacks and mindful of accidentally killing the Yemeni civilians roaming all over the battlefield in the dark. In a particularly creepy development, Houthi fighters could be seen up to their necks in the sea, sometimes escaping northwards but sometimes silently emerging from the surf to sneak up on UAE positions. Note the Mk. 19 grenade launcher, which equipped one out of every four Oshkosh.

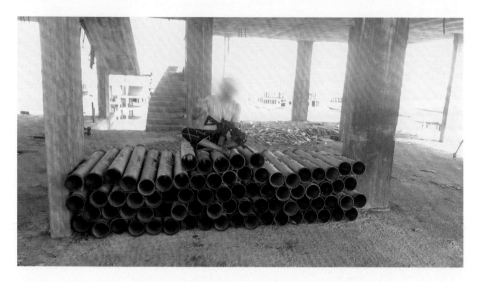

59. Spent ammunition from a Kornet Interdiction Team on the Ghazi Alwan front. In the two days of fighting, one of the two Kornet teams fired 68 rounds at enemy vehicles and personnel. Out of a total of 90 rounds fired on the axis, 47 vehicle kills were confirmed, including numerous spectacular high-speed crashes as Houthi drivers lost control as they tried to dodge incoming Kornets.

60. Brigadier Saleh al Nokhbi at the airport immediately after liberation. He had served as the former commander of the southern Yemeni army before reunification in 1994, and he was selected in May 2015 to lead the Sea Line axis in the first and second airport battles. Unable to achieve results in this role, he gave up being a leader and fell in with the normal fighters for the rest of the Aden campaign. He finally made it to the airport on 14 July 2015.

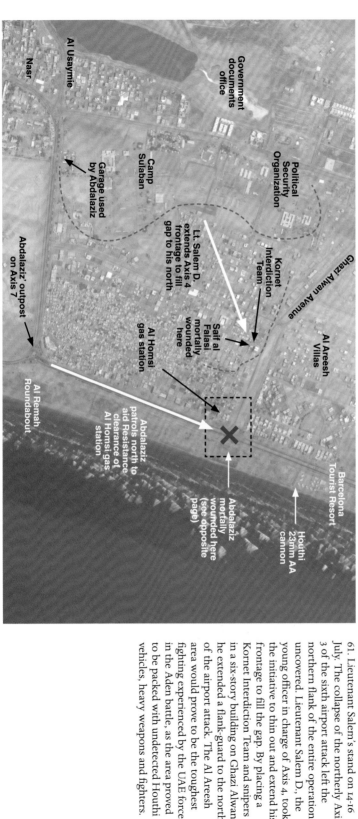

**Government documents office**

**Al Usaymie**

**Nasr**

**Political Security Organization**

**Camp Sulaban**

**Garage used by Abdalaziz**

**Kornet Interdiction Team**

**Lt. Salem D. extends Axis 4 frontage to fill gap to his north**

**Abdalaziz' outpost on Axis 7**

**Saif al Falasi mortally wounded here**

**Al Homsi gas station**

**Ghazi Alwan Avenue**

**Al Areesh Villas**

**Al Remah Roundabout**

**Abdalaziz patrols north to aid Resistance clearance of Al Homsi gas station**

**Abdalaziz mortally wounded here (see opposite page)**

**Barcelona Tourist Resort**

**Houthi 23mm AA cannon**

61. Lieutenant Salem's stand on 14-16 July. The collapse of the northerly Axis 3 of the sixth airport attack left the northern flank of the entire operation uncovered. Lieutenant Salem D., the young officer in charge of Axis 4, took the initiative to thin out and extend his frontage to fill the gap. By placing a Kornet Interdiction Team and snipers in a six-story building on Ghazi Alwan, he extended a flank-guard to the north of the airport attack. The Al Areesh area would prove to be the toughest fighting experienced by the UAE forces in the Aden battle, as the area proved to be packed with undetected Houthi vehicles, heavy weapons and fighters.

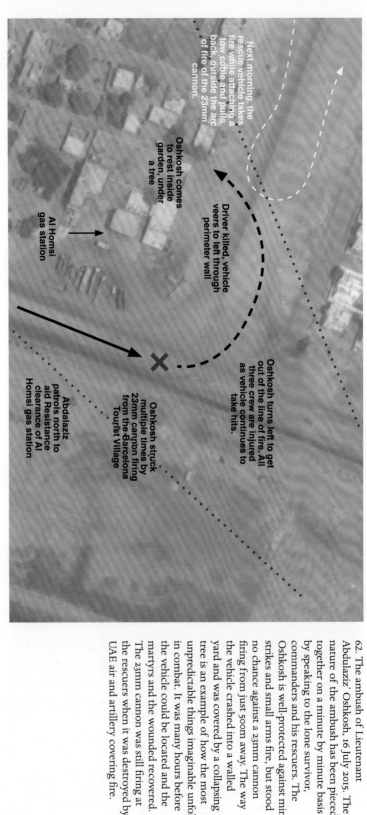

**Next morning, the rescue vehicle takes fire while attaching a tow cable and pulls back, outside the arc of fire of the 23mm cannon.**

**Oshkosh comes to rest inside garden, under a tree**

**Al Homsi gas station**

**Driver killed, vehicle veers to left through perimeter wall**

**Oshkosh turns left to get out of the line of fire. All three crew are injured as vehicle continues to take hits.**

**Oshkosh struck multiple times by 23mm cannon firing from the Barcelona Tourist Village**

**Abdalaziz patrols north to aid Resistance clearance of Al Homsi gas station**

62. The ambush of Lieutenant Abdulaziz' Oshkosh, 16 July 2015. The nature of the ambush has been pieced together on a minute by minute basis by speaking to the lone survivor, commanders and his rescuers. The Oshkosh is well-protected against mine strikes and small arms fire, but stood no chance against a 23mm cannon firing from just 500m away. The way the vehicle crashed into a walled yard and was covered by a collapsing tree is an example of how the most unpredictable things imaginable unfold in combat. It was many hours before the vehicle could be located and the martyrs and the wounded recovered. The 23mm cannon was still firing at the rescuers when it was destroyed by UAE air and artillery covering fire.

63. Fighting during the clearance of Khormaksar in June. In this sequence of pictures taken by intrepid photographer Saleh al-Obaidi we see a 'section' of Resistance fighters manouevre in cover. By June, some Resistance forces were fighting more like regular light infantry. Here they take cover – an innovation learned throughout the battle – while their tactical leader lays his plans. Note the tactical leader has a LAW-72 disposable anti-tank weapon, a sign of his prestige and a morale-booster in case a Houthi armoured vehicle was encountered.

64. Fire and movement, Yemeni style. In another shot by Saleh al-Obaidi, the same section moves forward. Each man is using the cover available and there seems to be some (slightly unsafe) covering fire being given by a prone fighter at the rear. Battlefield successes by the Resistance provided sufficient confidence to attack that quickly snowballed into wild overconfidence on many occasions. This underlines the manner in which momentum is a powerful and dangerous force in skirmish warfare by small emotionally-driven forces. Tightly-controlled manouevres with limits of advance are often not possible.

65. UAE Oshkosh's entering the Qaluaa Tunnel via its northern entrance, after the liberation. Back in early May, the area surrounding the tunnel entrance had been stubbornly held by 30 or so tough defenders led by Sheikh Ahmed al-Busairi, who retreated underground after 'final defensive fire' – the last salvoes possible, almost called down on top of friendly troops to stop them being overrun – failed to stop the Houthi assault. Thereafter the Houthis used the southern entrance of the tunnel to hide a 122mm artillery piece that they used to shell UAE ships until a Mirage pilot put a guided bomb straight into the tunnel's mouth and silenced the gun.

66. The UAE armoured bulldozer given to the Resistance to help them to clear Greater Aden The old Yemeni driver became a hero after manouevering the bulldozer around numerous explosive-rigged Houthi barricades. His favourite trick was to carve a path around the massive barricades by driving straight through the houses just off the road. Note the bullet marks in the armoured glass of the dozer.

67. Two 'write-offs' from the Oshkosh fleet. The vehicles served their purpose of providing 'protected mobility' to the Resistance and the losses suffered by the Oshkosh fleet underline how much enemy fire they soaked up. Of 121 Oshkosh's used in the sixth airport battle, 34 would be rendered unserviceable by the end of July 14 due to heavy machine-gun, sniper and RPG impacts on tires, radiators and armoured windscreens. Other Oshkosh were knocked out after the airport battle, during the pursuit operation towards Al Anad airbase. The two Oshkosh's shown here were disabled by mine strikes in the push on Al Anad. In a testimony to the value of these Mine-Resistant Ambush-Protected (MRAP) vehicles, none of the occupants of these two trucks were killed or seriously wounded. Note the blue and red cable-cars that place this photograph at the Oshkosh storage beach next to the Al Ghadir Fish Farms.

68. A BMP-3 of the Khalifa Bin Zayed 2nd Mechanized brigade north of Aden city. The UAE operated modernized BMPs with 100-mm guns capable of damaging main battle tanks. These infantry fighting vehicles demonstrated variable reliability and proved highly vulnerable to the large Houthi land mines encountered north of Aden. Three Emiratis died on 8 August when their BMP-3s detonated a huge 'daisy-chained' explosive array of seven massive 155mm artillery rounds.

69. UAE Leclerc main battle tanks on their way north to liberate Al Anad. The sixty-ton Leclerc could kill any enemy tank in Yemen before the adversary could even see the Leclerc, and it could take almost any punishment the Houthis could hand out. The Houthis tried to counter with landmines (aimed at the vehicle tracks) and used Iranian-made AM50 anti-materiel rifles to damage the tanks' optics, remote weapons stations, and even the smoke extractors used to vent the fumes from their main guns.

70. One Leclerc was lost to an EFP and was recovered to Little Aden for technical analysis. Precise burn holes in the Leclerc, edged by melted copper 'spalling', showed that the Houthis were using EFPs, the Iranian-designed armour-piercing roadside bombs that were employed by Lebanese Hezbollah to kill scores of Israelis and by Iranian-backed militias in Iraq to kill 196 Americans in Iraq. The EFP strike on the Leclerc was a mobility kill that damaged the propulsion but caused no injuries.

71. The author holding a Houthi Explosive-Formed Penetrator (EFP) on the Red Sea coast of Yemen at a later stage in the war. These devious roadside bombs fire an armour-piercing dart of molten copper, triggered by a passive infrared motion sensor, and camouflaged inside a spray-painted foam 'rock'. They were designed by Iran and Lebanese Hezbollah and can cut through the armour of all known main battle tanks. These devices began to show up north of Aden and were effective in slowing the initial UAE-Yemeni advance.

72. The Yemeni forces grew in confidence and size after the airport battle. Thousands of fighters flocked to join the mechanized attack on Al Asad and the clearance of the districts north of Aden. But the southern fighters stopped as soon as they reached the edge of the old People's Democratic Republic of Yemen. Liberating the north was a job northerners could do for themselves.

73. A partial reunion of the Aden team that was photographed by the UAE Ministry of Defence for public release in the *Al-Bayan* newspaper in June 2018. In the intervening three years between the Aden battle of 2015 and the photograph, the UAE would go on to liberate Marib Dam, Mukalla, energy-rich Sbabwa, the strategic Bab el-Mandeb strait, and much of the Red Sea coast. Many of the same cast of characters would lead these operations and some of the key officers were deployed overseas on the Red Sea coast of Yemen at the time of the reunion. Nevertheless, it was still an unprecedented gathering of the incredible team that led the liberation of Aden.

eastwards right along the airstrip until they reached the sea, whereupon the force would consolidate on an arc from Al Nawas Tourist Park to the Al Remah Roundabout. This smaller, final force was led by Lieutenant Khalifa M. and included a dozen Oshkoshes and a heavy complement of Javelins and Kornets to cut the Houthi line of supply, reinforcement or retreat on the coastal road and beach.

In contrast to the previous attacks, there would be much more focus on support services in the sixth airport battle. A 'reserve axis' of 23 Oshkoshes, 10 Nimr MRAPs and 200 Resistance fighters would be commanded by the UAE's Captain Mohammed M. and included 32 UAE troops. This force would be held near the May 22 stadium. This site also served as the hub for all logistical support to the attack. A large fuel tank was hidden between two houses and was used to refill two fuel bowsers that could be towed to any place fuel was needed to create a pop-up fuelling point for the gas-guzzling Oshkoshes. A UAE-funded field kitchen was set up, as was an ammunition distribution point. A field maintenance workshop for the Oshkoshes was also placed in the May 22 area, including a team of eight UAE mechanics and their truckload of tools. To supplement this capability, the ever-resourceful Adenese mechanics all over the city opened their doors free-of-charge to any UAE and Resistance forces who needed their help.

In anticipation that the Houthis would suspend cell-phone service from the Sanaa end as soon as the attack began, the UAE installed powerful radio repeaters at SH5 and, covertly, at several points close to the Houthi areas, to boost the signal used by 500 new Motorola handheld radios distributed among the attacking force. In combination with the hundred or so vehicle radios in the Oshkoshes, the attacking force would have a more robust radio net than ever before.

In terms of command and control, Ali A. would be at SH5, in front of the wide-screen TVs, with an Olympian view of the battlefield and good communications with Abu Dhabi. While Ali A. managed the overall battle, Salem got to pick his viewpoint from which to watch the battle unfold. He and a JTAC would be perched up an unfinished multi-storey building 900 metres south-west of the May 22 stadium, with long-range optics and a broad view over each of the axes, all of which were fanning out in front of his position.

Another difference in the sixth airport battle would be the level of medical support available to the UAE and the Resistance, which was vital due to the elevated exposure of the Emirati troops. Dr Ayesha had spent most of June doing daring covert reconnaissance of the hotels and clinics in the Resistance-held areas. On these trips she wore a full abaya and was accompanied only by a Yemeni driver, sometimes the red-haired Resistance leader Hashim Sayyed, with her UAE quick reaction force trailing some distance behind in a second car. Protection was minimal: she wore no body armour and did not travel in an armoured car. But she was a natural at this work and quickly gauged what needed to be fixed by seeing Aden's hospitals with her own eyes.

Dr Ayesha's trips into the hospitals of wartime Aden revealed nightmarish scenes: wounded men, women and children lined the floors of every corridor and stairwell. In a scene familiar to many war zones, Popular Committee fighters threatened doctors and nurses with death if they refused to bring wounded fighters to the front of the line for treatment. The wards were filthy and most surfaces were speckled or smeared with blood. Emergency wards and intensive care units would be her focus, and they needed to be close to the front line and with an assured power supply if lives were to be saved and the number of avoidable amputations reduced. Four hospitals were prioritised: the

Al Naqib and Al Wali hospitals serving the Dar Saad and Bir Ahmed fronts, and the Sabr and May 22 hospitals serving the airport front.

Essentially operating as a medical OMLT, Dr Ayesha and her four nurses trained tens of Yemeni volunteers, almost all women, to stabilise patients, stop bleeding with tourniquets, and issue medication, sedatives and intravenous drips. When Ayesha first came, ambulances were just morgue trucks, driving around the town stacked full of civilian bodies, with their doors swinging open for all to see. She changed this, prioritising medical evacuation of the living and ensuring that nurses stayed with patients throughout their ride to monitor their condition and keep them calm. To make head wounds more survivable, two retired neurosurgeons were found and paid five times a normal monthly salary to be made available for battlefield surgery.

## The Diversionary Attack on Imran

Ali A. wanted to start the battle on 14 July, which was the twenty-seventh day of Ramadan. Many of the fighters, but particularly the Salafis, would draw extra determination from the battle beginning on Laylat al-Qadr, the holiest night of Ramadan, known as the Night of Destiny. But one supporting operation would start on the twenty-sixth day of Ramadan instead. This was a diversionary attack intended to draw Houthis' attention away from the airport, and it was dreamed up not by Ali A. but by a Yemeni general. This man was Brigadier General Jaafar Mohammed Sayyed, who had been part of the abortive advance on Al Anad in March and who had re-emerged late in the Aden campaign as the newest military man to be put forward by the Hadi government.

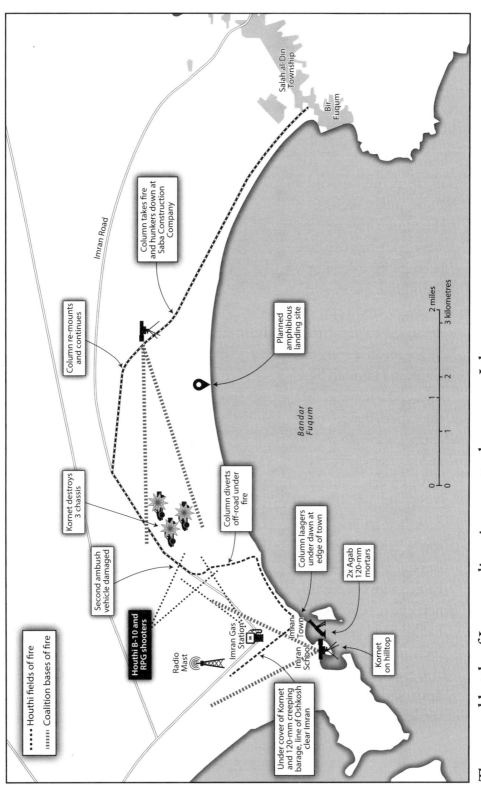

Salah al-Din
Township

Bir
Fuqum

Imran Road

Column takes fire
and hunkers down at
Saba Construction
Company

Column re-mounts
and continues

Planned
amphibious
landing site

Kornet destroys
3 chassis

Bandar
Fuqum

Column diverts
off-road under
fire

Second ambush
vehicle damaged

Column laagers
under dawn at
edge of town

2x Agab
120-mm mortars

Houthi B-10 and
RPG shooters

Radio
Mast

Imran Gas
Station

Imran
Town

Imran
School

Kornet
on hilltop

Under cover of Kornet
and 120-mm barage,
line of Oshkosh
clear Imran

Houthi fields of fire
Coalition bases of fire

| 0 | 1 | 2 | | 2 miles |
| 0 | 1 | 2 | 3 kilometres |

The second battle of Imran – diversionary attack on 12–13 July 2015

Jafaar had come to Ali A. with a plan to liberate Aden, and it was certainly better than previous Resistance ideas. However, when Jaafar heard Ali A.'s concept of operations, the general literally took his own plan and theatrically threw it in the trash. They were in alignment, and Jaafar would contribute importantly to the final attack plan with a suggestion he made late in the planning process. He dreamed up a deception operation to be undertaken the night before the main attack, to reinforce the sense that the Resistance had given up on the airport and were starting to attack on the Imran front instead. Ali A. had been looking for a new twist to add to his plan and now he had found it.

Near midnight on 12 July, a force of ten Oshkoshes was detached to serve the diversionary effort, which would be led by the most senior of the Presidential Security Group snipers, Captain Hamdan N. Hamdan was one of the most level-headed soldiers to serve in the Aden operation, with some grey hair and the experience to match. He had been promoted from the ranks and was close to the ordinary soldiers. An orders group was held at SH5 involving Hamdan, two Kornet teams, two snipers, the UAE vehicle commanders and the two Agrab-mounted mortar teams. Many of these men and machines were temporarily detached from the other axes and would fight on those fronts too when the airport attack came. They would be joined at Imran by the 80-man Popular Committee of Brigadier General Fadhil Hassan Khalil, the sole escaping commander from the first effort to retake Al Anad back in March. Brigadier General Fadhil had been spoiling for a fight since then, lobbying for just such an attack on Imran and the Aden Steel Factory. Fadhil had also frustrated efforts by some Resistance officers to negotiate deals with Saleh officers to surrender the western defences of Little Aden, the old British military canton that had been called

Falaise Lines and was now called Salah al-Din camp. Tonight, he and his 80 men would join Captain Hamdan's attack, and they would even be given three UAE-donated Oshkoshes to mount their command group.

It was a very dark night and there was no manmade light to the west of Salah al-Din, the scrubby *sabka* desert on which Abdullah Y. and the first SOC JTAC had decimated Houthi armour in mid-April. The UAE–Resistance column must have been visible or audible from a distance, however, because accurate small-arms fire quickly began to send the Resistance fighters diving for cover behind a wall at the Saba Construction Company, about 4 km out from the line of departure. Hamdan searched for the source of fire with a night-vision device as a Kornet crew set up the launcher. There were three *chassis* with 23-mm cannons or Dushkas on their flatbeds, firing short bursts and single shots at the column. One after another, three Kornets whooshed away in the dark, their red exhausts disappearing into the distance. The little dots of fire followed down the laser beam projected by the Kornet post, then disappeared with a *crumppp* that echoed across the desert. In a couple of minutes, the three *chassis* burned in the distance.

The column mounted up and got moving again. About 3 km further on a new source of cannon and Dushka fire from the north began to strike the column as it reached the intersection of the coastal highway and the Imran Road. The column moved off another 3 km closer to Imran on the road while aerial assets were brought in to look for the enemy heavy weapons. Every street corner and landmark of Aden city was now familiar to the UAE JTACs, but this was just featureless desert on a dark night and the Air Tractor and the 'fast air' – F-16s and Mirages – was working far to the north, hunting Houthi armour and reinforcements being drawn to the fight.

As the column approached the Imran gas station, Hamdan's vehicle was rocked back on its powerful suspension by a heavy impact, perhaps an RPG detonating on the cage armour. A second vehicle – one of those operated solely by Yemenis – was knocked out by another strike and began to burn. The column wheeled off-road and south through the desert, not seeing the inky sea until the vehicles were almost in the surf. They followed the shore west and laagered the vehicles for all-round defence at the edge of Imran town. There, some local Resistance fighters who had kept outposts in the small fishing village told them that the diversionary attack had run headfirst into a Houthi probe. They had just fought what was known as a 'meeting engagement' or an 'encounter battle', when both sides attack at the same time.

Just before dawn on 13 July, the UAE troops reconnoitred the town and its environs to familiarise themselves with the terrain they would attack. Hamdan woke up Brigadier General Fadhil and deployed their forces. The Kornet teams set up on a 40-foot-tall rocky outcrop just south of Imran town. The two Agrab mortar carriers were nearby, just east of the small school. Advancing under the cover of these supporting fires, the line of Oshkoshes and their following infantry swept north through the town, past the gas station and up the coastal highway for a kilometre until they reached a radio mast that was their first objective and their limit of advance.

They had now pushed 15 km beyond the Little Aden perimeter, but General Fadhil kept going. The G-6s at Ghadir could support his probe all the way out to the Aden Steel Factory, another 20 km to the north. Air and artillery fire were picking off Houthi vehicles and artillery before they could reinforce. So, he kept going another 4 km to the junction of the coastal highway and Route 66, then another 10 km up 66, past the old wrecks from Abdullah Hammer's first airstrikes, plus new wrecks that were still burning. Then, before long, Fadhil's men were at the Aden Steel Factory, which had been abandoned and which was full of unused Houthi ammunition stocks.

By the time Fadhil's patrols had fanned out and found the new Houthi frontline at Waht, they had covered nearly 35 km, halfway to Al Anad and just short of the Houthi main supply route north of Aden. The diversionary attack indicated that, once the hard crust of the Houthi frontline was pierced, friendly forces could exploit quite long distances before they encountered new blocking positions. Best of all, it had been a great proof of concept for the OMLT teams and for protected mobility. Six Resistance fighters had been killed, 25 wounded, and one of their Oshkosh's had been disabled by a missile or rocket, but the morale effect of the diversion attack was tremendous. Twenty-eight dead Houthis were recovered from Imran and eight were captured, along with numerous heavy weapons including a SA-7 shoulder-launched Man-Portable Air Defence System (MANPADS). As the story would be told, General Fadhil had fought and defeated the Houthis, delivering the first unmistakable territorial victory for the Resistance.

## Main Attack on the Airport

The Resistance went into the sixth airport battle with a victory under their belt, but still nothing was left to chance by the UAE forces. This was a time of careful final preparations – some of which went well and others not. One success story was the use of the Sabr drones to do route reconnaissance for the attack axes. The drivers and UAE vehicle commanders sat in the command suite at SH5 and watched recordings of the routes they would drive on the wide screen TVs. This provided a much better appreciation of potential obstacles, fields of fire and the methods needed to maintain the spacing between vehicles.

To ensure the drivers were ready to go – even those who stayed up chewing *qat* too late into the night – they slept next to the vehicles in Little Aden the night before the attack. Dr Ayesha similarly kept her key medical staff at the Sabr hospital with her the night before, though she had to improvise a series of staff briefings to justify them staying: 'I seemed like a crazy woman, deciding to review all our plans at 3:30 a.m.,' she remembered, 'but I was the "crazy woman" with all the money, so no one argued.'

Getting the Yemenis to assemble for an attack was still a complex routine, requiring careful planning and coaxing. However, the Emiratis and Resistance Council leaders had by now done it five times and they had learned from experience. H-Hour for the attack was nominally 05:00 hours but everyone knew the Yemenis would not be ready then. Instead, the real H-Hour was expected closer to 09:00. To keep the Emiratis nice and relaxed while they waited for the Resistance to show up, the Resistance Council had learned to bring the UAE officers delicacies such as frozen mangoes. As it happened, the Emiratis also needed more time, for once, as the newly established radio nets were not working smoothly. By 08:00 things were a little less relaxed and the commanders were really earning their pay, begging, pleading, cajoling and threatening to get Yemeni troops on the move. General Jaafar was using rough Bedouin's and soldier's swearwords to spur the Resistance into fighting. In contrast, Ali A. used guilt and shame; when some Popular Resistance complained that they had been moved a couple of kilometres south of their own neighbourhood front, Ali A. scolded them:

'You complain you were moved from Dar Saad to May 22? I moved from the UAE to Yemen!'

'You left the UAE to come here?! Why?!' one fighter asked incredulously.

'This is our duty; this is our task. You are our brothers,' replied Ali A.

It was hard to argue with Ali A., a man who clearly invested every atom in his body and his every waking thought in the success of his mission. The Yemenis moved to the assembly area at Little Aden.

It was at this point that the mood changed and a powerful energy began to build in the attacking force. In previous airport attacks, the Resistance had been supported by one or two old BMPs and these had typically broken down after a few hours, leaving the attack to unarmoured Hiluxes and infantry on foot. This time there was a 1,500-metre-long column of over 100 brand-new Oshkoshes uncoiling on the highway between the Khor Ghadir beach and the Farsi Bridge over the Khor Bir Ahmed . Despite some mild protests from the Emiratis, the Resistance had decked out many of the vehicles with the old People's Democratic Republic of Yemen flag – a symbol of southern independence. 'These are your vehicles, but this is our land, and the southern flag will not go down again,' the fighters told their Emirati allies.

The morale boost brought by the armoured vehicles was everything the planners had hoped and more. Participants described a strange feeling coming over the scene as the column mounted up. The line was so long that vehicles at the other end appeared stretched and distorted by the unusually strong mirage effect on the hot road. The column began to pick up civilian followers as soon as it started its 15-km approach march to Caltex Roundabout. Wild excitement began to grow. Tribal women were ululating – making high-pitched warbling sounds with their tongues. Running alongside the vehicles were young

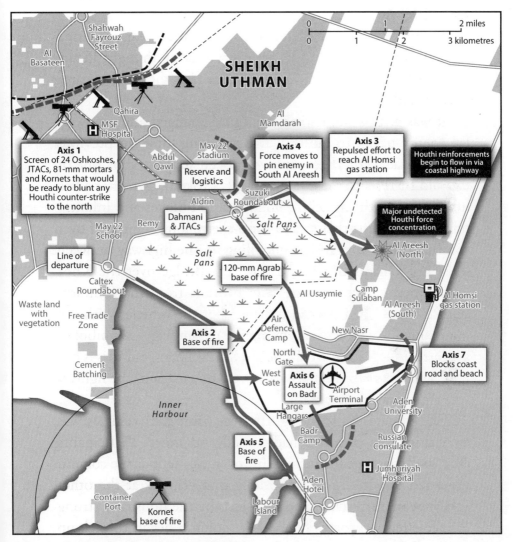

**The sixth airport battle, 14 July 2015**

Yemeni men lacking even guns and carrying only sticks or knives. Others were just desperate to see and to snap pictures and videos with their phones. Like the days of the Battle of Waterloo, when civilian onlookers would come to view the battle from a safe distance, this airport assault would also have an audience.

But there was no safe distance in this battle and, despite the best efforts of the UAE and the Resistance Council, civilians streamed down the Sea Line causeway behind the Oshkoshes. These were the refugees from Tawahi, Mualla and Khormaksar and they were going home. From having too few attackers, the UAE suddenly had too many to handle, and the very concept of protected mobility was strangely twisted by the presence of large numbers of people who were suddenly willing to rush unprotected to the front line, even clinging onto the anti-RPG cages of the Oshkoshes – which were sure to become 'bullet magnets' in the coming fight.

By the time the column began to branch off into its separate axes at Caltex Roundabout at about 09:30 hours, the fire plan had already been unfolding for nearly four hours. Unlike in early iterations of the airport assault, Salem and his JTACs had learned that the Resistance could not exploit pinpoint timing to descend on the enemy just as the bombardment lifted. Whereas Salem's first airport attack had been planned to start with a 'fire strike' – ten minutes of very intense fire support that would suddenly lift – the sixth airport battle instead began with hours of 'free hunting' for dynamic targets. There were fairly few fixed targets these days. The Houthis had learned to stay mobile and under cover. But an impending ground assault forced the Houthis to reposition and that was when the unprecedented roster of half a dozen JTACs could hunt. The artillery support available to the battle was also reaching its apex, with four G-6s, and four Agrab 120-mm rapid-firing mortars. Badr Camp, the CSF complex at Sulaban, and Labour Island were pulverised by 2,000-lb bombs, radiating huge overlapping concussion waves and thunderclaps outwards. The battle had never been this loud before, civilians across the city realised.

At 10:00 hours, the screen of Axis 1 had fanned out to the north and Oshkosh columns were all stacked up at their lines of departure at Caltex. Off went Axis 2 down the Sea Line, headed for the old stone British-built wall of the airport. Almost immediately, the young axis commander Lieutenant Nasser K. was tested: his very first vehicle began to suffer loud but harmless hull impacts from small arms fire and immediately made a U-turn, speeding past him back towards Caltex. Lieutenant Nasser took over a point vehicle and led his axis up to the low wall, which provided them with good hull-down cover and the expected lines of fire into the airport. His turret guns, mortar and Kornet went into action.

With his left flank denied to the Houthis, Major Seghayyar and the seven Oshkosh of Axis 5 immediately drove down the Sea Line, machine-gunning to keep RPG gunners from taking accurate aim on his vehicles. Major Seghayyar intently watched Labour Island to his front for any sign of 23-mm anti-aircraft cannons readying to fire. The island, formerly a tourist resort and – long before – a holding pen for the slave trade, had become notorious as a fire base for the Russian-made ZSU (pronounced 'z-juu') guns. No matter how many times the air force had knocked out the guns, more magically popped up to sweep the Sea Line with cannon fire. Though an MRAP was well designed to survive a mine strike, a 23-mm ant-aircraft round would punch right through the Oshkosh. Yet, as Axis 5 secured the entrance to Labour Island, no guns fired. The air force had made Labour Island too costly for the Houthis to maintain as a firebase. The western edge of the runway was secure. It was 10:10 hours.

At 10:17 hours, Lieutenant Colonel Mohammed K.'s Axis 6 was in position on the Sea Line at the western gate to the airport runway. Like an electric prod, this stimulated the Houthis to open fire from the white and light grey multistorey buildings around the airport perimeter and the southern edges of Badr Camp. The G-6s and their newly arrived laser-guided 155-mm rounds began to surgically pick off these threats, using 'impact fuses' to detonate micro-seconds after striking the building, to only demolish the rooms around the enemy strongpoint but not drop the whole structure.

All the while, Lieutenant Colonel Mohammed K. calmly directed the components of his large column to prepare for the assault. He could see crowds of Yemenis beginning to follow the axes down the Sea Line, scurrying behind and using the vehicles for cover. Lieutenant Colonel Mohammed K.'s problem was chaos; he wanted to fight a clean, orderly battle, but the Yemenis were swarming everywhere, and it would soon be hard to differentiate Yemeni fighters, civilians and enemy forces. At 10:30 his vehicles began to move onto the runway. From his high-rise observation post, Salem D. could see them through the high-power optics carried by the JTAC: due to the mirage effect of air rising off the hot runway, they looked tall and almost like they were flying across the airport.

Lieutenant Colonel Mohammed K. drove his vehicles along the runway and then turned them 90 degrees to face south towards Badr Camp. The precise manoeuvre was reminiscent of a fleet of battleships coming 'line abreast' to engage the enemy. His battle line began deliberate probing fire on assigned buildings using their 12.7-mm heavy machine-guns. Over the secure radio net, his calm commands could be clearly heard by other

Emirati commanders: 'Move ... stop ... shoot ...' It reminded many of them of an exercise at Sandhurst, his technique was so polished and controlled.

A creeping barrage of 120-mm mortar shells fired by the Agrabs began to move ahead of the battle line but Yemenis began to edge backwards to the north when a 'drop shot' landed among the Oshkoshes. Lieutenant Colonel Mohammed K. called for the mortars to cease fire. It was 10:50 hours. Momentum could be lost and there was no time to lose: Lieutenant Colonel Mohammed K. detailed 8 of his 24 Oshkoshes to assault the first line of hangars and the rusting ruins of the old British Royal Air Force quarters with its tennis courts, destroyed swimming pool and cinema. The other Oshkoshes would protect his flanks and serve as a reserve. The eight vehicles rolled forward, led by Lieutenant Colonel Mohammed K.'s Oshkosh. Every structure in Badr Camp was burned out or half destroyed after three months of airstrikes. The gruesome evidence of recent strikes was all around – bodies on fire, palm trees snapped in half and ash floating in the air. Lieutenant Colonel Mohammed K.'s instructions were to bypass enemy strongholds – to mark them for destruction but keep pushing to the limit of advance at the southern edge of Badr Camp.

The noise was tremendous. Yemeni turret gunners were hosing down Houthi snipers out of ragged palm trees and off the corrugated iron roofs. Other Houthis burst out of cover and leapt onto the anti-RPG cages of the vehicles, too low for the gunners to depress their heavy machine-guns, forcing the drivers to jerk the vehicles left and right to shake them off and then run over them. Lieutenant Colonel Mohammed K. heard an urgent call over the Resistance's Motorola radio net: 'Tank! Tank!' someone was shouting. Lieutenant Colonel Mohammed K. pressed the send button and spoke reassuringly: 'Be calm:

use your LAW,' referring to the should-fire disposable anti-tank launchers. Then a heavy airstrike pulverised the Houthi counter-attack before it could even begin moving. The attack rolled onwards.

The limit of exploitation – the stop line – was reached at the southern side of Badr Camp, and Lieutenant Colonel Moham-med K. ordered all vehicles to halt. The fighters dismounted from the backs of the Oshkoshes and spread out to avoid the sniper fire from low-rise buildings in the adjacent Khormaksar neighbourhood. This was real battle: unbelievable chaos. Lieu-tenant Colonel Mohammed K. saw Resistance fighters trying to build a huge pile of tyres and trash. Their plan was to set fire to it and hope that the smoke would force the Houthis out of a building overlooking their position. 'No,' Lieutenant Colonel Mohammed K. explained, pointing at the heavy machine gun on the nearest Oshkosh. 'Use the 12.7 on it.' His foot disturbed a grenade in the pile of trash they were about to set fire to. 'Take this, throw it in, then assault.' They nodded and he stalked off to check the next group, shaking his head in disbelief. Before long, Lieutenant Colonel Mohammed K. could tell he was running out of steam, staring blankly at the two Motorolas in his hand, unable to work out which connected him to which radio net. It was just 10:59 hours: the assault had seemed to take an eternity but it had actually been nine minutes. His throat was too dry to talk. Enough was enough: he had to break his fast. He needed water, something to eat and above all a smoke. He would add a day of fasting after Ramadan when the battle was over.

At this moment, the northern axes were launching after some delays on Axis 3, which hooked over the eastern edge of the salt pans at 11:04 hours and began moving in a single-file column of vehicles down the wide avenue of Ghazi Alwan, leading to the coast at the Al Homsi gas station. This avenue was intended to become the north-east-facing defensive shield against Houthi counterattacks, but the enemy was not being cooperative. The parts of the Al Areesh neighbourhoods north of Ghazi Alwan were positively crawling with Houthi reserves, including tanks, BMPs and 23-mm anti-aircraft cannons. Many of these had not been detected by the deep ISR 'soaks' of the area, so effective was the Houthi camouflage and so disciplined was their husbanding of such reserves.

Within minutes, five Oshkoshes were lost to heavy weapons fire that opened up all along the northern flank of the column. The Oshkosh could take a beating and these tough vehicles could still keep moving on flat tyre rims for tens of kilometres at low speeds. But they could not endure this weight of fire. Houthi snipers with anti-materiel rifles were proving adept at puncturing the tyres of the Oshkosh and the vehicles were being chewed up by high-calibre cannon roads to the wheels and radiators. The Houthis spotted the extra aerials on the axis leader's vehicle and concentrated fire on it. Turret gunners were forced back inside the Oshkoshes and more than one was saved by their Ops-Core helmets, which successfully diverted head strikes. Axis 3 recoiled back a few hundred metres along Ghazi Alwan with many vehicles limping back to the rally point at the May 22 complex. Half an hour into its attack, Axis 3 was stalled.

Just to the south of Ghazi Alwan, Lieutenant Salem D., the Axis 4 commander, had achieved his tactical objective of creating a defensive line anchored on the CSF base at Sulaban. It was 11:39 hours. Yet Lieutenant Salman could sense that something had gone badly wrong on his left flank, with no friendly forces where Axis 3 should have been. Lots of fire was coming from northern Al Areesh. If the Houthis counterattacked towards the

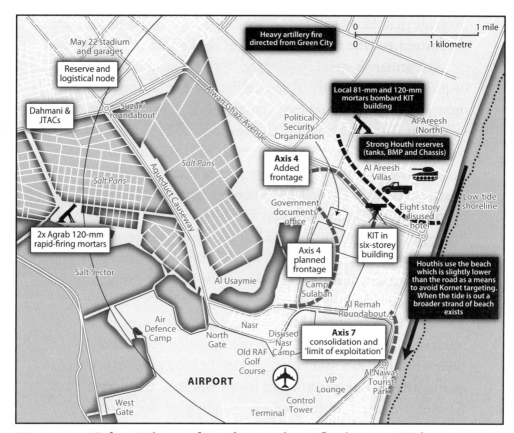

Lieutenant Salem D.'s stand on the northern flank, 14–16 July 2015

airport or May 22 from the north-east, they could collapse the whole operation. At this moment, despite having been drilled to stick to the plan and not cross the agreed 'limit of exploitation' at the CSF base in Sulaban, Danhany assessed the situation and used his initiative. He would send two of his OMLT teams northwards into tall buildings on Ghazi Alwan to cover the frontage that Axis 3 had been allocated. He would become both the eastern *and* the northern shields of the airport. Ali A. agreed.

Al Danhany's stand in Al Areesh would be one of the most inspiring vignettes of the Aden battle and it would be a hell of a fight – some of the toughest combat the UAE would experience in Yemen. The lynchpin of his defence would be a six-storey tall, partially finished building on the Ghazi Alwan avenue, about 400 metres west of the Al Homsi gas station. Two Kornet firing posts and two UAE snipers would be placed on the upper floors of the building and would constantly move between different firing points. The Kornet teams would fire an astonishing 90 rounds in the fight to hold the northern flank, resulting in five observed 'catastrophic kills' on enemy armoured vehicles – with their turrets flung into the air amid huge, oily fireballs – and 42 other 'mobility kills'. Many of the hits took the form of near misses on fast-moving *chassis* on the coastal highway that nonetheless resulted in a number of spectacular high-speed turnovers as the drivers lost control. To try to suppress the devastating Kornet fire, the Houthis heavily bombarded the strongpoint with Dushka and RPG fire, tank main-gun rounds, and mortar and Katyusha strikes. Forty-five 122-mm Katyushas fell in one hellish bombardment of the building, with a steady *whoosh-whoosh-whoosh* of launches coming in from the main Houthi artillery base at the Green City housing development 12 km to the north.

Back at the airport complex, the final part of the attack

unfolded. Axis 7, under Lieutenant Khalifa M., drove down the Sea Line and then onto the runway. His Oshkoshes fanned out at the eastern end of the runway and rolled up on their objectives: the Al Remah Roundabout to the north-east and the Al Nawas Tourist Park to the south-east. An armoured bulldozer trundled down the length of the runway after them and began to create roadblocks on the coastal highway and also defensive berms to allow the Oshkosh to adopt 'hull-down' fighting positions that left only their turrets showing. The airport had been sealed off from all sides and Resistance fighters were streaming into the terminal and the air traffic control tower. It was exactly 12:00 hours.

## The First UAE Martyrs of the War

The airport had been taken and sealed off from enemy counter-attack on all sides. Surprise seemed to have been complete. Ali A. opened a line to MGM back in Abu Dhabi. 'We took the airport!!' he shouted, slamming his hand on the table for emphasis. A roar went up from the Abu Dhabi end. Finally. And then straight back down to earth. MGM's mind turned immediately to holding what they had seized. He directed Ali A. to stick strictly to the planned limits of exploitation and not let the Yemeni Resistance fighters disperse. The Greater Aden neighbourhoods of Crater, Mualla and Tawahi were not today's objectives, nor even the adjacent Khormaksar. The Houthis were bound to punch back and the situation up in Al Areesh was already tough enough. Salem D. also felt that the seizure of the airport was too good to be true. He had been dreaming of this moment for months but he could not relax: 'I did not want to be happy'. He remembered thinking: 'If I did, something would go wrong. We could get hit by artillery while all the Emiratis were close together or the front could collapse. We didn't have a firm frontline and we still had no idea who was inside the areas we had captured.'

The Yemeni Resistance fighters and armed refugees did not recognise any limit of exploitation. A great mass of people, mainly the refugees of Khormaksar and Greater Aden, streamed southwards into the no-man's land beyond the limit of advance. They would be coming and going all night, desperate to get back to their homes to find out who was still alive and what of their possessions was left. Other Resistance fighters went to take back the bodies of their fallen comrades: a miraculously low figure of ten Resistance fighters were killed in the assault, and around a hundred were wounded – about one in ten of the assault force. Even more disconcerting, the Resistance also left in the afternoon – even the fighters trained by the UAE. Most of the Yemenis left to go and spend iftar – the fast-breaking meal – with their families and to attend *qat* chews and tell war stories of the great battle. They all swore they would be back the next morning, although not *too* early. The UAE axis commanders were now stretched tight. After fighting the battle, about 70 Emiratis would now have to hold the new 7-km urban frontline all night, and then fight again tomorrow. This was the moment that all the realistic training had led up to.

The exhausted UAE troops consolidated their positions, raising berms and digging shallow foxholes in the hard-baked earth. Captain Mohammed M. began to bring logistics forward from the May 22 logistics hub to the airport, driving a water truck himself. At the eastern end of the runway, Lieutenant Salem D. built a fighting position facing the sea, overlooking the strand of beach which was the Houthis' last way to get vehicles in or out of Greater Aden. The Oshkoshes were deployed in pairs, nose-to-nose, watching each other's rear quadrant, and their UAE commanders stood watch in the turrets.

It was a nerve-wracking night, with Yemenis crossing the lines in both directions. Houthis were also prowling around. In a particularly creepy development, Houthi fighters could be seen up to their necks in the sea, sometimes escaping northwards but sometimes emerging from the surf to sneak up on UAE positions. Lieutenant Colonel Mohammed K. was haunted by the risk that his men would shoot Yemeni civilians and fighters, mistaking them for Houthis attacking in the night. He walked the front lines constantly, keeping everyone awake and alert, and running the risk that he would be gunned down by his own men in the process. But his duties did not end there. Houthi prisoners had to be guarded by the Emiratis, or the Yemeni Popular Resistance would kill them. And then, deep into the night, the Yemenis would make pitiful calls for assistance, drawing UAE fighting patrols out to rescue the wounded or even recover dead bodies for burial. This situation clearly was not sustainable. At the crowning moment of their success, the UAE soldiers were not celebrating by breaking iftar with their family and friends, nor were they resting. They were peering into the night, waiting for a counterattack, dehydrated and heading towards sleep deprivation if a solution could not be found quickly. Only one thing could keep the Yemenis with them: the leaf that they craved so badly. The Houthis had long recognised that if you did not bring the *qat* to the frontline, then the frontline would move to the *qat*. Lieutenant Colonel Mohammed K. made the call: 'I need 1 tonne of *qat*,' he radioed. 'What?!!' came back the shocked reply. 'Not for *me*, for *them*,' he shot back, 'to keep them with us at night!'

The next day, 15 July, would bring the first UAE fatality. On the Axis 7 frontline, the Emiratis had been up all night due to the risk of Houthi raids from the sea. One of these vehicles at Al

Remah Roundabout was commanded by Lieutenant Abdulaziz Sarhan Saleh Al Kaabi, a 24-year-old Al-Forsan officer. Lieutenant Abdulaziz did not have to be there; he had been allocated to an OMLT in the reserve at the May 22 gas station but had begged Ali A. to let him join the main attack. Like all the other UAE soldiers, Abdulaziz had just spent a long night peering into the darkness but at least he had a friend from home to keep him company – an Emirati sergeant called Saleh A. who had volunteered to replace a Yemeni and gun for him the previous day. Sergeant Saleh A. destroyed three Houthi *chassis* on the beach and held off a number of Houthi infantry probes during the night. Abdulaziz's Oshkosh had one flat tyre, shot out on the day of the assault, and it would need a special jack to do a tyre change on the 16-tonne vehicle. The team drove west to the garage as soon as Abdulaziz' Yemeni driver returned from home on the morning of 15 July. The garage was located a kilometre west of Al Remah Roundabout on the main supply route back to the May 22 gas station.

After a tyre change, he was back at his station at Al Remah Roundabout by 11:00 hours on 15 July. Resistance outposts just north of Al Remah were trying to secure the Al Homsi gas station, to fill in the right flank of the six-storey redoubt where Salem D's Kornet teams were operating. Abdulaziz eased the Oshkosh forward, watched from above by a Sabr drone, and ordered Saleh A. to be ready to engage targets with the 12.7-mm to cover the Resistance advance. Suddenly, as they reached Al Homsi gas station, heavy blows began to rock and punch holes in the Oshkosh, one after another. The front windshield was punctured by 23-mm rounds. Al Ameri was badly wounded through both legs. Then Abdulaziz was hit in the chest and his body armour penetrated. The Yemeni driver accelerated past Al Homsi gas station only to be killed instantly by a high-calibre round through the head. He slumped forward and the Oshkosh veered left and rolled through the outer wall of a small walled compound and into a tree, which fell on the vehicle, hiding it from above. The Houthis continued shooting into the area throughout the afternoon, holding off other Oshkoshes from entering, while UAE aircraft and drones unsuccessfully scoured the area for the missing vehicle and its three crew, which had suddenly and inexplicably disappeared.

That night a search and rescue mission was sent out. At the crash site, Saleh A. had managed to drag himself out of the vehicle despite his two leg wounds, caused by a single through-and-through shot from a high-calibre round. Like most of the contents of the Oshkosh, his own M4 carbine was destroyed so he took the dead Yemeni's rifle with him. Saleh remembered hearing Abdulaziz's calm voice coming from inside the vehicle, ordering him to secure the site and stand guard. He heard an Emirati vehicle at one point but, to his horror, it came and went without finding them.

As darkness fell, some of the older and most experienced UAE soldiers – Salem D., Lieutenant Colonel Mohammed K. and Hamdan N. – took over the hunt for the missing vehicle. They gathered intelligence from the Resistance and sent out search parties but the Salafi foot patrols did not discover the part-buried vehicle until dawn on 16 July. By then, Saleh was half-dead from blood loss and desperately searching the ground for something to drink, finally finding a water bottle in the dark. It was then that he heard his rescuers: an Oshkosh commanded by Lieutenant Colonel Mohammed K. A Resistance fighter clambered over the wrecked vehicle and found Saleh. When asked years later how he felt at that moment, he welled up with emotion, saying, 'I had no hope, I was dying. God gave me a new start.'

The UAE team carried him out. They could see the driver

was dead and, upon checking, so was the other Emirati, the commander Abdulaziz. Neither could be freed from the vehicle, so Lieutenant Colonel Mohammed K. tried to hitch a tow cable to the Oshkosh to pull it out but, just at that moment, the same cannon that had destroyed Abdulaziz's vehicle opened up again from the seafront. The undamaged Oshkosh pulled away: one Emirati was dead, and they were not going to lose Saleh A. and other soldiers to the same ambush. Once the vehicle was safely sheltered, Lieutenant Colonel Mohammed K. pulled out his tablet with its cracked screen and calculated, using the angle of incoming fire, where the enemy gun was located. He cued a drone onto the area and the JTACs readied an airstrike. The 23-mm anti-aircraft cannon was exactly where he thought it would be, inside a beach chalet in the unfinished Barcelona Tourist Resort, which was swiftly demolished with GBU-12s and G-6 artillery. Under this covering fire, the Resistance recovered the two soldiers – one Emirati and one Yemeni. As Hani bin Braykh would later proudly remember: 'We carried the UAE martyr on our shoulders.'

For Saleh A., a long road to recovery was just beginning. Heavily medicated against the pain, he suffered awful hallucinations about Houthis all around him as the ambulance carrying him was loaded onto a landing craft at Little Aden. As he was being loaded onto the craft, he became lucid and looked up at Ali A., who was overseeing his evacuation: 'Did we win?' he asked. Seeing how badly injured he was, Ali A. tried to boost his morale: 'Yes we did, we destroyed the enemy!' Salih gave thanks to Allah and slumped down in his stretcher. The landing craft sailed out to meet the *Al Shareeah*, which would take Saleh to Assab. There he would be visited by MBZ and many senior officers.

The body of Lieutenant Abdulaziz was quickly returned to the UAE. Driven to Little Aden in an Oshkosh, he was carefully carried by his comrades onto a RHIB and sped out to a waiting corvette. The Puma helicopter on the ship then carried him to Assab, where a C-17 would shortly land and turn straight around. Late in the evening on 16 July, Abdulaziz came home, received at Al Bateen airbase. The next day, MGM visited Abdulaziz's family on Eid Mubarak, passing on the Presidential Guard's condolences to his stoic father, brothers and son.

Sadly, though, he was not the last fatality of the airport battle. Also on 16 July, just a few hundred metres away from Abdulaziz's crash site, Sergeant Saif Youssef Ahmed al-Falasi was helping with the defence of the six-storey Kornet firing position on Ghazi Alwan avenue. Al-Falasi was a 35-year-old Presidential Security Group sniper from Dubai and a father of five. He was a popular soldier, professional and eager to fight, and he was loved by his comrades. Saif used to prepare the urns of coffee for the iftar fast-breaking at SH5. On the day of his injury, he was carrying 60-lb Kornet missiles from the street below to the upper floors but, as he emerged at the base of the building to gather another Kornet tube, he was struck in the head by falling debris from the floors above. The wound was extremely serious, and he lost consciousness immediately, triggering a desperate evacuation under fire to take him to Dr Ayesha's neurosurgeon at the Saber hospital. He battled for life for five days but never regained consciousness. After being attended 24 hours a day by Dr Ayesha and another military doctor, Dr Ali G., he finally slipped away on 21 July 2015.

Death in combat is random, and never more so than in the case of Saif al-Falasi. But fate could also favour the Emirati soldiers. Weeks after the liberation of the airport, UAE engineers found rows of anti-tank mines buried in the sands north of the runway. They had not been detected and numerous Emirati vehicles had driven right through them. It was a miracle that no one had detonated them.

# XIV

# PURSUIT AND STABILISATION
# OPERATIONS

As the UAE forces were mourning their martyr and serving their wounded, the Adenese Resistance was spreading out across the city like floodwater bursting from a broken dam. On 15 and 16 July, the Resistance rooted out remaining Houthi snipers and diehards in Khormaksar. Each morning, at a leisurely 09:00 hours, the Popular Committees would gather in greater and greater numbers now that victory, revenge and probably also some looting were all realistic options. The supply chain established by the UAE out of the May 22 gas station and the airport functioned smoothly: ammunition, food, water and fuel were provided in the morning to sustain the day's fighting. On 16 July alone, the Coalition distributed 10,000 rounds of 12.7-mm ammunition and 300,000 rounds of Kalashnikov ammunition, all of which would be quickly expended due to the terrible fire discipline of the Resistance and their tendency to squirrel away ammunition as a kind of currency. Then, in the evenings, *qat* was provided to groups who had fought that day. Those evenings, some Resistance fighters even began to camp with their UAE team-mates, letting the Emiratis finally rest after days of constant activity and sleep deprivation. Lieutenant Salem D. was relieved to allow the warfighter to finally get some well-deserved rest.

The UAE forces did not want to get drawn deeply into the

liberation of every corner of Greater Aden. Their role had always been to cut the Houthis off at the airport and coastal road, and the Adenese could do the rest. Instead, the UAE supported the Resistance advance remotely, with drone reconnaissance, fire support and resupply. The line of departure for the clearance of Greater Aden ran along the base of Jebel Hadid, as would have been the case in the sieges of old. Logically enough, there were two axes of attack. On the western side (Mualla, Qaluaa and Tawahi) was one group of about 300 fighters who had been gifted ten Oshkoshes to provide fire support and protected mobility for the operation. A UAE Kornet crew, sniper and JTAC in the Container Port and on the now-liberated Labour Island provided overwatch in support of this axis across the small inner harbour. On the eastern side (Crater and the Mashiq Palace) was another group led by Hashim Sayyed, with the same number of fighters and Oshkoshes. Each axis was supported by a UAE-provided armoured bulldozer to remove the many barricades that the Houthis had erected throughout the town.

The Resistance poured into Mualla via the coastal road that ran around the western slopes of Jebel Hadid and into Crater via the Main Pass, under the follies built to resemble a historic gatehouse that was demolished when the pass was widened. An armoured bulldozer driven by an old bearded Yemeni engineer created diversions around booby-trapped Houthi barricades by driving straight through small buildings and shops on the verges of the avenues. This column seized Arab League Roundabout, drove straight down the urban canyon of Mualla Street, and then split up at Hedjuff Roundabout below Jebel Hedjuff. The column of Oshkoshes shouldered its way through vehicle wrecks and rubble in the Qaluaa Tunnel, breaking through the the Gold Mohur Valley.

The other Resistance fighters pinned the Houthi defenders

at the Hedjiff defile while the armoured force swept up behind them clockwise, via the coastal road in Tawahi. On the other side, the Emiratis watched full-motion video from the Sabr as Hashim Sayyed fearlessly lead the fighters to the centre of Crater town. It was agonising to watch, for they could see the snipers aiming at Hashim and men falling around him, but none of the Resistance fighters were answering their phones or radios to receive the warning. Hashim survived to besiege the Mashiq Palace, where the Houthis would make their last stand.

After suffering an estimated 1,620 Resistance fighters martyred and an unknowable number of civilians killed in action since March, the Resistance rooted out the Houthi snipers and holdouts in three nights and three days of rough justice. The Houthi leaders had long since abandoned their troops. UAE intelligence and navy personnel believed they caught a tantalising glimpse of the 'Houthi Houthi' command group fleeing by speedboat from Crater. The Sabr drone watched a well-secured Houthi leader – most commonly believed to be Abdalkhaliq – a full brother of the Houthi leader Abdalmalik – as he was evacuated from the Mashiq Palace. The UAE Navy tried to give chase but his powerful speedboat outpaced the UAE corvette and escaped to Shuqra, 90 km to the north-east. Houthi leaders could not spare so much as a bandage for their cannon fodder but they never seemed to lack the resources to protect themselves.

The fighters, and the files they left behind, were revealing and tragic. Some of the stay-behinds were true fanatics who had chained themselves to their anti-aircraft guns with bone-dry intravenous drips in their arms, crazed with dehydration and the cocktail of the amphetamine Captagon, blood clotters and powdered milk that they lived on. In one case, Houthis tried to deter an assault on their location by holding hostages, slitting one woman's throat in the street as a warning to Resistance pursuers. Intriguingly, some dead and wounded Houthis had their blood groups tattooed on their right shoulder and the sole of their left foot, for which no explanation was ever found. Most were just illiterate northern tribesmen, small and wiry, weighing around 60 kilograms (130 pounds). Many were boys between the ages of 12 and 15 who the Houthis had bought from their families for as little as 1,000 Yemeni Riyal (under five dollars). They cried for their mothers now.

Those foot-soldiers abandoned in Great Aden had been told by their supervisors to defend their sectors until the Houthi Houthis returned, which they never did. In some cases, they did not know what city they were in, and most of them believed they had been fighting Al Qaeda, or the Americans and Israelis, or some strange mix of all the above. Only small pockets of Houthis remained at the western tip of Tawahi and in the Qaluaa Tunnel as Ramadan ended and Eid began on 17 July.

After finding a Houthi operations room, the UAE used captured radios to listen to a dwindling number of local Houthi cells calling desperately for help and then going silent, one by one. Northern Salafi Resistance fighters were used as they could easily understand the northern accents of the Houthis. For eight hours straight, the last transmitter begged his Houthi Houthi commanders to rescue him, until his voice gave out. No one will ever know how many Yemenis the Houthis sacrificed in their effort to take Aden for they scrupulously removed their dead and sent the wounded north without treatment, many to die along the way. The Resistance found scores of boxes full of paper sheets listing the deaths of Houthi troops, but they too disappeared from history and were lost.

As the last streets of Aden were liberated, Salem D. was finally called home to the UAE. He had been constantly engaged since March with the Aden battle. As he embarked on a ferry to the *Al Shareeah*, Naif al-Bukri gathered up a jar of the soil of Aden to give to him. He would take a little piece of Aden with him.

## Exploitation in All Directions

The command staff of Ali A.'s Amphibious Task Force always had one part of their mind on the fighting of the day and another part on tasks that needed to be achieved in order to facilitate future operations in the coming days and weeks. This concurrent activity is what allowed the force to move fluidly to the next stage of operations without noticeable pauses. To the casual observer, this was invisible or just looked serendipitous but there was no luck involved. MGM, Ali A. and their teams put a lot of effort into thinking ahead.

On 16 July, the UAE chain of command had directed an immediate breakout effort towards Al Anad airbase, in order to exploit the shock effect of the victory at Aden airport. This effort would soon become doubly urgent for a different reason altogether: the escalating Houthi artillery bombardment of Aden city. As soon as the Houthis recognised they had lost Aden, they seemed to lose what little restraint they had previously shown, as if determined to punish the city and fire off all remaining stocks of mortar, artillery and rocket rounds. Mosques, markets and water distribution points were precisely hit at crowded times with 120-mm mortars, with Human Rights Watch and Médecins Sans Frontières reporting over 100 civilians killed on a single day, 19 July. The airport, now reopened and receiving humanitarian flights, was also being struck by 122-mm rockets fired from the Houthi artillery canton at Green City. As a matter of growing urgency, the Houthis had to be pushed out of artillery range of the city.

On 18–19 July, the Presidential Guard commander and the Assab logistics officer Major Hamid K. arranged the fast-track airlift to Assab of a platoon of six Leclerc main battle tanks and a full company of BMP-3s from the Presidential Guard's Khalifa bin Zayed Mechanised Brigade. As always, the air force came through, lifting the 60-tonne Leclercs in the bellies of the C-17s, sometimes two at a time, and the navy loaded them onto landing craft and ferried them across the Bab el-Mandeb to Little Aden. On 20 July, PG commander MGM made his one and only visit into Aden during the operation, part of a conscious effort to ensure that only Emirati nationals served ashore in the Aden battle, contrary to the unfounded rumours that foreign contractors were being used in combat.

In his congratulations visit with Ali A., MGM relayed Mohammed bin Zayed's directive regarding the seizure of Al Anad. Making a quick study of the terrain, it seemed obvious that a left hook through the desert would be far preferable to a direct thrust up either highways N1 or 41, which ran through vegetated 'green zones' that could hide ambush sites. In keeping with Ali A.'s principle of triple-redundancy and MGM's preference for always presenting the enemy with 'tactical dilemmas', they quickly sketched out a three-pronged advance on Al Anad that would include demonstrations against the N1 and highway 41 axes, but which would favour a main effort through the desert to the west of the highway corridors.

Ali A. began to move his headquarters from SH5 to Shaab's Qasr Hotel (known as 'the palace') in order to shorten communications and flight ranges for the Sabr drone. The man who would tactically lead the mechanised force would be Al-Forsan officer Major Seghayyar N., who had led Al-Forsan forces during the attrition phase, the clearance of Labour Island, and now at Al Anad. Though not a mechanised warfare officer, Major

Seghayyar was battle-tested and held Ali A.'s trust. To support the first phase of the pursuit operation, a G-6 howitzer and a JTAC with a short-range tactical drone was pushed forward to Bir Ahmed under the command of a Land Forces artillerist, Lieutenant Ali D. Dr Ayesha began to move her medical team up to a new field hospital near Waht. Two 120-mm Agrabs were set up at the Qasr Hotel, with the range to support the frontline just north of the city.

The first phase of the Al Anad operation began on 27 July and involved a characteristic three-pronged assault through the northern suburbs of Aden city. Pinning attacks up the N1 Highway and towards Green City were intended to draw the enemy's attention while the main attack – a 'short hook' around the west of the Houthi defences – captured Waht and positioned the Resistance to cut the Houthi line of reinforcement and supply at Sabah. The airport battle and the Imran diversionary attack had resulted in 34 Oshkoshes being made unserviceable, leaving 87 of the MRAPs still serviceable. Ten BMP-3s and five Leclercs were landed at Colonel Saeed's jetty and moved north to reinforce the attacking units.

The two demonstration attacks ran into trouble almost immediately. The Green City axis included around 1,300 Resistance fighters – on paper, at least – in UAE-commanded Oshkoshes led by Hashim Sayyed and a Khalifa bin Zayed Mechanised Brigade officer, Lieutenant Ali M. In addition to running into minefields covered by RPG teams and mortars, the four BMP-3s suffered repeated breakdowns. Four UAE troops were lightly wounded by a mortar in another close call.

On the N1 corridor, another similar-sized force under a Khalifa bin Zayed Mechanised Brigade officer, Lieutenant Mohammed M., was supported by Leclerc main battle tanks and six BMP-3s. In a short time, three vehicles were immobilised by

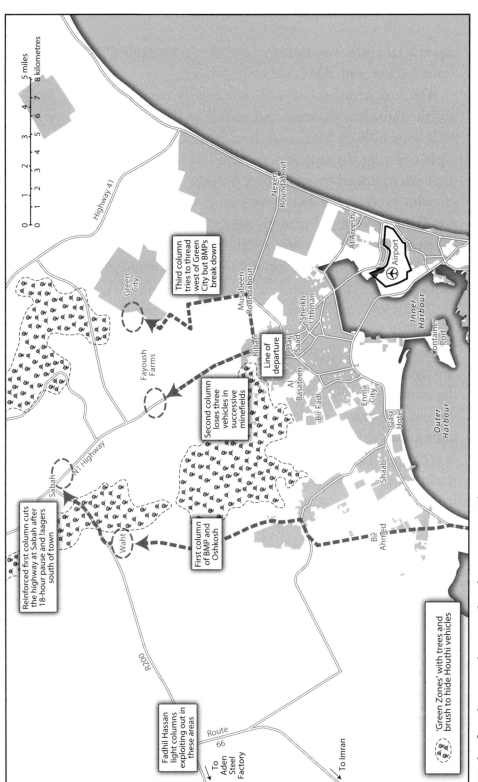

**Fight for the northern suburbs, 27–30 July 2015**

Map labels:

5 miles
8 kilometres

Highway 41

Nexen Roundabout

Al Areesh

Green City

Airport

Third column tries to thread west of Green City but BMPs break down

Musabeen

Ribat

Ribat Roundabout

Sheikh Uthman

Dar Saad

Inner Harbour

Container Port

Fayoush Farms

Line of departure

Al Basateen

Bir Fadl

Emma City

Second column loses three successive vehicles in minefields

Qasr Hotel

Outer Harbour

N1 Highway

Sabah

Waht

Shaab

Reinforced first column cuts the highway at Sabah after 18-hour pause and laagers south of town

First column of BMP and Oshkosh

Bir Ahmed

R200

Fadhil Hassan light columns exploiting out in these areas

Route 66

To Aden Steel Factory

To Imran

'Green Zones' with trees and brush to hide Houthi vehicles

expertly laid mines and advanced anti-armour explosive devices – one Leclerc, one BMP and one Oshkosh.

The loss of a Leclerc was particularly disconcerting as it was the most heavily armoured vehicle in the UAE's inventory, with large bolt-on blocks of composite armour and anti-RPG cages covering the thinner rear armour. Precise burn holes in the Leclerc, edged by melted copper 'spalling', showed that the Houthis were using Explosively Formed Penetrators (EFP), the Iranian-designed armour-piercing roadside bombs that were employed by Lebanese Hezbollah to kill scores of Israelis and by Iranian-backed militias in Iraq to kill 196 Americans in Iraq.

The science of the EFP is ingenious and diabolical: high explosives propel a concave copper dish forward, forming it into a hypersonic slug of molten copper that can instantly burn through the strongest armour. To ensure this inch-wide slug hits the vehicle, the EFP warhead is emplaced to cover a narrow area such as a road and is triggered by a passive infrared beam, the same kind used to trigger external security lights if movement is detected. To hide the device, it is placed inside a synthetic rock made out of painted foam. The UAE had been lucky not to lose lives and the EFP threat confirmed the importance of the flanking movement through the desert, away from predictable road corridors.

While both the central and eastern axes became bogged down, the western axis succeeded beyond expectation. Led by Al-Forsan Major Seghayyar N. and 4th Military Regional Command Commander Brigadier General Ahmed Saif Mohsen al-Yafaei, the force included around a thousand Yemeni fighters in *chassis* and a half-dozen BMP-3s. The force bypassed Houthi defences and linked up with Fadhil Hassan's Resistance patrols in Waht. On this flank the BMP-3s proved decisive, rolling straight into Sabah, cutting the Houthi line of supply to the N1 corridor defences.

It was then that the exploitation operation hit its first hitch. The link-up between the salient in Sabah and the highway N1 central axis would take days, requiring a methodical combined arms-breaching operation led by UAE combat engineers that would clear more than 250 mines. This left the UAE's Sabah axis dangerously isolated and it was heavily counter-attacked from Al Anad on 27 July. Houthi snipers with AM50 anti-materiel rifles got so close to the Leclercs on the perimeter of the pocket that the vehicles began to suffer equipment damage to their optics, remote weapons stations, and even to the smoke extractors used to vent the fumes from their main guns. Houthis with B-10 recoilless rifles were stalking the BMP-3s with their armour-piercing rounds. For two days, a relay of Sabr drones were kept constantly overhead, calling down Mirage and F-16 strikes and G-6 artillery salvoes on the 'green zones' to keep Houthi tank-hunter teams and infantry assaults at bay. The force of 600 Resistance fighters sustained an all-round defence for three long days on 28–30 July before the Houthis evacuated the N1 Highway south of Sabah.

As August began, the UAE force had grown to a full tank battalion of 45 Leclercs plus their armoured recovery vehicles and a mechanised infantry battalion with 30 BMP-3s. Another Agrab platoon of four 120-mm rapid-fire mortars had been landed as well as a new SOC company of 60 operators. Ali A. had planned a new three-pronged advance to employ this force of 1,700 UAE troops. Protected by a Al-Forsan team under Lieutenant Mohammed A., the G-6 and JTAC group would be pushed forward again to the desert northwest of Sabah, where they could engage targets as far away as Al Anad. The two highway axes – the N1 and Highway 41 north of Green City – would again pin down enemy forces on the predictable lines of advance. Meanwhile, a column under Major Seghayyar N. and Brigadier General Ahmed Saif Mohsen al-Yafaei were sent on a wide flank march to Al Anad, well beyond the visual range of Houthi forces guarding the highway approaches of the airbase.

The flanking force comprised a company of 14 Leclercs, a company of 15 BMP-3s, plus 2,200 Resistance fighters in UAE-commanded Oshkoshes and *chassis*. Halfway to Al Anad the column linked up with around 800 local tribal fighters gathered locally by Brigadier Mahmoud al-Sobaihi and UAE agents and SOC operators.

On 3 August, the three axes converged on Al Anad. The attack was overseen from the Qasr Hotel headquarters via Sabr drone and the movements were carefully controlled by Ali A. The first tactical objective was not the sprawling airbase of Al Anad itself, but rather the army camp of the 201st brigade on the high ground 9 km north of the runway. This was seized in a double envelopment by the converging forces of the three axes. Employing 'times ten' magnification thermal sights, with the ability to sense hot vehicles and weapons through light cover, the Leclercs mapped the Houthi defences and then employed pin-point fire from their 120-mm main guns to surgically destroy Houthi strongpoints. The G-6s made a new firebase 5 km outside Al Anad so they could range far beyond the base and cut the reinforcement routes by fire.

With the high ground of the 201st brigade base under Resistance control, the Houthis could not reinforce the base and UAE tanks could sweep the lower ground of the airbase with devastating fire and spot targets for the stack of airpower circling overhead. In methodical clearance operations, Ali A.'s team liberated Al Anad by the end of 4 August 2015. They found 130 Resistance prisoners who were barely clinging to life in a

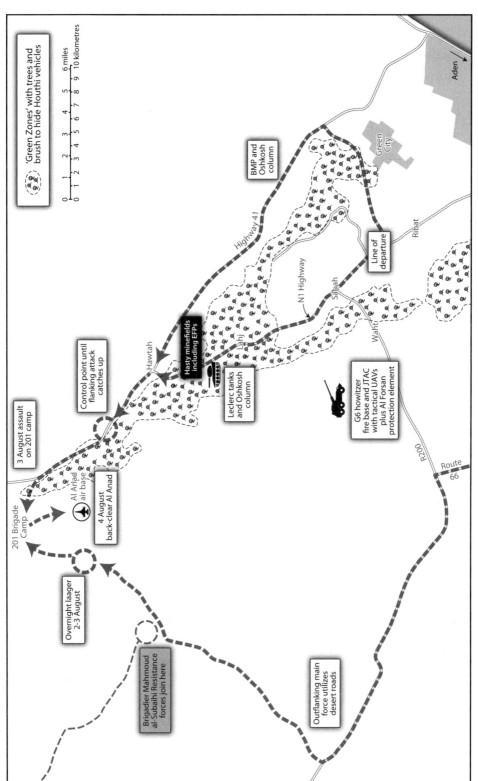

**Pursuit operations to Al Anad and beyond, 1–3 August 2015**

'Green Zones' with trees and brush to hide Houthi vehicles

0 1 2 3 4 5 6 7 8 9 10 kilometres
0 1 2 3 4 5 6 miles

BMP and Oshkosh column

Green City

Highway 41

N1 Highway

Line of departure

Sabah

Ribat

Wahti

Hawtah

Lahj

Hasty minefields including EFPs

Leclerc tanks and Oshkosh column

3 August assault on 201 camp

Control point until flanking attack catches up

201 Brigade Camp

Al Anad air base

4 August back-clear Al Anad

Overnight laager 2-3 August

Brigadier Mahmoud al-Subaihi Resistance forces join here

G6 howitzer fire base and JTAC with tactical UAVs plus Al Forsan protection element

R200

Route 66

Outflanking main force utilizes desert roads

Aden

medieval prison, many with their ear lobes cut off as a lifelong humiliation of the defenceless captives.

Then, on 6 August, Ali A. finally got the call he had been half expecting with a mix of dread and relief. Mohammed bin Zayed and Deputy Chief of Staff of the UAE Armed Forces Lieutenant General Issa Al Mazrouei told him that he had done a fine job, but it was time to rest. He would return to his family and then to staff college at the Australian Defence College in Canberra. But he would be back, multiple times: this would not be his last major command in Yemen.

In the days after Ali A. left, the Resistance and UAE forces (now under Presidential Guard Colonel Nasser O.) opened a new front against the Houthi bases at Zinjibar, Jaar and Lawdar. One axis involved 1,500 Resistance fighters in *chassis* and Oshkoshes driving directly eastwards from Al Anad. A second axis drove north from Aden along the coastal highway, numbering about a thousand Resistance fighters in *chassis* and six BMP-3s and a G-6. Once again, mines and improvised explosive devices (IEDs) proved to be the Houthis' best delaying tactic. In one tragic mine strike on 8 August, two UAE BMP-3s were destroyed by a massive buried IED made up of seven 'daisy-chained' 155-mm artillery rounds. Three UAE soldiers died in the explosion and five more were wounded.

The three martyred soldiers were first corporals: Juma Jawhar Juma Al Hammadi, a 31-year-old father of two from Sharjah; Khalid Mohammed Abdullah Al Shehhi, a 33-year-old father of two from Ras Al Khaimah; and Fahim Saeed Ahmed Al Habsi, a 33-year-old with five children, also from Ras Al Khaimah. MBZ visited the families of the three martyrs, as he would visit all the families of the fallen UAE service members during the war. On 11 August, he told the families:

All martyrs are our sons. We share the same loss, but we remember with pride the sacrifices they made so our flag will continue to fly high. History will immortalise the Emirati sons who stood by their brothers and defended our country against those who target its stability and national unity.

The Yemeni forces pushed on for 150 km, remotely supported by Sabr drones and UAE airpower, naval gunfire support and, now, AH-64D Apache gunships flying from Aden for the first time, all overseen by Lieutenant Colonel Mohammed K. from the Qasr Hotel. These Yemeni columns liberated the coastal plain all the way to the mountain passes at Mukhayris, where the high-altitude operations strained the Sabr's engines and the Houthis were dug in to the rocky cliffs. To the west, the UAE–Yemeni forces at Al Anad pushed northwards a further 40 km until they reached Kirsh, in the foothills of Taizz governorate. The Houthis were now in their favoured mountain terrain and the defence thickened. But, as importantly, the southern fighters said they could no longer advance as they had reached the edge of the old People's Democratic Republic of Yemen and the liberation of Taizz was a job northerners could do for themselves.

## Stabilising Aden, Hunting Al Qaeda

With the Presidential Guard-led battlegroups in pursuit mode, the UAE sought to ensure security and restoration of basic services in Aden by deploying a Land Forces brigade battle group to the city. The roots of this stabilisation initiative stretched far back into the first week of May, when Land Forces commander Major General Saleh A. was tasked to prepare a battlegroup for insertion to Aden after the city's liberation. The plan was to prepare a stabilisation presence that would remain in liberated Aden for up to 12 months, with lines of effort focused on the development of security forces and police forces, provision of emergency humanitarian support, restoration of infrastructure and the reintroduction of stable governance. The effort would be led by a capable UAE officer, Colonel Rashid G.

On 23 July, the battlegroup sailed from Fujairah on three leased ships, which arrived in Assab on 1 August, whereupon they were reunited with the battlegroup's 1,200 troops, who had been flown in to Assab. The battlegroup was landed at Little Aden on 2–3 August, a remarkably speedy amphibious landing aided by both the non-stop shuttling of landing craft but also by the arrival of the High-Speed Vessel *Swift*, a former US naval landing ship that MBZ had leased way back on 19 May from an Australian dredging company, another example of his foresight and ability to move resources where they were needed. The *Swift* was more than twice as fast as the UAE's other landing craft and could carry 50 per cent more cargo, meaning that it could deliver a load and return at the same time it took a normal ship to make one leg of the Assab–Aden journey.

The Training and Civil Military Operations Centre (TCMOC) plan developed since May was put into operation by the battlegroup. The core staff of 50 was split into six sections. The training cadre and military coordination cell aimed to professionalise four brigades of Yemeni forces from the Popular Committees as a permanent security force operating under the government of Yemen. Under the rule of law and police coordination cell, Abu Dhabi's police service would lead on the rehabilitation of Aden's police forces.

Humanitarian relief and the restoration of government services was equally important. On 16 August, a UAE infantry company – including National Service conscripts for the first time – was detailed to secure Aden airport, where the UAE brought in a modular air traffic control system to allow humanitarian flights directly into the city. Large container ships had begun to dock in Aden's Inner Harbour from 21 July, with one World Food Programme ship alone delivering 5.4 million daily food rations and another UN ship bringing the first civilian fuel delivery to Aden in months. Though not suffering famine, the population was overcrowded, malnourished and vulnerable to disease after months of being supplied by small boats run by food merchants.

In addition to donating and installing 24 diesel-fuelled generators, the priority infrastructure restoration cell ploughed funding and technical assistance from the UAE conglomerate Mubadala into reconditioning the 100-megawatt power station at Al Hiswa, which lay close to the UAE's old safe houses in Shaab. The cell also provided spare parts and fuel for the city's smaller power plants. Sewage, water and health systems were the next priorities. In an effort to return the government to Aden, five Yemeni government ministers were emplaced at the Mashiq Palace in August, though President Hadi himself would never make good on his promise to return to rule from Aden. Sadly, true stabilisation of Aden – systematically starved of resources since the 1990s civil war, abandoned by a fleeing government, plunged into a destructive urban battle, and then subject to local and international power struggles – could not be assured by any external actor, no matter how well intentioned or generous.

Against this backdrop, the old tumour of Al Qaeda came out of remission, feeding on chaos 'like cancer feeds on sugar' in the words of MGM. From the beginning of the Popular Committees, some Al Qaeda fighters or sympathisers had always been present in the Resistance, but the terrorist group was never allowed to run whole committees or whole fronts on their own.

Their greatest concentration of fighters was rumoured to be in Tawahi, and many of these had relocated to Sheikh Uthman upon the fall of Greater Aden in May. The counter-terrorism mission against Al Qaeda and the Islamic State had always been at the forefront of UAE planning. A counter-terrorism fusion and targeting cell in Abu Dhabi had been preparing for post-liberation operations for over three months. As the liberation unfolded, both the terrorists and the UAE eyed each other cautiously until Al Qaeda struck first on 3 August, when a bomb was discovered hidden in the room that Ali A. was due to occupy in the Qasr Hotel – built into his bed, in fact. Other rumours caused a scare that Al Qaeda was also planning to poison the food being delivered to the Qasr Hotel headquarters. By 12 August, the UAE was ready to start counter-terrorism operations and a forward fusion and targeting cell was set up in Aden on 18 August. On the same day, the US intelligence community and Joint Special Operations Command asked the Emiratis for help getting re-established in Aden, and they were assisted in returning to their old site at Al Anad.

And in the background, something even more ambitious was brewing: a sequel operation to the Aden battle, but this time against Al Qaeda forces to the east, which had cooperated with deserting Saleh forces to take over the port city of Mukalla in Hadramaut province. Despite everything it had done in Aden, the UAE had never taken its eye off Al Qaeda in Yemen. Many nations would have taken a breather or just focused on the Houthis but, in Abu Dhabi, an important conversation was happening between Mohammed bin Zayed and the head of the Presidential Guard's Special Operations Command, Brigadier General Musallam R. The UAE would now accelerate its parallel war against its other enemy, Al Qaeda, even as it took on new battlefield responsibilities against the Houthis in Marib and at the Bab el-Mandeb. For as long as the Aden operation had lasted, Musallam's Joint Task Force East had been working quietly to the east to marshal the tribes of Hadramaut, Shabwa and Marib against all invaders – Houthis or Al Qaeda. Now 291 would be charged with knocking the terrorists out of the famous port city of Mukalla and collapsing the Al Qaeda mini caliphate on the Indian Ocean. But that is another story.

# INDEX

Page references in *italics* indicate images.

22–3, *63*, 64–8, *69*, 71, 72, 78, 79, 83–4, 87, 89, 115, 118, 121
Doraleh Container Terminal 65
dynamic targets 61, 76, 180

**E**
Egab coastal artillery boats (P203 and P206) *130*, 140–1, 150, 158
Emirates Red Crescent 121–2
*Ever Given* 44
Explosively Formed Penetrators (EFP) 9, 203, *206*

**F**
Falasi, Sergeant Saif Youssef Ahmed al 194
*Farragut*, USS 9
Farsi Bridge *xix*, *69*, 71, *74*, *85*, *86*, 178
Fateh (Victory) base 20
F-15SA Strike Eagle 46, 59–60, 64, *130*
Fiver Shia Muslims 7
Al-Forsan (commando) units 47, 50, 116, 118, 127, 142, 150, 151, 152, 166, 167, 168, 190–1, 200, 203, 204, *206*; enter conflict 83–106, *100*; interdiction teams 143–9
Front for the Liberation of South Yemen (FLOSY) 25
F-16 46, 48, 50, 68, 71, 77, *130*, 138, 174, 204
Futaisi, Wissam al 55

**G**
Gargash, Anwar 39, 44–5
GBU-10 Paveway II 94
GBU-12 Paveway II 59, 104, *130*, 140, 193
General Headquarters of the Armed Forces, UAE 121
General People's Congress (GPC) 3
Geneva peace talks 153–4
Ghadir *xix*, *69*, *74*, *85*, *86*, *130*, 141, 142, 157, 161, 162, 175, 178
Ghannatha 140
Gold Mohur xvii, *xix*, 40, *69*, *85*, *86*, 107–8, *109*, 110, 196
Greater Aden *xix*, 29, *32*, 33–4, 54, 59, 60, 61, *69*, *85*, *86*, *93*, 107, *109*, 110, 111, 127, *130*, 161, 188, 189, 196, 211
Greater Salil *69*, *74*, 79
Green City *18*, *86*, *130*, 147, *186*, 187, 199, 201, *202*, *206*
G-6 self-propelled howitzer 83, 89, 90, 91, 125, *130*, 141–3, 145, 161, 180, 182, 193, 201, 204, 205, 207
Gulf Cooperation Council (GC) 39

**H**
Habsi, Fahim Saeed Ahmed Al 207
Habtour, Abdel-Aziz bin 119
Hadi, Abd-Rabo Mansour al- 5,

Hussein, Saddam 12, 13, 43
Hwasong-6 missiles 12

**I**

Illyushin IL-76 58
Iman University 10
Improvised Explosive Device
  (IED) 27, 207
Imran *69*, 72–3, *74*, 75, 77, 81, 90,
  99, 135, *202*; diversionary attack
  on 171–6, *172*, 201
infrastructure restoration 209,
  210
Inner Harbour *xix*, *32*, 34, 59, *69*,
  *85*, *86*, *93*, 99, *100*, 108, 110, 112,
  *130*, *179*, 196, *202*, 210
Intelligence, Surveillance
  and Reconnaissance (ISR)
  capabilities 127–38, *130*, 185
Iran xv, xvi, xvii, *xviii*, 7, 22;
  Houthis and 8–9, 11, 14–16,
  29, 37, 43–5, 46, 133, 134, 203;
  nuclear deal 44; UAE, threat
  to 43–5
Iran-Iraq War (1980–8) 43, 137
Islamic Revolutionary Guard
  Corps (IRGC) 9, 14–16, 43;
  Quds Force (IRGC–QF) 8,
  16
Islamic State 42–3, 45, 64, 211
Israel 9, 44, 87, 122, 198, 203
Issa, Ahmed xv
*Iwo Jima*, USS (LHD-7) 66

**J**

J., Captain Khalifa 142
Jaar 14, *18*, 28, 42, 56, *63*, 140, 207
Jabr, Ali 29
Jaifi, Major General Ali al- 12
Jalab, Ahmed 55
Javelin anti-armour missiles 97,
  99, 102, 144–5, 146, 150, 169
Jebel Hadid *xix*, *32*, 34, 59, 60, *93*,
  108, *109*, 196
Jebel Hedjuff *93*, 108, *109*, 112
Jihan-1 dhow 8–9
Joint Arab Defence Treaty 45
Joint Aviation Command (JAC)
  70
joint fires 51, 118, 127–8, 132,
  138–43, 147, 168
Joint Fires Initiative 51
Joint Task Force 291 64, 211–12
Joint Terminal Attack
  Controllers (JTACs) 50–1, 65,
  66, 71, 73, 75–6, 78, 91, 94, 97,
  98, 103–4, 112, 118–19, 124, 127,
  128, 129, 131, 132, 139–40, 142,
  143, 147, 150–1, 167, 170, 174,
  *179*, 180, 182, *186*, 193, 196, 201,
  204, *206*

**K**

K., Major Hamid 88–9, 121–2,
  200
K., Lieutenant Colonel
  Mohammed 151, 168–9, 181–4,
  190, 192–3, 203, 208

# PICTURE CREDITS